Praise for
Contagious Optimism

"No matter how difficult or easy your life may be at any given moment, it is possible to experience meaning and happiness. Read *Contagious Optimism* for yourself. Read it for your teams at work. Read it for your family. It will help you improve your life, your outlook, and your behavior."

—Marshall Goldsmith,
New York Times bestselling author of *Mojo: How to Get It, How to Keep It, How to Get It Back If You Lose It*

"Reading *Contagious Optimism* will allow you to appreciate and understand the principles that people of all races, religions, and socioeconomic backgrounds live by through their life's adventures."

—Daniel P. Tully,
Chairman Emeritus, Merrill Lynch & Co., Inc.

"Filled with triumphant and fascinating stories from people all over the world as well as life coaches and other authors, *Contagious Optimism* offers you encouragement to trust yourself and forge ahead in the midst of confusion and fear. This book has a contagious vibration that sparks courage, self-love, and personal empowerment. Be prepared to open yourself to new perspectives that place you outside the box and into a place of trust and love!"

—Laurie Martin,
author of *Smile Across Your Heart: The Process of Building Self Love*

CONTAGIOUS OPTIMISM

CONTAGIOUS OPTIMISM

Uplifting Stories and Motivational Advice for Positive Forward Thinking

DAVID MEZZAPELLE

Foreword by Marshall Goldsmith

VIVA EDITIONS

Published in the United States by Viva Editions,
an imprint of Cleis Press, Inc.,
2246 Sixth Street, Berkeley, California 94710.

Printed in the United States.
Cover design: Scott Idleman/Blink
Cover photograph: Ann Cutting/Getty Images
Text design: Frank Wiedemann
First Edition.
10 9 8 7 6 5 4 3 2 1

Trade paper ISBN: 978-1-936740-41-3
E-book ISBN: 978-1-936740-45-1

Library of Congress Cataloging-in-Publication Data

Contagious optimism : uplifting stories and motivational advice for positive forward thinking / [compiled by] David Mezzapelle ; foreword by Marshall Goldsmith. -- First edition.
     pages cm
  ISBN 978-1-936740-41-3 (pbk. : alk. paper)
  1. Optimism--Miscellanea. I. Mezzapelle, David.
  BJ1477.C66 2013
  158--dc23
                                        2013009245

To my family for teaching me the value of hard work, honesty, respect for others, and giving back to the community. To our Contagious Optimism team for your confidence in this project and your dedication to seeing it through. This has been a great endeavor and I look forward to continuing our mission.

TABLE OF CONTENTS

FOREWORD

When David approached me to write the preface in his new book, *Contagious Optimism*, I wondered, "Why me?" As I pondered the answer it became very clear: "Why not me?" I've been positive and optimistic all my life. I'm a "glass is half full" type of guy.

It seems predetermined that I worked all my life with Merrill Lynch, which is noted for its motto, "Bullish on America." I remember back in the 1950s when Bob Suydam, a Merrill Lynch partner, asked our class of future operations managers what philosophy we would espouse. He called on me for a response and I answered, "Do unto others as you would have them do unto you." He liked my positive attitude and that I lived my life like that in all endeavors—family, sports, business, etc.

Since I was a teenager I have been collecting positive, uplifting anecdotes that I try to live by. Examples include "I never met a rich pessimist" from Bill Schreyer and "The optimist finds opportunity in every difficulty, not difficulty in every opportunity" from Winston Churchill. One of the simplest and most important maxims for success was presented by Wayne Gretzky: "You miss 100 percent of the shots you never take." The premise of *Contagious Optimism* is the same as many of these uplifting anecdotes—positive thinking, inspiration, and motivation but across many facets of life and compiled from people all over the globe.

Years ago a business magazine said I exude positive thinking so much that I even have *The Optimist Creed* framed on my wall. This creed was written in 1912 by Christian D. Larson. His goal was clear: to attract good into your life and to share good with others. While this may have been written a hundred years ago, it still holds true today and is unaffected by time.

THE OPTIMIST CREED

Promise yourself:

To be so strong that nothing can disturb your peace of mind.

To talk health, happiness, and prosperity to every person you meet.

To make all your friends feel that there is something in them.

To look at the sunny side of everything and to make your optimism come true.

To think only of the best, to work only for the best, and to expect only the best.

To be just as enthusiastic about the success of others as you are about your own.

To forget the mistakes of the past and to press on to the greater achievements of the future.

To wear a cheerful countenance at all times and to give every living creature you meet a smile.

To give so much time to the improvement of yourself that you have no time to criticize others.

To be too large for worry, too noble for anger, too strong for fear, and too happy to permit the presence of trouble.

As humans, many of us have principles we live by. Organizations generally have principles as well. At Merrill Lynch, we have five principles we call the "Five Commandments."

These are Client Focus, Respect for the Individual, Teamwork, Responsible Citizenship, and Integrity. If you notice, all of these have a positive, uplifting connotation. None are negative, counterproductive, or pessimistic. Shortly after becoming chairman, I had these principles chiseled in our lobby floor at our world headquarters in New York and posted in every office around the globe in the local language. Our leadership teams are evaluated on how they interpret and carry out these principles. Similarly as humans, we have to act on our principles as well. Having them is not enough unless you live by them.

Reading *Contagious Optimism* will allow you to appreciate and understand the principles that people of all races, religions, and socioeconomic backgrounds live by and have exhibited during their life's adventures.

Daniel P. Tully
Chairman Emeritus, Merrill Lynch & Co., Inc.
Hobe Sound, Florida

POSITIVE FORWARD THINKING

Once during an executive development session with a group of investment bankers, I was describing the process of helping successful leaders achieve a positive, long-term change in behavior. One banker asked, "How will this stuff help us make more money?" I replied, "This process will help you make more money, but that is not what is most important."

I then got up the nerve to say, "My mission is to help you and the people around you have a happier life." I looked at the faces of the executives, expecting some kind of challenge. Then I asked, "Does anyone have any objection to this mission?" No one objected. So far, no one has ever objected.

I feel the same way about this book. *Contagious Optimism* is inspired by the idea of "positive forward thinking" created by David Mezzapelle. Positive forward thinking is the ability to find the silver lining in every cloud no matter how difficult yesterday or today may be. David has since developed his idea into this great book of stories and tools for readers worldwide.

In today's competitive world it's difficult to remain optimistic and focused. Without a positive attitude we can face many obstacles to happiness. It's easy to get caught in a "poor me" cycle if we dwell on the negative aspects of life and work—the fast pace of our lives, the constant barrage of emails, a 24/7 workplace, and so on.

That's why we all need a little inspiration sometimes, and the uplifting message of *Contagious Optimism* does just that. If you are experiencing a difficult situation at work or at home, this book can help. Each chapter relates to a theme such as goals, talents, relationships, finance, jobs, aging, wellness, relaxation, jealousy, and more. The sections are filled with the wisdom, philosophy, and experience of many contributors. In addition to the wealth of information and encouragement provided by professionals, there are stories included from a variety of contributors. These are real people sharing real solutions to real problems. And these stories make this book very intriguing!

No matter how difficult or easy your life may be at any given moment, it is possible to experience meaning and happiness. Read this book for yourself. Read it for your teams at work. Read it for your family. It will help you improve your life, your outlook, and your behavior. Enjoy!

Life is good.

Marshall Goldsmith
Bestselling Author, Motivational Speaker
Rancho Santa Fe, California

WELCOME

I can happily say that my life has been powered by the concept of "contagious optimism" long before I ever dreamed of writing a book or even establishing the concept. Having lived through challenging events and experiences, no different than many of you, I wanted to share how my contagious optimism has made it all worthwhile and continues to do so every day—for myself and for many others around me. The key was my ability to anticipate positive results in advance of them happening, thus making difficult circumstances surmountable. I call this "positive forward thinking." The anticipation of the positive results I call "Life Carrots."

So what is a Life Carrot? Quite simply, a Life Carrot is something great out in front of you that you can reach. This personal philosophy has made my life a pleasure no matter what obstacles have stood before me. When I experienced financial setbacks, I found opportunities. When I experienced loss and grieving, I found life. When I became engrossed in materialism, I found simplicity. When I experienced rainy days, I found sunshine. These are all positive results from negative situations.

I am fortunate to have been given the ability to radiate this optimism to others and to help them get through difficult situations in life with a smile and confidence in the future. Apparently my enthusiasm for positive thinking is contagious. I receive thank you messages daily from people who want me to know that I have added zeal to their lives.

One example took place several years ago in Jacksonville,

Florida. I was conducting interviews for a satellite office we were opening there. One of the candidates was a woman named Jennifer. Unfortunately Jennifer was not qualified for the position but I encouraged her to stay positive and gave her some good advice that would make her more marketable in the future. She thanked me profusely and her correspondence included one of the nicest thank you letters I have ever received. She mentioned that she was down about her unsatisfactory job search and financial situation before we met but that my contagious optimism had altered her frame of mind and outward demeanor for the better. I wrote her back and wished her well.

Seven years later Jennifer was reading the *Wall Street Journal* and saw an article about our company. She recognized my name and decided to track me down through our website. She wanted me to know how much our meeting had impacted her life and that she continued to have the sparkle of optimism that was generated from our interview seven years earlier. After her failed interview, but with her newly gained outlook, she was able to secure a part-time job to fund the balance of her college education while building work experience in the process. Ultimately she was able to land a position with another technology company and had been promoted several times over the years. She was now married and had children. I was touched that our brief time together had such a profound impact.

Many people ask me to bottle this optimism. I frequently receive calls from people I have known for years, and others I just met briefly, letting me know they are "psyched." They are sharing with me their positive outlook that they didn't have before we met.

Over the years many friends, family members, colleagues, and teachers have asked me to write about positive forward thinking in order to help people worldwide feel good about themselves and to find optimism in any situation. In summary, that is how *Contagious Optimism* was conceived.

For people in a good state this book will help you appreciate what you have and how you got there. Some people lose sight of that and need a little boost once in a while. For people in a bad state this book will help you realize that not far away is something real, something tangible, which makes today worthwhile and necessary. To better illustrate, each of the following chapters breaks down common themes in our lives and how optimism and positive forward thinking can make those themes a pleasure as well as a means to something greater.

Each chapter contains a series of essays written by a wonderful team including lay people, life and career coaches, medical professionals, wellness experts, financial experts, social workers, and spiritual professionals (across a variety of faiths). The purpose is to allow the reader to benefit from the uplifting stories, outcomes, and advice offered by our *Contagious Optimism* team.

I am confident that this book will help you achieve a positive outlook and appreciation for today, no matter how difficult it may be. This book will help you find balance in your life and lift that proverbial weight off your shoulders.

Thank you for reading. Stay positive and make it contagious!

David Mezzapelle
Jupiter, Florida

CHAPTER ONE
TALENT

Ignore thinking that you are bad at something.

Nothing is impossible and you can learn anything in the area where you wish to excel.

Lacking talent only means you have the ability to recognize what needs practice.

My parents always reminded me that practice is the only way to excel at something such as sports, hobbies, music, school, etc. They also reminded me that shortcuts are just a means of cheating yourself, only further delaying the attainment of your goal. The true leaders in any field have exhausted what is necessary to understand the subject and then have developed the necessary skills that led them to their pinnacle point. We all have that capability and simply need to apply ourselves.

Many before us have paved the path that provides us the wisdom and insight to carry on. We can take advantage of their legacies to build our own talents. There is always going to be the next Mickey Mantle, the next Pavarotti, the next Ronald Reagan, etc.

If you dream to be great at something, but lack the skills to reach that dream today, this is a good thing. Your mind and perhaps your body recognize the need to practice in order to improve those skills. No excuses! Just patience, persistence, and perseverance.

David

"I believe that true talent is being able to cut it when the chips are down."

—Kim Solomito, Watermill, New York

"I don't admit to failure because I believe an admission of failure is a concession to defeat. I embrace the idea that I haven't yet succeeded."

—Joel Heller, West Chesterfield, New Hampshire

# NEVER, EVER GIVE UP

TINA MONTEZ

First, you have an opportunity. Next, based on that opportunity, you create a vision. And when you execute that vision, you meet your opposition. It is here on the battleground, facing the opposition, that success is either realized or relinquished.

R. H. Macy started seven businesses that failed before finally hitting it big with his store in New York City.

After his first audition, the casting director told Sidney Poitier, "Why don't you stop wasting people's time and go out and become a dishwasher or something?" Poitier went on to win an Oscar and become one of the most highly regarded actors in entertainment.

Jimmy Denny, manager of the Grand Ole Opry, fired Elvis Presley after just one performance, telling him, "You ain't goin' nowhere son. You ought to go back to drivin' a truck."

Walt Disney started a number of businesses and went bankrupt several times. He kept plugging along, however, and eventually built Disneyland.

Bill Gates dropped out of Harvard and the first business that he cofounded, Traf-O-Data, flopped. Undaunted, Gates went back to work and created the global empire that is Microsoft.

When E. E. Cummings did not find a publisher for his book, *70 Poems*, he got the money from his mother and published the collection himself. The dedication, printed in uppercase letters, read, "WITH NO THANKS TO..." followed by the list of publishers who had rejected his manuscript. Perhaps this was Eddie's way of illustrating that nobody loses all the time.

Who could ever forget the Nike commercial in which basketball legend Michael Jordan recounts, "I have missed more than 9,000 shots in my career. I have lost almost 300 games. On 26 occasions I have been entrusted to take the game-winning shot and I missed. I have failed over and over and over again in my life. And that is why I succeed!"

Michael is right. If you are encumbered with the fear of failure it will thwart your efforts, neutralize any enterprise, and make success impossible. The next time a failure attempts to form a stranglehold on you, keep this list handy and remember that sometimes failure is the first step toward success.

CONTAGIOUS BY EXAMPLE

When you think you're failing at something, read a biography on one of your favorite people in history. You'll find that their path to success was filled with bumps as well.

ACHIEVEMENT BY MIND AND WILL

ALAN MALIZIA

The human mind is a wonderful gift and a powerful tool. It can lead us to success or failure. It can exalt or humble. It can strengthen or weaken us in the face of adversity. Maxwell Maltz in his book, *Psycho-Cybernetics*, recounts an experiment carried out at the University of Chicago that proved the power of imagined experience:

A number of people were divided into three groups, then were tested on shooting basketball foul shots. The groups were given the following instructions:

Group 1—Do not practice foul shots for 30 days.

Group 2—Practice foul shots every day for 30 days.

Group 3—Practice foul shots only in their mind (imagined experience) for 30 days.

After the thirty-day period the three groups were tested again and their results, compared to their initial performance, were as follows:

Group 1—Showed no improvement at all.

Group 2—Showed 24 percent improvement.

Group 3—Showed 23 percent improvement.

It's interesting that Group 2 had been practicing for a month and Group 3 had not touched a ball for a month. The above are effective examples for the topic at hand: talent seeking. The first is of the mind and the second of the will. By mind, will, steadfast effort, and faith one can accomplish that which one sets out to accomplish.

Our minds are capable of great things: self-awareness, appreciation of beauty, talent to analyze and create or look to tomorrow. Dr. Norman Vincent Peale, the famed minister and writer, tells a story in one of his books, *You Can If You Think You Can*. Dr. Peale's college professor, a strong and imposing man, yet quite approachable, was very influential in his students' development. His goal was to inspire his students to be confident and stand firm in the face of life's obstacles. The world then, as it is today, was challenging. On entering class from time to time, as a test to his students, he would write one word on the blackboard: CAN'T. Without missing a beat all that had been instilled in them came forth in a unified shout, "Erase it!" He would reply, "Erase what?" The students, even louder would respond, "You know! Erase the 'T!" And when he did, CAN'T became CAN.

When I was stricken with polio at the age of four the one thing I wanted to do most was walk. Although I was initially paralyzed, enough of my strength returned to allow me to do just that. In time, with the aid of leg braces and crutches, I was on my feet again. When life knocks you down, the only thing to do is get back up. As a handicapped person, falling was an unavoidable fact. My memory of being paralyzed was motivation enough not to stay down for long. I brought this attitude with me to all aspects of my life.

Ever since Russia successfully put a satellite into Earth orbit, namely *Sputnik* in 1960, I dreamed of being an astronaut, as most of the ten-year-olds of my time did. I read all I could on the subject, never missed a space launch, manned or unmanned, joined a model rocket group that participated in national competitions, and entered the annual school science fair emphasizing space science or rocketry. My passion directed me to major in mathematics in college and eventually to secure a job as a Systems Analyst with a company that designed and built helicopter and jet flight simulators to train naval pilots.

Obviously my disability did not allow the dream of being an astronaut to come to fruition. However, there are alternative ways to participate in any field of endeavor. I'm sure there were those who would have sacrificed much to be the first to set foot on the moon. Yet without the support of scientists, engineers, and technicians, no one would have had the privilege to represent mankind in the historic effort.

I finally had achieved all that I had sought after for so many years. Or, so I thought. In actuality, the monotonous work involved was not what I had expected. My job yielded no sense of fulfillment. Endless research, flow charts, and computer syntax errors were on the menu of each tedious day. I began to realize my dream had become a nightmare. I never enjoyed the moment of admiring a completed project before embarking on another. Just because something strikes our fancy doesn't mean it is in our blood. An attractive want is not necessarily our true need. With government contract cuts, and a mutual agreement between me and the dream field I chose, I parted from the company.

While still at my job, my mom encouraged me to accompany her to a new girl's recreation basketball league meeting. She was interested in managing and I could be her coach. I had become interested in sports during my later years in high school and in college, but had no opinion with regard to the ability of girls in athletics. I am not chauvinistic by any means; however, skepticism was in the back of my mind.

After our first practice I was a changed man. The level of play was challenging to coach and the kids were great. I finally found what I was looking for: feedback. Immediate return from my efforts. Win or lose, the teaching and learning exchange between player and coach was very fulfilling. The same passion I put into my earlier scientific interests was applied here with equal energy. This program became the stepping-stone to a successful career in education as a teacher and athletics coach on the high school level. Despite coaching a number of sports, the one that was most successful was girl's volleyball.

By the time I retired we had won four state, one county, numerous city and division championships and regularly qualified for postseason play in Connecticut even though we were the smallest school in our conference. In 1988 we won what would be our last state championship. What I treasure most was the lasting relationships developed with my players over the course of each season. Many, to their own credit, received individual honors as well as athletic college scholarships. There were many challenges and setbacks, but the difference between success and failure is the difference between faith and doubt.

Bishop Fulton J. Sheen, the great Catholic preacher, writer, and television personality in the 1950s, once wrote the following: "Believe the incredible and you can do the impossible." His thought was based upon the biblical account of Matthew 14: 22–33. A summary of the passage states, "Christ during a storm at sea was walking on the water as He approached the boat which held the Apostles. Peter, inspired by this sight, stepped out onto the sea to meet Christ. Peter then looked around and about him and saw nature raging. In a momentary lack of faith, Peter took his eyes off Christ and began to sink." If our faith is strong and our love stronger, fear, doubt, and failure have no place.

One day at school I received a letter from a most unexpected source. My doctor who had treated me for polio as a child wrote that my success as a volleyball coach had reached him down in Florida where he had retired. His note read: "I always knew you would accomplish what you set your mind to. You proved that to me while at the hospital convalescing from polio." Among being named coach of the year in Connecticut in 1988 and inducted into the Connecticut Women's Volleyball Hall of Fame, his letter is cherished the most. He was with me when things were the worst. His congratulations validated all that was achieved from polio to this moment.

Whatever it is that you choose to do in life know that your mind and will are the tools to see you to success. Know that the passion with which we put forth effort will ensure that we leave no stone unturned in the pursuit of the goal. Be prepared to face hardships, obstacles, frustrations, and endless adaptations to the constant emergence of Murphy's Law that seek to block you from reaching your goal. But remember, "You can if you think you can," and the true value in any achievement can only be measured by the level of struggle one must endure to attain it.

CONTAGIOUS PRACTICE

In striving for your goal, take a "hand to the plow" attitude. Be focused straight ahead with your eye on the target. It is mind over matter. You will not MIND the deterrents that attempt to discourage you, because you will not allow them to MATTER.

I NEVER FAIL

JOEL HELLER

I never fail in life. I know that sounds conceited, but it is true. I don't always succeed in everything I attempt, but I never fail. I have learned that if we believe in failure we are holding ourselves back from success. One of the definitions of failure is "a person or thing that proves unsuccessful." I have had many experiences and outcomes in life that meet the definition of failure but I never admit to it.

If we admit to failure we are overlooking success. We are provided with an opportunity for growth and learning each time things don't turn out as we would like. Each time we do not succeed we are given an opportunity to evaluate our goals and our actions. We can learn from what worked well and what we can change to have different outcomes. By always evaluating the steps we take to achieve a goal we are continually learning how to improve in our lives. When things don't turn out as planned I ask myself one question: "What could I have done differently to impact the result that was achieved?"

I have learned that this is a powerful and effective exercise. Instead of focusing on the outcome, focus on the decision-making process and actions taken. By shifting your focus, you make yourself a better person and embrace success. By undertaking an honest assessment, we discover what skills we need to develop, what strengths we possess, and how to plan better.

By focusing on what we can do better or differently we grow as individuals. Life is about learning, improving, and making positive steps forward. I don't admit to failure because I believe an admission of failure is a concession to defeat. I embrace the idea that I haven't yet succeeded.

You may be asking, "Why do you make the distinction between lack of success and failure?" I make the distinction because when I don't succeed in something I embrace the challenge of improving my skills so that I am successful in the future. When we are learning to ride a bike, do we give up the first time we fall and skin our knee? No, we keep getting back on the bike until we master the balance and coordination needed to roll around the neighborhood. We are not failures; we just haven't succeeded yet!

CONTAGIOUS INSIGHT

•• ● ••

Today you should make it a point to embrace the world in the same way you did when you were learning to ride a bike. You didn't stop until it was mastered. You didn't give up because you fell.

TALENT BUILDING 101

DAVID MEZZAPELLE

"Luck is opportunity meeting preparation."
—Unknown

Please don't tell me that you don't have what it takes to be the next golf sensation, musician, athlete, executive, or anything else. Contrary to what you think, you absolutely do have what it takes. I know it with 100 percent certainty.

There is no secret or special formula for building talent. There is no "right place at the right time" luck that is required. Building talent is one of the few tools for success that is not contingent on anything other than hard work. Your talent is the direct result of the hard work and practice you put in. Sure, there are some people that may excel faster. Sure, there are some people that get the unfair advantage of knowing someone already in the field. All that just falls in line with "the grass is always greener." Forget all that stuff and start applying yourself. The more you make excuses that you are not cut out for the job, the more you prove you really just don't want it in the first place.

There is one tool that is equally important to practice. That tool is your brain. You need to convince yourself that you are improving as you move forward. You need to visualize yourself at the pinnacle of talent. Whatever it is you are working toward, picture yourself already there. It will materialize but not through magic. It will materialize because you have the confidence to picture yourself reaching the goal, and at the same time you are taking all the physical steps necessary to get there. These are mutually inclusive steps that are surmountable.

There are many scholars, theologians, motivational speakers, athletes, philosophers, and industry titans that have proven this. It is not some oracle or quest. It is simply the art of applying your entire self to whatever it is that you want to succeed at doing. Good luck and don't lose sight of the goal.

CONTAGIOUS COMMITMENT

Having a tough time getting to the top of your sport, career, relationship, etc.? Stop whining and stop blaming others. Acknowledge where you are lacking and prioritize what it takes to improve. The brain and body together will accomplish the rest.

DISCOVERING YOUR PASSION, DISCOVERING YOUR TALENTS

MARINA TONKONOGY

Do you know what your talents are? If not, you are not alone. I didn't know mine for a long time and, even now, I am sure I have not discovered all of them. As a child, I was not allowed to freely explore different activities. My parents didn't want me to overexert myself, and, consequently, took my childhood away by confining me to a home prison. I was not allowed to attend afterschool classes, camps, physical education in school, and, sometimes, was even banned from other children's parties. Having this childhood experience, I know very well what it is like not to be able to find out what you love and are good at. It feels as though a large part of your soul is missing and that you won't be able to achieve inner peace until you find it.

Discovering my gifts as a psychotherapist and an educator allowed me to recover a large section of this lost piece. In addition, I enjoy writing and want to try acting, dancing, singing, painting, and anything else that would help me express myself in the world. Does that mean that I am gifted in all those areas? I don't know. I may or may not be, but that is of little importance. I explore different things because there is a playful and curious little child in me that wants to come out and live her life to its fullest.

Talents are an essential part of who we are. When we are searching to find our true self, we are finding our talents along the way. And when searching for talents, we are getting closer to our true self. This search is not an easy one; it requires us to take risks and to put our time and energy into something that may not bring immediate results. But it is significant because it brings us closer to who we truly are. Sometimes, it may even require us to deviate from an established path and to change our career. In my case, I abandoned the computer technology field and began a master's program in Psychology. Turning my life around was frightening; however, had I not made that change, my life currently would be dull and devoid of meaning.

Our talents are directly connected to our passions. I believe it is possible to be gifted in something that you are passionate about. Talents give birth to passion, because talents are meant to be discovered and put into use. Our passions are the vehicles through which our talents try to come out into the world. When we have the courage to follow our passions, we will excel in what we do because we invest our whole energy into it. We work day and night in order to master the necessary skills without getting burned out. Confucius once said, "Find a job you love and you will never work a day in your life."

You might say: "I can't afford to spend time and effort on this talent search, and I can't afford to quit my stable job because I have to support myself and my family." Of course, we are restricted by external demands that life imposes on us, and we have to do what's necessary to survive. But this life is not just about survival. It is also about joy and fulfillment, growth, and a search for meaning, inner peace, and giving back to the world. Under very difficult circumstances we should find the time to discover what we love. I know from experience that if we invest in this process, it will start working and new exciting opportunities will come our way.

CONTAGIOUS BY EXAMPLE

Make it a point to try something new, whether it's painting, dancing, golf, tennis, pottery, art, cooking classes, wine education, etc. Also, make it a point to encourage others to do the same with you. You will broaden your horizons and build camaraderie in the process.

TAKING ON SOMETHING WAY ABOVE ME

KIM SOLOMITO

"It's not getting what you want. It's wanting what you got."

—Sheryl Crow

I never believed that what we saw was all there is. There is another dimension that we, as humans, can't describe, understand, or relate to. For the scientific types, it doesn't exist because it defies the laws of physics and the universe as they know it. Even the philosophy of metaphysics can only attempt to explain the fundamental nature of "being" and the "world," but only on a plane that humans can decipher. For many people, myself included, we have faith in that other dimension. That faith is really an inner strength that allows people to believe there is so much more and it also motivates us to do amazing things. It allows us to be taught, allows us to learn, and allows us to build. It tells us that our mind, in conjunction with the universe, can do anything it wants as long as our faith and confidence is strong enough and not distracted from its mission—whatever the goal.

My first job was in a restaurant while I attended college. The boss was tough on me and only me. I performed, brought in the most money, had the largest number of repeat customers, and had never missed a day. When I asked him why he was so tough on me, he said that I have all the potential—not the others. He wanted me to apply that potential to my studies and observe my professional and personal growth. And so I did! My passion and career focus was in horticulture and floral design. These were natural paths for me even though many people in my life thought they were way above me.

When I was twenty-six, I met a woman named Hollis who was on a metaphysical path of her own. She gave me a wonderful book, *Way of the Peaceful Warrior,* by Dan Millman. This book, along with many other forces in my life, drove me to excel even further at everything I did. I believe that you can recognize when something is right or wrong. Your inner self talks to you and tells you which path to take. It is up to you if you want to see and hear it. My inner self led me, with no doubt whatsoever, to the path I stayed on for more than twenty-five years and I could not be happier for it.

Rita, my mother, always said that she had no idea what I would be when I grew up, but she was certain that I would be happy. She felt that I had the ability to apply happiness and confidence to everything I touched. She also knew this ability would ensure my career, my relationships, and my hobbies.

Together with my wonderful husband Jon, we have built a successful floral business in the Hamptons in New York. We have wonderful friends, a terrific home, and what I consider the perfect life. It is not perfect in everyone's eyes, but it is perfect for me. I smile every day for it and would not change a thing. I love my economy car and I love seeing mansions every day. Do I need a new car? Do I need a mansion on the ocean? Not at all.

My point to all of this? Anybody can do anything, anytime. A person can be talented or become talented. Either way it will happen if you let it. There is no reason for anyone to ever consider themself a failure. You need to know you have "it" in order to achieve "it." Without that belief it just won't happen. I took on many things "way above me" from starting a floral shop, to building that perfect centerpiece, to mastering yoga. Each one of those endeavors took study, practice, repetition, "homework," perseverance, and persistence. It also took significant patience because some things come more naturally than others. But I achieved them all and have the scrapbooks and track records to look back on with pride. Even my reputation as the "wild flower lady" in the Hamptons was a term to describe the uniquely beautiful and innovative style of my work.

CONTAGIOUS ACTION

Take on anything you want that is above you. Do it with confidence in yourself, belief in the universe, and your ability to succeed. It will happen.

INTERVIEW:
DAVID DI FRANCESCO,
THE LIVING WARRIOR

SUSAN YOUNG

How many times have you asked yourself the questions, "What do I want to be when I grow up?" "How do I master a talent?" or "How can I be number one?" These are questions that require a great deal of self-knowledge. In my interview with David Di Francesco, David reveals the elements required for selecting a profession or mastering a talent that gives your life meaning and purpose. David is the founder of The Living Warrior, a world-renowned program for training the body and mind.

David says that the original thought that we dreamt about as children seems to be the best fit. It is learning to trust yourself, listening to your voice, and going ahead with your dreams. He says, "You're going into your fear. You're going into the unknown but at some point your passion and your desire outweighed that fear." David's original desire was to heal people.

He explains that each of us has some aspect of ourselves that needs to find a way to be expressed. You have to ask your heart, "What is the end result I desire out of my profession? What talents am I trying to master?" Physical and mental training are critical in finding yourself and your passion.

David says, "There has to be some reward and fulfillment. There has to be something that says, 'Okay, I feel like I'm being adequately rewarded to make this worthwhile.' What is that for you?"

In my interview with David you will discover the journey he

has taken and the lessons to be learned when you follow your passion. Below are some highlights of that interview:

Susan: "In my heart of hearts I always knew I wanted to be in communications but I became an accountant. It's totally not me and I've been miserable ever since."

David: "The people that I've worked with, whether they're in the midst of a career transition, thinking about it, or actually having already done it, what I found to be the best fit seems to be the original passion and the original thought that they dreamt of as children.

"It was learning to trust themselves, listening to their voices, and going ahead with it. They had no understanding that they were going to be successful or that they were going to be able to financially take care of themselves.

"You're going into your fear. You're going into the unknown but at some point your passion and your desire outweighed that fear."

Susan: "How about living in regret?"

David: "Regret is a major element that can blur your original dreams and goals but it is not a rock wall, it can be overcome."

Susan: "So tell me about your journey. I always start with anchoring where you are and what it is you do."

David: "I am a physical trainer and coach. I get people ready to become Navy Seals, FBI, CIA, Rangers, Secret Service, policemen, firemen, and even athletes. I work with people worldwide. I get them ready for deployments and different task units as well."

Susan: "Doesn't the military or these other professions train these people?"

David: "I work with people who want to pass the test to enter the Academy. I also work with people that are already on board but need to be trained for a new deployment, which is usually an advancement in their career. For example, I work with people to train for food and sleep deprivation, cold-water immersion and all sorts of things related to sports as well.

"Here's the critical part that connects all this together: The physical performance of the human body is predicated on the beliefs and the thoughts going on in the mind. These are mental training techniques that tie in with the physical."

Susan: "In terms of the people you work with, what do you believe is the key to making them look good and feel good about themselves and their decisions—and act accordingly to sustain them?"

David: "I found that in order to get people successful about their bodies, I had to get them successful about their minds and their belief systems. I can tell how you feel about yourself by how I see you, how you look, etc. Your physical body is an outward expression about how you feel about yourself. I've never seen it otherwise. The physical nature cannot exist differently, or at least not for very long, with what you are believing about yourself."

Readers are welcome to contact me to obtain the rest of this interview. It is motivating, inspirational, and something I recommend reading to everyone that is trying to achieve the best in themselves in order to meet a goal or obstacle.

CONTAGIOUS INSIGHT

•∙●∙•

To be physically healthy you need to be mentally healthy as well. To start, believe in yourself and consider that mind exercise is just as important as physical exercise.

TALENTS AND ACHIEVEMENT

LISBETH CALANDRINO

I think we all have many talents, but talent isn't enough. There are many talented people in the world who have achieved very little. On the other hand, there are many not so talented folks who have soared to amazing heights. I think they call them "overachievers." In my mind, overachievers are the survivors of this world; always knowing on some level they must continue to achieve if they are going to remain competitive.

One of my friends is eighty-five and just hired me to become her life coach. At first I laughed when she approached me. What did she have that was unfinished? Our conversation informed me it wasn't a question of unfinished business; it was a question of new business. Recently diagnosed with cancer, she felt the need to hurry and learn more things. Her Facebook account needed tending to and her LinkedIn experience was just starting. I don't know how much talent my friend has, but I do know that she is always living life to the fullest.

Talent is a funny thing and in many ways, holds people back. Talent can make people feel satisfied with mediocrity. Talent is not the end of the world, but can be if it is left to fester and grow mold. I remember a friend told me his wife was a Rockette dancer at Radio City Music Hall. After further investigation, I found out she had auditioned for the Rockette summer program when she was seventeen. She didn't get the job but had been talking about it as if she had been on tour all these years. Ah, more talent left to grow mold.

The real talent worth having is the talent to be inquisitive and mindful. Wondering about the world and taking every possible opportunity to create excitement and meaning. I don't remember anyone ever saying I had talent. The only talent I had in high school was annoying teachers and talking too much. Despite my inability to stand out from the rest of the students, I never worried about the future and that seemed to be a problem for the teachers. Once I got out of high school and through my first year of college, I realized my life's journey was about the journey itself.

I was brought up in a very competitive household and my dad expected the best from me. In his mind, education was the key and my job was to fulfill his dreams. Fortunately, my dreams were the same as his and learning is one of my core values. I always feel better when I'm learning. Some days I have the desire to compete with what I've learned and other days I just enjoy doing.

As I age, I find myself most interested in the importance of my life on earth. My mother gave me this opportunity of life and I often wonder if I have fulfilled my purpose. I believe the key to living life to the fullest is to always be recognizing opportunities and following your own path. To enjoy every minute, whether it's writing a novel, giving a speech, or petting the kitties, it's your life.

There will always be more to come—if that's what you're wanting. Every day is to be enjoyed, every thought to be cherished. Instead of making every day count, make every breath and every thought count. Remember that if you do what it takes today, tomorrow will take care of itself.

CONTAGIOUS PRACTICE

Do what you can to the best of your ability, and then do one more thing!

TALENT—A PERCEPTION

PAULA SNYDER

What is talent, anyway? Is it the perception of one's self, or the perception of others? The trick is to feel that something you do can be useful to someone else, whether for pleasure or for pay. In my eyes, everyone has a talent of one kind or another. You might tell a good story. You might be a genius at math. Talent doesn't mean creative expression, nor does it mean star-quality fame.

For me, music has always been a part of my life. Though I loved to sing, people did not recognize me as a star, but I enjoyed it anyway. My family used it for recreation. But somewhere along the line, I decided to get some guts and use it for vocation. Not only did I want to sing, I wanted to make money singing.

No longer satisfied in harmonizing with the chorus, I wanted to have my own voice. I listened to my favorite singers at the time, practiced their recordings, and picked up their vocal nuances, mannerisms, and styles. I could be Barbra Streisand's *Funny Girl*, Maria in *West Side Story*, sing folk songs like those of Joan Baez and Joni Mitchell, or pop-rock like Linda Ronstadt. Somewhere along the line I decided that I needed to have accompaniment. Bands were difficult to pull and keep together, so the most reliable solution was to do that myself. I had learned basic rhythm guitar at the age of fifteen and piano by twenty-one. I kept the accompaniment simple to enhance my vocals. Singing was my main thing, but I still had to find my own voice.

On a hitchhiking trip "going west," I started writing my own music. I found a way of expressing my thoughts and feelings in a more universal style. Not only did I get some therapeutic value from writing and performing my own material, I touched other people with these songs. As I continued on, singing in campus coffee shops, restaurants, and local pizza hangouts, I became pretty good at expressing myself publicly through music. People began to compliment my voice and my ability to accompany myself. They liked the music I wrote. I got hired and I got paid. Was it talent, luck, or guts? No matter which one, it became an integral part of my life.

I eventually left music behind to raise my daughter. She didn't sing with the family or have the same joy in music when we started out, but she later found her own voice and there was no stopping her. She competed vocally with high ratings, participated in auditioned choral groups, and led her high school choir. When she was sixteen, my daughter asked me to perform with her for Christmas at the coffee shop where she worked. I agreed, and we became a seasonal mother-daughter duet. For the last ten years, we have performed together annually during the Christmas season creating some beautiful harmonies.

After being bitten again by the "music bug," I brushed off the dust and started all over. The joyous feeling came back in full force. Presently, I am performing regularly for pay. People rave about my ability to sing and are impressed with my ability to accompany myself.

Do I feel talented? Sometimes I do. Singing still feels good. I pursue opportunities and get them because I have the guts to ask, because I charge a reasonable price and because I've become a reliable businessperson. I also try to provide quality music and entertainment. I believe I sing better now than I ever have before. The people I perform for now seem to see me as a star. They get misty-eyed when I sing a torch song, tap their feet to fun, upbeat rhythms, whisper-sing along, share their memories, and remember life through what I bring to them.

Talent is relative and, in my opinion, just self-perception. No matter what it's called though, it feels good and I have found a way to make it work for me.

CONTAGIOUS COMMITMENT

Not everyone is born talented. Most people need to practice hard. Consider your aspirations and instead of saying, "I am not gifted in that area," ask yourself, "What do I need to practice to reach the pinnacle?" Then make the commitment to do so and never give up.

EMPOWERING TALENT

IRA SCOTT

We all have talents—the question is which talents we choose to utilize. The challenge is we often fail to recognize our talents. We forget all that we have already achieved. We tend to view past "successes" as things that just sort of happened to us. And we look around at "successful" people and think that they were just lucky, or that they had some special talent that we could never have. Those thoughts inside our heads are simply lies told by the ego mind that strives on creating conflict and fear. Some people fear failure while others fear success.

We all inherently know if we are honest that fear is the only thing to fear. We also fail to recognize what successful people had to do, the work they put in, and the sacrifices they made to get to where they are. A classic example is Michael Jordan. Most people think he was born with some God-given talent that made him an NBA superstar. What most people do not know is that Jordan was cut from his high school basketball team because he was not considered good enough. He raised his own standards and worked hard and that is what led to his success. You too have talents and you too have been successful. If you looked back at several of your life successes and you gave some serious thought to all that you had to put in to make those prior successes a reality, you will realize that not only do you have resources but also resourcefulness.

The only thing stopping you now is yourself and the limiting beliefs you have about what you think is possible. If you want to expand and grow, the first thing you must do is eliminate false beliefs about who you are and expand the empowering beliefs as to what you think you are capable of. And then you must take ACTION.

CONTAGIOUS INSIGHT

Focus not on what you think you're lacking, but rather on all the resources and resourcefulness you have. Give yourself a strong enough WHY and you will figure out the HOW.

A MOTHER'S GIFT

JOEL HELLER

Mothers provide their children with many gifts. They bring us into this world, nurture us as we grow, and act as a sounding board through life. Mothers play numerous roles in our development and in our lives. We all share one common denominator in life: we all have a mother. The relationship we share with our mother is, however, as varied as the world's population.

You would never describe the relationship between my mother and I as one of being "best friends." We had very different world-views, goals, and demeanors. Regardless of our viewpoints, however, I would always be her son and she would always be my mother. My mother passed away a few years ago, but the gift she left will always be with me.

During my sophomore year in college I came home for a visit and received news that no one wants to hear. My mother had been diagnosed with mouth and throat cancer. My mom and my dad walked me through the surgery and the treatments that would be forthcoming. As part of the surgery a portion of my mother's tongue would be removed and her ability to speak would be impacted. After the surgery she would have a speech impediment and the doctors weren't sure to what extent it would limit her speech. This didn't sound good and my mind raced with all types of thoughts, concerns, and fears. As we concluded our conversation, she told me how she was looking forward to attending my graduation from college and saying "Congratulations."

I was a bit puzzled by how she had ended our conversation and the comment ran through my head as I drove back to college. Why was she setting this goal? Was she trying to tell me to put down the beer and pick up a book? In the years that followed I came to understand the comment, the goal, and the gift.

My mother was a psychiatric social worker and her ability to work depended upon her ability to speak. She was a very driven and motivated person. Although she was going to lose part of her tongue, she vowed it was not going to impede her ability to continue to speak and work. What happened after her surgery showed me just how strong she was as a person.

After her surgery she went out and bought a tape recorder and stack of children's books. For the next few months she taught herself to speak again. She would read the children's books and record herself. She would listen to the recording and read the words over and over again until she figured out how to pronounce the sounds of each letter and each word. Each day she worked at retraining herself how to speak. This was a very slow and tedious process, but she didn't stop until she learned to speak with no impediment.

It would have been very easy for her to accept her circumstances and live with a speech impediment, but she had set a goal and there was nothing that was going to stand in her way. I learned a lot about goals and perseverance from my mother. If she could learn to speak again, surely I could graduate on time. I never complained about an assignment or a class after seeing my mother's strength. Having to write a term paper was easy compared to what she had undertaken. She taught me that no goal is impossible to reach. With time, persistence, and some creative thinking we are capable of achieving any goal we establish.

On a breezy day in May of 1990 I was able to give my

mother the gift she had wished for years earlier. After receiving my diploma I walked up to her and we exchanged a great big hug. Simultaneously, in perfect pronunciation, we both said "Congratulations." I will always carry that moment and my mother's gift with me. Whenever I think things are impossible, I open my mother's gift and persevere.

CONTAGIOUS INSPIRATION

Next time you're pushing yourself and not quite there yet, consider the persistence and perseverance of Olympians or top composers. Hard work and sacrifice will yield long-term positive results and success—in all areas of life. Push yourself. You'll be glad you did.

TALENT

When I was young I had a great talent
For bitching and moaning,
Lamenting my errors
Lost in self-pity's groaning.

And now as the leaves on my branches grow dark
The life force within me ignited a spark,
Can do it, will do it
Talent—that's all there is to it!

A poem by Karen Lyons Kalmenson

CHAPTER TWO

GOAL ANALYSIS

Where am I? Am I where I thought I would be?

Remember that part of the fun is the ride to the destination.

What am I doing to achieve my goals? Am I living my dreams?

The excitement of change, something new—don't hesitate if it's what you want.

Passion and dreams can always be monetized if income is your concern.

*"If opportunity doesn't knock,
then build a door."*

—Milton Berle

I am one of those people that believe you can do anything. The difference is that I apply optimism to the process of getting there as well as to the end result. Most people have a habit of picturing the goal but will allow negativity and failure to cloud the process. I am sure you have heard of "second guessing," "devil's advocate," or "cynicism." These common traits can cause many to abandon their dreams.

It is important to embrace a stumbling block on the journey as a milestone and not as a mistake. Do you remember how psyched you were when you first learned how to ride a bike after several attempts? Imagine how many chefs ruined a meal when they were in culinary school. I am sure they experienced soufflés that didn't rise, burnt pans, bland sauces, grease fires, etc. I guarantee they learned from every one of those milestones. Some of our greatest bonds and memories are made during tough times or during periods when we take for granted how great things are. Unfortunately it is years later when we look back and appreciate them.

I believe that the key here is to enjoy the ride no matter how difficult because any step can be a memory that stays with you for life. Louis Gerstner, former CEO of IBM, in his autobiography, *Who Said Elephants Can't Dance* (New York: HarperCollins, 2002), said, "Have you ever noticed how the past keeps getting better the further into the future you go? Someone once said that the only paradises we have are those that are lost."

Look at a rocky road as a challenge that helps you build strength similar to a good physical workout. Don't let the process cloud your goal—no matter what it is. It's all part of the fun.

David

"Communication, self-awareness, and planning are just three skills that can help you to change your picture and achieve your goals. But remember to enjoy this one life that you have been blessed with. Make the most of every day and each person. The effort will yield the life you were meant to have."

—Lynda Smith, Johannesburg, South Africa

"I had to pull into the parking lot when I saw the famous Nike billboard for the first time with the words, 'Just Do It.' All these years later, I still hate to admit my epiphany was a tennis shoe ad—but it was!"

—Jeri Hird Dutcher, East Grand Forks, Minnesota

 TURNING IMPOSSIBLE ON ITS HEAD

J. C. MONROE

If you're looking for a story that turns "impossible" on its head during these challenging economic times, look no further than the astounding account of a single British Mum named Joanne, or Jo, as those close to her call her.

Her meteoric rags-to-riches fairy tale seems every bit as magical as the character that rocketed her from welfare to billionaire. Her happy ending was shaped by her very real motivation to always get up after being slapped down hard, yet again, by life.

One day Jo boarded a Manchester train bound for London only to find the departure was delayed four hours. Perhaps it was the hustle and bustle of the station that inspired her. By the time Jo arrived home that day, her hands raced against her mind to get thoughts down on paper. In that inexplicable rush of creativity a literary star was born.

That same year Jo's mother died after a long battle with MS. The loss devastated Jo, and she wove her feelings of grief into her story with powerful effect. She moved to Portugal to teach English and shortly after fell in love with a Portuguese TV journalist whom she eventually married.

They had a daughter, Jessica, in July of 1993, but their marriage quickly crumbled. By December Jo was left heart-broken, unemployed, and clinically depressed.

Jo (and her infant girl) pulled up roots for Edinburgh, Scotland, to live near her sister. To teach in Scotland, however, Jo would need the equivalent of a master's degree. The required program was a full-time, yearlong undertaking. She opted to first finish the story she'd begun writing prior to her mother's death. She became a fixture at local cafes, writing longhand on yellow lined pads while Jessica slept tableside in her carriage.

Jo pounded out her completed manuscript on a manual typewriter and hired a literary agent to shop her work. The first twelve publishers rejected it out of hand. Then, the story goes, the chairman of Bloomsbury, a tiny British publishing house, asked his eight-year-old daughter to read the first chapter of Jo's book. The young girl clamored for more. Thirteen proved to be Jo's lucky number.

The Bloomsbury editor assigned to Jo's book presented her with a fifteen-hundred-pound advance and advice: "Get a real job; there's no money in penning children's books." In June 1997, a thousand copies of her book were published and five hundred were shipped to libraries around Britain. The Scottish Arts Council admired Jo's work well enough to endow her with an eight-thousand-pound grant to keep writing.

That autumn, while she was toiling away on her sequel, Jo's first work was awarded the Nestlé Smarties Book Prize. That following winter she was awarded the esteemed British Children's Book of the Year. The following spring, Scholastic, Inc. successfully bid for the U.S. publishing rights. Jo never looked back. In March 2010, Forbes estimated her wealth at one billion dollars. By now you may have figured out that Jo is J. K. Rowling and her famous character is Harry Potter.

Her philanthropy is legendary. She has amassed a record-breaking string of awards and has been decorated with numerous honorary degrees from prestigious universities, including Harvard. Hers is a story in perseverance and follow-through, best expressed by Jo herself in her 2008 Harvard University Commencement speech: "It is impossible to live without failing at something, unless you live so cautiously that you might as well not have lived at all—in which case you fail by default."

CONTAGIOUS INSIGHT

····•••● ●••···

The next time you find yourself behind or down and out, look around for a wizard in your midst.

PUNCHBALL

J. C. MONROE

Children are genius inventors of admirable persistence. We all began as children so we can all lay fair claim to that as part of our personal history. With little coaching we taught ourselves to walk despite falling hundreds of times. We mastered language and learned how to discard the odd noises adults "coo" and "goo" at us for much of our first year of life.

As older kids we created complicated games from the simplest of objects. Take Punchball. It probably came into being one day when two or more kids found themselves standing around on a paved street with a small pink Spalding ball as the only toy among them.

Punchball fundamentals are loosely inspired by the MLB rulebook but many key pages are missing. There are no bats, mitts, uniforms, spikes, or protective gear. No leagues, seasons, pitchers, or catchers.

Before play commences, agreement must be reached about what will constitute the field's parameters. Often a manhole cover in the middle of the street is home plate. Second base is usually a flat dollop of asphalt in line with home plate and roughly one hundred feet away. First and third bases are variously curbs, tree trunk knots, or maybe a parked car's door handle or rear bumper. Once the foul lines are determined the playing field is established.

I recently happened upon a modern-day anomaly. A group of kids were playing a lively game of Punchball; three on each team with nary a single helicopter parent hovering. There was a girl on first, another at home plate, and a boy sitting on the curb waiting to hit. Three more boys were scattered in the pavement field.

The girl at home plate held the ball about eye level in her left hand. She let it drop and swung mightily with her fisted right. BOOM! It soared then bounced toward third. She took off for first and her teammate sprinted toward second.

"Foul!" cried one of her opponents.

"No way!" shouted the girl as she charged toward the asphalt dollop. "That was totally fair!"

"Foul!"

"Fair!"

"Foul!"

Back and forth it went until the puncher yelled, "Do-Over!"

With that, the field fell silent. The runner returned to first, the puncher to home plate, and the fielders moved into positions they thought held greatest promise to get the puncher out.

Punchball has no umpires so the "Do-Over," another genius invention of childhood, is the conflict resolution tool employed. In a close-call situation, either side may call a Do-Over. Both sides agree to repeat the play at issue, whatever it may be, so the game can progress.

In the particular Do-Over I observed, the puncher nailed the ball straight at second base. A fielder caught it on a bounce and tagged the runner out. The puncher was safe at first.

As he tossed the ball to the boy who was next up, the fielder called, "That's two away!" I could swear I heard the kid within me whisper, "Remember?"

Somewhere during the process of laying aside childhood games to take on adult responsibilities, we also walked away from some of the abiding genius of their rules. We lost our sense of fair play and sportsmanship for what we can get away with and one-upmanship. We traded patience and understanding for restlessness and intolerance.

The result is, as adults we too quickly label endeavors as failures when first results are not what we anticipated. We also quit too readily on relationships when someone acts in unexpected ways. The destination is attainable, don't stress about the ride. Just work through the bumps.

CONTAGIOUS BY EXAMPLE

Are you at odds with another person or disappointed with yourself? Take a break. Go on a meditative stroll. Ask your inner child-genius to join you, the one who taught you how to walk in the first place by dint of sheer persistence and unwavering faith. Then get back to what you were doing and call a "Do-Over."

CREATING A VALUE-BASED RETIREMENT

DEE CASCIO

We often hear people talk about values and what they feel is important to them. Values are consistent ideals that are personally important to each of us and give our life true meaning. We all have them and many of us share common values that affect how we live our lives. As we transition into our retirement, it is not unusual to begin to explore the question, "What is really important to me?" Or ask, "What are my values and how can I become more conscious of living my life making sure that my behaviors are in alignment with my values?" By acting consciously, you can be sure that living by your values in later years will reflect your life's true meaning and purpose.

WHAT ARE YOUR CORE VALUES?

While in coach training, one of the courses required us to do a Values Inventory Exercise. As I reflect back on this experience, I remember being impressed with the fact that this concept was explored, inventoried, and then discussed among our training group. For the first time, I looked carefully at this list and quickly identified those that I was currently living by. This exercise is something that many of us do unconsciously, but this process brought it to a whole different level for me. Here are some of the values that I follow:

1. Relating and appreciating family and friends and experiencing a sense of community.

2. Having high standards in my personal and professional life.
3. Volunteering my time and contributing to my community through Rotary membership and other groups.
4. Supporting, teaching, and encouraging others.
5. Learning new skills, concepts, and activities.
6. Maintaining a healthy lifestyle by exercising, eating well, and getting enough rest.

What values would you list? Are you currently living by these values or do you need to explore this concept in your life? Who in your life is modeling core values that you might like to incorporate into your life?

ALIGNING YOUR VALUES WITH YOUR LIFESTYLE NOW AND IN RETIREMENT

As a therapist as well as a life and retirement coach, I have been exploring these issues with my clients. I have used this exercise as a foundation for the discussions about what is truly important to them. Are your life goals, planning behaviors, ideas, and projects in alignment with your core values? If not, you may experience difficulty generating the energy that it takes to reach your goals, complete a project, or stay with an idea. If you are not in alignment with your values, you may be headed in a direction that will lead to a less satisfying transition if that hasn't happened already.

For example, if you value friends and family yet you plan to move away from them, will you be truly happy in your retirement? I have talked to many who have moved away, only to miss the community, family, and friends that they left and move back to be closer to those they love and care about. Relocating remains a choice, and you can make visits back to your roots and have friends and family visit you. This can work well while you establish new relationships in your new home. This is called phasing into your new lifestyle.

Some say that they value their health and will start to make changes when they are no longer working and have the time. If this is a value, isn't it time to start making those lifestyle changes now that will lead you to your goal? I encourage you to explore your core values and determine what is important to you. If you need a tool to help facilitate this, check out the Life Values Self-Assessment Test at www.whatsnext.com to identify your core values.

CONTAGIOUS INSIGHT

What will give your life meaning in your retirement (whether you are in that transition now or will be in the future)? Listen to your thoughts, feelings, and level of motivation and you will find out if your lifestyle reflects these values or not.

POSITIVE STRENGTH

SAM LIEBERMAN

When you ask someone to identify what they believe to be the strongest thing in the universe, you get answers ranging from a piece of iron to Superman. Of course when we think of strength we always focus on something physical. There are different ways to measure strength: absolute strength (maximum force), dynamic strength (repeated motions), elastic strength (exerting force quickly), and strength endurance (ability to withstand fatigue).

However, there is another type of strength: the power of the human mind. I believe that with the proper training and enough time, the mind can accomplish anything. Of course, a lifetime may not be enough to train the mind for certain tasks (i.e. moving a physical object). But, if we channel our energies into positive thought, there should be very little that we cannot accomplish in our day-to-day living. I have found that approaching a daunting task as if "the glass is half-full" as opposed to "half-empty" allows me to view any situation positively. Looking at a problem as a challenge allows me to think clearly and concisely. Of course, the best result may not always be the first result, but when tackling the problem head-on, results do occur. Although some tweaking may be necessary, at least I have moved to the point that allowed me to see the errors I have made so I can correct them.

CONTAGIOUS ACTION

···•• ● ••···

Putting off a task under the guise of trying to think of the best way to reach the stated goal will never result in an accomplishment. "I DID" trumps "I WILL" every time!

ENVISION THE PERFECT DAY: A VISUALIZATION EXERCISE

JERI HIRD DUTCHER

Sometimes the hardest thing about getting what we want is figuring out what that is. When deciding on goals, we can get caught up in the lists of pros and cons, the rational reasons to work here or live there, and the benefit packages offered. We end up more confused than ever.

If that's where you are, use this simple visualization exercise to move through the left-brain patterns to the right-brain play. Let your imagination take you anywhere it goes. Just be sure to record your experience electronically or on paper as you imagine it because some of your observations may be surprising, especially to you!

Close your eyes. Breathe deeply for a moment and relax. Imagine yourself just waking up in the morning. It's a good day and you're excited. You can do anything you want. Anything. Now, write or record your voice describing in the greatest detail possible the rest of your day, including work, family life, personal and spiritual pursuits, relationships, and your environment.

Where are you?

What are you doing?

Who is with you?

What do you see?

What do you hear?

What smells meet you?

When you feel pleasure or accomplishment, what is happening?

Is something missing? What is it? Where or how would you find it?

Continue moving through your day from morning until night, keeping these questions in mind about each scene.

CONTAGIOUS REFLECTION

When the above lesson is complete, note what surprised you and what did not. Did you learn anything about yourself? Did you learn anything about what you want? This is a simple yet powerful practice.

RIDE WITH THE WAVES

ANABELA OLIVIER

My family and I had a good life, a bustling life. Both my husband and I worked full-time at medical device companies in the San Francisco Bay area. Our son came along and we hired a nanny. We also had a housekeeper, luxury cars, vacationed often, and shopped at Nordstrom. Who wouldn't want the life-style we had?

Unfortunately, it all ended one day when I was laid off. I had been with that employer for six years and wasn't expecting it. The economy was hanging by a thread and employment applications were many but to no avail. A year passed and we lost our home, our cars, our nanny, our housekeeper, and, of course, shopping at Nordstrom. I believe we would have lived that way forever if the layoff never happened. "Keeping up with the Joneses" seemed easy.

"Materialism rules!" was the attitude I had, along with the rest of the country. So what happened then? I thought I would drop into a severe depression. I thought I would be extremely unhappy. Most of all, I thought I would feel ashamed and try to avoid friends and colleagues. But none of these were the case. Of course the transition period was difficult, especially when I began cutting coupons, but I realized I was more resilient than I thought.

I don't have a magic formula to help others get through such painful times. What I can say is that when many of us are pushed against the wall with difficulties, we may do either of two things: 1) Ride with the waves, or 2) Ride against the waves.

So what do the two choices bring?

Let's begin with riding against the waves. The waves represent all those outer factors that are not within our control, such as the economy, illness, death and even those who are plagued by ignorance and spite. So then why would you want to go up against and fight these factors? Ask yourself whether certain things in your life are truly as dire as you perceive them. As Mark Twain said, "My life has been filled with terrible misfortunes—most of which never happened." Oftentimes, when you ride against such waves, there is the possibility that you will drown. The sense of poor self-esteem, a jaded sense of reality, hatred and animosity for the world, and many more experiences, can make your new life a terrible one.

I prefer spending time in the positive. Turn your surfboard 180 degrees in the other direction and now you are riding with the waves. See your life realistically. It is all about being realistic, being accepting, learning life's lessons (i.e. the dangers of being 100 percent materialistic), making the journey a sweeter one, and finally, MOVING ON!

When not job-hunting, I suggest picking up a book—any book. Exercise, meditate, and volunteer helping those in need. Spend more quality time with your children and family. They deserve it! Make some changes to your lifestyle with as little pain as possible (cutting coupons is not as bad as you think!). Contemplate the important things in your new life such as being peaceful, positive, having good health and true happiness—what else could one ask for?

So, my family and I have a different life now, a good life!

CONTAGIOUS INSPIRATION

"At birth all people are soft and yielding. At death they are hard and stiff. All green plants are tender and yielding. At death they are brittle and dry. When hard and rigid, we consort with death. When soft and flexible, we affirm greater life."—Tao Te Ching 76

WHERE ARE YOU ON YOUR LIFE JOURNEY?

MARINA TONKONOGY

Where are you on your life journey? Did you imagine yourself being where you are now ten years ago? Did you achieve the goals you set for yourself five years ago? Did you make your childhood dreams come true? I did not and I am happy that I didn't.

Since I was ten, I imagined myself becoming a world famous scientist, which never happened because that desire was being produced by my ego that craved recognition of my abilities that I never got from my parents. I was not naturally inclined to think as a scientist. I am not a left-brain-oriented thinker, but I was still pushing myself to do well in math, physics, chemistry, and biology throughout my school years and was, in fact, doing well. However, my academic achievements never made me happy. When I started college I chose computer science as a major, only to discover later that my true nature was as far from computer science as I could imagine. This helped me find my true calling—psychotherapy and psychological education.

My life has always been navigated by a force that contained great wisdom. That force, which I call my "Life Force," has put me in situations where I would learn some tough lessons. It has prevented me from being stuck in situations and relationships that ultimately were not good for me. It has also provided me with opportunities to unfold my potential and, along the way, has sent me people who were helping me become the best I could be. My Life Force has spoken to me through my feelings, instincts, intuition, visions, night dreams, and unexpected events that altered the direction my life was taking. It has prevented me from holding jobs that I hated, on one hand. On the other hand, I wanted to keep them for a variety of reasons: in order to have financial independence and stability, to get approval and recognition from others, and to fulfill the cultural image of a successful individual.

I had to struggle with two forces in me that were fighting each other and tearing me apart: my Life Force and my Fear.

My Life Force would tell me that I needed to quit certain jobs because they did not match my true self, therefore, preventing me from discovering my gifts and unfolding my potential. It would also tell me that I needed to end certain relationships because they were not healthy.

My Fear of being judged by others, being seen as a failure and as someone who does not contribute to society, as well as my own moral judgment of myself, would tell me to stick with any job regardless of how much I hated it. My Fear of not being liked or loved would tell me to tolerate things in some of my relationships with others that should not have been tolerated.

In the end, I always chose the Life Force and did what it told me no matter how scary it felt. And I never regretted it later. Making this choice has brought me to where I am right now. It has made my life as interesting, exciting, and fulfilling as it has made it full of challenges, hard-learned lessons, and necessary losses. My strong inclination to follow the guidance of my Life Force helped me let go of the desire to control things in my life and not get crushed.

So, do you find yourself where you wanted to be? Have you become the person you wanted?

CONTAGIOUS INSIGHT

Take a moment to reflect and be honest with yourself. Does your motivation come from the fear of being judged, rejected, or abandoned? Or does it come from the desire to fulfill your need for self-expression, your need to genuinely connect to other human beings and to give to the world? Make a habit to ask yourself these questions often and answer honestly. Your answers will define what direction your life will take and what you will become.

JOURNALING AS A GOAL-SETTING TOOL

DR. BARBARA SEIFERT

Goals help us to achieve. Goals help us to find purpose and to act on this purpose. We all need goals in our life. If we didn't, we would be living on autopilot. Life would get very boring. Our journeys would lead us nowhere.

When we talk about goals, we often think about big dreams we want to achieve. We think goals take a long time to achieve or they take a lot of work. But we all accomplish goals every day, whether we know it or not. Did you have a set time you woke up today? Did you plan what you wore or ate today? Did you have a time to leave for work? These are goals, even though we don't think of them as such. A goal can be defined as a point or an end place that one strives to reach. Anyone who does anything worthwhile has either consciously or unconsciously followed through on goals.

But not everyone has goals or knows how to set them. Not everyone knows how to break past barriers to make the cognitive shifts from "following" to "leading" and to reach desired levels of success. Not everyone knows how to tap into their deepest levels of insight to uncover their strengths and to recognize the answers to their "burning" questions.

One way to start this journey to get to the destination is through a very simplistic tool—journaling. Journaling is a technique that was originally taken from the therapeutic world in order to help clients identify their thoughts and feelings from a psychoanalytical perspective. But it has implications across a variety of fields. Writers and authors use it to help them document storylines, meditators use it to find inner peace, and teens use it in the form of a diary.

A journal can take several forms, such as a hardbound journal or book, or a spiral notebook, either large or small. You can use a voice recorder or the voice application on your cell phone. You can write on the computer through a word processing document or an online journal. No matter what the form, journaling gives you a platform in order to:

Set goals and action steps; record your accomplishments or blockages,

Capture your thoughts and feelings you want to hold onto or to let go,

Release anger or hurt feelings in a safe manner,

Make decisions,

Reaffirm your goodness,

Document your personal and professional growth and progress,

Release thoughts you might never tell others, such as fears or angry thoughts,

Resolve your past and give hope for your future.

If you are ready to experience the benefits of journaling, here are some guidelines:

1. Decide what format you will use to journal (i.e. book, computer, voice recorder).
2. Decide when you will write—make it a part of your day and schedule it in your calendar.
3. Practice mindfulness—you need to be open to your thoughts and emotions; meditate beforehand or call on your higher power to release your thoughts.
4. Create a flowing atmosphere—choose or create an envi-

ronment that is quiet and calming, such as nook in your bedroom, a comfy chair, or a place at the beach.

5. Free-write—allow your thoughts and feelings to flow; don't hold back and write whatever comes to mind.

6. Review—but not often; look at your journal entries every other week or longer so you can see thought patterns or themes and areas of growth.

7. Share—only if you feel able; you may want to share with someone, such as a friend or a coach, who can help you to clarify and validate your breakthroughs and successes.

CONTAGIOUS PRACTICE

Take the time and make the commitment to this journaling technique to set and reach your goals. It is easy, inexpensive, and can make all the difference to having a great life.

THE GREATEST POWER

DR. CARLOS GONZALEZ

We use it every time we get out of bed. We use it every time we go to work. We use it every day. Did you know that each and every one of us has it? What is it? It is the power to CHOOSE.

Think about this for a minute. Each day when you wake up you may feel like you have to go to work. But going to work is a choice. You could choose to not go to work and not make any money. It's obviously a better choice to go to work than not, but it's still a choice. In fact, everything in life is a choice.

Just like it's a choice to go to work, we can choose what kind of attitude we're going to have. We can choose to be happy or grumpy. We can choose to be upset or we can choose to look at problems as opportunities and learn from them. From the moment we wake up the only thing we have to do is make choices. We choose what we're going to wear, who we hang out with, what we eat, who we accept phone calls from, and the list goes on and on.

We have the power to choose so many things that affect our lives. Many doctors worldwide acknowledge that the majority of what people get sick from, and eventually die from, are lifestyle choices such as the things you choose to eat and drink every day. I have taught my kids from very early on that, for example, candy, soda, and snack foods taste good but are not good for you. A choice to eat or drink less of these the better their health will be.

I know of a three-year-old girl that started having ear pain and the pediatrician thought it was an ear infection. After a couple of months and different antibiotics, this little girl developed other symptoms. At one point she became hospitalized for eight weeks. She had CAT scans, MRIs, spinal taps, blood work, urinalysis, and was put on many different prescription drugs. Her parents incurred thirty thousand dollars in medical bills and the doctors still did not have a definite diagnosis.

The culprit was artificial sweeteners (aspartame). It was one of the main ingredients in their little girl's chewable multi-vitamin. She was also consuming sugar-free yogurt that contained artificial sweeteners. Good news, now that her parents are aware of the dangers of artificial sweeteners, you can rest assured that they will be monitoring her diet closely.

You have the greatest power in the world, to choose. Decide and commit to make healthier choices. The number-one cause of death today is no longer heart disease; it is cancer. Most cases of cancer are preventable through lifestyle choices. Most cases of heart diseases are also because of poor lifestyle choices. There's that powerful word again, CHOICES. Make it your friend, not the cause of your demise.

CONTAGIOUS ACTION

By making better-informed and well-educated lifestyle choices, you are choosing to live a healthier, happier, and longer life. Exercise your greatest power by choosing wisely!

FINDING NEW CARROTS

FAYE LEVOW

"It's never too late; that's why they invented death."
—Walter Matthau

There are many reasons to step into new directions, both in careers and in relationships. One thing is for sure, if you are unhappy, it is time for a change. It doesn't matter whose "fault" it is. You deserve to be appreciated and treated with respect assuming, of course, that you appreciate and treat others that way.

There have been several times where I was disrespected and treated badly by bosses, relatives, or significant others. I kept thinking it was something about me that needed fixing, and did much soul-searching each time to correct the problem. While the work I did on myself paid off in numerous ways, it never changed the other people.

Emotional and mental abuse made it harder to realize that it wasn't about me. We have been taught that abuse leaves physical scars, but emotional and mental abuse can be just as bad, or even worse, because it's not so obvious. When someone else pointed that out to me, I was dumbstruck as I considered all I had been through each time.

While I appeared to be a very confident person and high achiever, there were holes in that confidence. These individuals seemed to be able to find the weak spots and prey upon them.

I allowed the abuse to suck away more of my confidence, as I groped for some magic change to make them appreciate me. I hate to give up. I will go to the mat for something that is important and I refuse to let anyone's stupidity get the better of me.

It seems that the universe gives us as many opportunities as necessary to learn our fundamental lessons. Each time, I had to find my voice and confidence in order to determine that I deserved better before I could leave the situation. I always thought I had the pattern licked, and then a similar circumstance would arise again.

What did I need to know in order to attract only positive, respectful people into my life? I had to know that I deserved respect. I had to believe in myself enough to walk away from disempowering situations early, rather than hoping things would change later. I had to learn that self-preservation is different from quitting.

I am also someone who likes everyone to "get along" and have amicable separations. I like to "stay in touch" or "get back in touch" and I'm very nostalgic. There's nothing better than some good old-fashioned "wool gathering."

Sometimes, though, it's best to just let go and move on. Create new carrots. Find a new goal, a new mate, a new project, a new job, a new career. Acknowledge your lessons. Reevaluate what you really want and how you want it to show up in your life. Focus only on what you desire.

CONTAGIOUS ACTION

Stand in your power and take action to be around people who deserve your presence, where there is mutual respect. You will be happier and more productive. The difference is truly enlightening!

REGALO

To *live a life of one's own choosing*
Is not about the winning or losing
It is living each day for the thrill of the ride,
Not what awaits on the other side.

Taking the process as the essence of what you
    do
Not what happens when the effort is through
The joy of each step, a source of elation
The greatest gift of God's creation.

A poem by Karen Lyons Kalmenson

CHAPTER THREE

TURNING ENVY AND JEALOUSY INTO SOMETHING POSITIVE

Energy wasted on envy and jealousy is just that—waste!

It is 100 percent out of your control so why bother?

Good news—you have the ability to channel that energy and convert your dreams into reality.

So many people, from all demographics, are financially strapped due to envy and jealousy. In addition to the "keeping up with the Joneses" syndrome, the fashion industry and tabloids have glamorized the lives of the wealthy to such a point that people with far less means are over-spending just to expedite the good life for themselves. Many neglect to realize that all these nice things have a price and should be earned, not leveraged.

I came from a family where we were taught the value of hard work, savings, and respect for people—both the less fortunate and the more fortunate. Growing up in Fairfield County, Connecticut (a suburb of New York City), I was exposed to many motivating things including the free market system in full force. I realized at an early age that hard work can yield success but I also witnessed the growth of many "trust fund babies." For some, like myself, growing up around wealth motivated me to succeed both in my studies and in business. I find it rewarding to build something and watch it flourish whether it's detailing cars, landscaping, or launching a technology company.

For many others around me I noticed a significant amount of envy and jealousy when their peers had more than they did. The intense pressure people would put on themselves, and their families, just to keep up was, and still is, out of control. I always tell people that they should find opportunity in their contacts and peers, not envy or a gravy train of leisure. If you admire someone's success consider asking for a few minutes of their time to discuss their life—in person or on the phone. It is a well-known fact that people like talking about themselves and you may learn something invaluable to help you steer your course.

Remember, it is one thing to desire success from achievement. It's another to allow money and materialism to blur your view of reality. This can quickly cause you to lose sight of what's important in life. Quite simply, the speed of the universe has nothing to do with money so don't let life pass you by.

David

"Resist the temptation to compare yourself to others who may seem more successful. Their journey is not your journey and your journey is not theirs!"

—Michele Nuzzo, Los Angeles, California

"We all are fulfilling a purpose in this life, no purpose more important than the next. It is only together that we make the world go round."

—Dr. Colleen Georges, Piscataway, New Jersey

THE GAME OF PERFECTION

DR. COLLEEN GEORGES

"Striving for excellence motivates you; striving for perfection is demoralizing."

—Harriet Braiker

We often compare others to ourselves. This is part of being human, but this concept can sometimes evolve into something that is too heavily focused on. This can lead to difficulty in relationships and negative attitudes about people and life. Feeling or speaking negatively about others is simply a mechanism to help us feel better about ourselves. When we think someone else is terrible, we believe consequently that we are better than them. But the more we allow ourselves to indulge in these feelings, the harder it becomes to see what is positive in others. And when we have trouble seeing the good in others, it gets harder to feel good about ourselves. This affects the general quality of our lives.

We all are flawed people. We should not cast judgment on the flaws in others, when we too have our own flaws. Instead, we should try to spend more time paying attention to the good in those we encounter. When we love others, we feel better. We begin to show ourselves the same kindness, focusing less on our own flaws. Our relationships flourish and our self-concepts improve.

None of us are perfect. The reality is, perfect has no actual definition. Perfect is a subjective, abstract standard that individuals create for themselves to live up to. And something that is created by an individual can also be changed by that individual. Thus, if we were ever to come close to our standard, we always possess the ability to raise the bar. This is something we do frequently. Have you ever noticed that when you reach one of your goals, you usually start looking to achieve more? It's hard for us to allow ourselves to be satisfied. We often forget that we are just human.

We make mistakes, sometimes we fail, and we are not the best at everything we do. And that's okay. A mistake does not signify the end of our journey. We must accept it, get up, dust ourselves off, and start again. When we are in a situation where we know we are wrong, we should admit it to ourselves, as well as to others, in order to learn from the experience. It is a mix of our strengths and our limitations that make us the unique people we all are.

Some of us will never be mathematicians or professional athletes. Others will excel in these areas. But we all are fulfilling a purpose in this life, no purpose more important than the next. It is only together that we make the world go round.

CONTAGIOUS PRACTICE

Don't waste time and energy comparing yourself to others. Make a practice of recognizing your strengths, forgiving your limitations, and readily extending the same courtesy to all those you encounter.

ONLY YOU SUFFER WHEN YOU ENVY OTHERS

ADAM FISHEL

There are going to be bad days. You may wake up in a bad mood; you may hear something that sets you off...who knows. This is a good thing because if we didn't have bad days, we would not appreciate the good ones, as they would be impossible to distinguish.

I remember a day when I attended a classic car show in Monterey, California, where I was living at the time. It was called a "Concourse" which generally includes cars from all over the world and from different eras. When I left the show I was in a funk because, due to financial constraints, I could not own a classic car or participate in an event like this. Those feelings brought me down especially due to the fact that I had been in a financial hole for ten-plus years with no end in sight. Nevertheless, it occurred to me (again) that I was working hard and trying to manage my finances. I knew my diligence and a strong work ethic would ultimately yield the financial goal I desired. And this would give me the opportunity to partake in such hobbies.

I remember another day when envy got the best of me. It was one of those days when I was fighting bill collectors. Sales were down, the economy was in the toilet, and we were cutting checks daily to pay interest just to remain afloat. I was pretty bummed out, constantly wondering how I could keep the business alive, pay the mortgage, pay employees, save for college tuition, and meet the next set of credit card bills and loan payments. It was nauseating every time someone said, "You should appreciate your life, there are so many people that have it worse than you." Or, "Life is short, money is not everything. At least you have your health." As much as I cringed, those sayings were very true.

When I thought the day could not get any worse, I received a call from a good friend. He was in a dilemma because he could not decide where to take his family on vacation with his recent Wall Street bonus. I did everything I could to not snap at his superficial quandary. The envy was boiling throughout my system, but it was my problem that I needed to get past, not his. In addition to being at rock bottom, my daughter wanted to attend a private college the following year instead of the local state school. Her grades and hard work earned her the ability to attend any school she wanted but, quite frankly, this was not financially possible for us.

It was difficult to watch my wealthy friends be more successful, earning enough so that their wives did not have to work, or at least not work as hard as mine. My wife was working seven days per week and at least twelve to eighteen hours per day earning very little. When she would leave her day job, she would clean people's condos in between tenants. All of this helped us survive, but it was a blow to my manhood.

Shortly after this horrible bout of jealousy and feeling sorry for myself I redirected my angst toward the future. My only other choice was to fall deeper into depression, which I couldn't let happen. The concept of being financially independent again and providing a wonderful life for my family was a positive step and very motivating. It literally made me want to run to the office and to be productive every day. I did my best to explore new markets, secure new clients, and create new sources of revenue. As I type this story, I have invested in several foreclosed properties and have created a wonderful stream of rental income. I have set my sights on several other properties and lined up investors as well. It finally seems to be coming together.

Why waste your energy on such negative things that are out of your control? Why not dream of a wonderful life for you and your family? Focusing on other people's success with envy is pointless and stressful. There is nothing good that can come from envy and jealousy—nothing!

CONTAGIOUS COMMITMENT

Success starts at some point. That starting point is risk followed by hard work, optimism, and confidence regardless of whether it's you, a rich uncle, or a grandparent! Be the catalyst of your success.

THE BIKE FROM HELL

LEE SHILO

We had not been in Victoria long after moving away from my abusive father. My mother was only getting part-time work at the General Hospital. At the same time, I really wanted a bicycle like all the other children. I was constantly being made fun of for not having one. As everyone can remember, being teased was the worst thing that could possibly happen to a child.

Money was tight and my mother shopped around for weeks trying to find a good deal on a cheap, used bicycle. I guess she could not take my whining any longer and finally bought the cheapest bike she could find. Okay, now most of you are thinking a normal, typical bike, right? Wrong, because this is where it gets interesting! This was a fold-up bicycle. The front tire folded back to the left, and the back tire folded to the right, just like an accordion.

The handlebars were a facsimile of the banana bar-type on normal bikes but much more stupid looking and smaller. They came out from the front prongs for easy storage and there was nothing to keep them tight when they were in. Each tire had a tightening lever to keep them from buckling once they were deployed. Then, it was a simple matter of just shoving the handlebars in and away you go.

I can't really say I was now popular, but I was certainly noticeable to the other kids. At that time I did not care, I had a bike to ride like everyone else and that was all that mattered to me. I enjoyed my bike, and not getting teased, right to the end of summer.

It was in the last good days of that summer when I was riding my bicycle back home. We lived three houses away from a busy intersection. I was making a left-hand turn at the traffic light when both tightening levers from the wheels decided to suddenly loosen. Trying to quickly adjust and regain my balance, I pulled up hard on the handlebars. And you guessed it—they came right out in my hands! Cars came to a screeching halt, horns began to blast from every direction, and obscenities were being hurled at me as if they were supposed to help me get out of the way sooner.

So there I was, in the center of the intersection, with my legs trapped between the folding wheels and the handlebars flailing in my hands. I was doing a balancing act trying not to fall over. I eventually managed to extricate myself from the evil clutches of my bike and hobbled to the side of the curb with the bike pieces in my hands. I would like to point out that no one actually left their car to try and help me. I curse them to this day! Once I got the pieces home I threw them with disgust into the garbage and explained to my poor, hard-working mother why I was not going to ride the bicycle anymore. Thank goodness she understood and I never again complained about not having a bicycle.

Since this episode took place, I resorted to walking and jogging everywhere. Consequently, I became one of the best track and field runners in my school. My popularity grew and no one made fun of me anymore for not having a bicycle!

CONTAGIOUS EFFECT

You'll be pleasantly surprised to know that other people probably envy something about your life as well.

ENVY TO GRATITUDE

SUSAN YOUNG

I was always envious of people who had great figures and were successful in life. Everything seemed to come easy for them, yet I was always struggling to keep up, and at times, I had given up on my dreams. For years, I never enjoyed eating because I was always thinking about how it would affect my weight. I ate to live, but I did not feel grateful for the food. As I ate all I could think was, "This will make me fat."

I was working with a health coach to improve my diet hoping to lose weight. She said something that totally changed how I looked at food. She said there is a physical component of every emotional feeling in your body, and when you have negative feelings while you are eating, it affects how your body digests food. She said you should always be in a place of peace and gratitude when you eat. Food should be a source of nourishment, not punishment to your body. She also encouraged me to eat food that was closer to nature and less refined because too much sugar prevents you from thinking clearly and making good decisions.

At the time, I was eating too much sugar and butter. I began making smarter food choices and I would consciously feel grateful for the food I was eating. I would also be aware of how I felt while eating. I no longer ate unconsciously or felt bad because I overate. That was a vicious cycle that ate away at my self-worth. I replaced those feelings, and food now represents power not punishment.

Envy is a negative emotion, and gratitude is a positive emotion. By thinking of food as nourishment and being grateful, it gave me the energy to make better decisions in my life. Then I got to thinking: if this works in my diet, maybe it will work for other areas of my life.

I began applying the same principles to my business (which is helping people choose the right profession). I realized the way I was approaching my business did not feel right. I remembered I had taken an assessment test years ago, but I did not understand what it said about my personality. I found a coach who was able to explain what the assessment said about me. The lightbulb went on when he gave me his insights, which made it clear why I was struggling with my business. I was going against my natural tendencies. My personality is intuitive, and I needed to create systems from actually interviewing people. That made total sense to me, because at the time I knew what I was doing was not working. I shifted my approach and one person after another allowed me to interview him or her. When people know you have a greater purpose for what you are doing, they are inspired to help you with your dreams.

This shift in focus from envy to gratitude helped me develop a system that will in turn help others. What do you want to accomplish? Instead of being jealous and envious, start from a place of gratitude in the area you most want to grow and develop. Find something to be grateful for and look for ways other people can help and support your dreams. That is how I turned envy into gratitude—and you can too.

The four steps to turn envy into gratitude: 1. Focus on an area of your life you desire to grow. 2. List all the things you are grateful for in that area. 3. Look for ways to grow your gratitude by building on what you already have. 4. Get a clear grasp on gratitude. Being grateful is not the same as being content. Content means you have no desire to grow. Gratitude is about appreciating and being open to receive.

Envy and jealousy create resentment and close your heart. Gratitude attracts appreciation and opens your heart.

Having a jealous heart tells the universe that you need what someone else has in order to be happy. Would you be inspired to give to someone like that? Think of the people you enjoy giving to the most. Are they the ones who say "thank you" or are they the ones who are satisfied by nothing and always want more from you? They are the people who are positive, happy, and inspire you to want to give to them.

Jealousy will eat you alive if you let it. When your focus is on the external world, you are always waiting for something to fill the void. It is like trying to put a band-aid on a cut that is on the inside. You know something is hurting but you do not see the wound, you only feel it. The wound is the condition of your ungrateful heart, which can never be satisfied.

Be grateful for what you have, look for opportunities to grow from a place of gratitude, and your cup will soon overflow with a lifetime of love and blessings.

CONTAGIOUS PRACTICE

Wish blessings on those you once envied and your life will be blessed too.

ON ATTACHMENT AND AVERSION

ELLEN KRATKA

Recently I have been playing with the realization that attachment and aversion are one and the same. It follows that both tendencies can be overcome or "healed" the same way. In the case of the twin demons of envy and jealousy this is quite transparent, so let us explore from that vantage point. First, some definitions...

In the case of jealousy, according to Wikipedia, "We're holding onto (guarding) someone or something that we feel might be taken away from us." So there's both an attachment to the object of jealousy and an aversion to the idea of losing them (or perhaps to the person we believe will take our love object away). Envy, on the other hand, is a desire for something we believe we don't have. In this case, the attachment is to the idea of something that has not yet been experienced and the aversion is to the current state of perceived lack. So we can already see that attachment and aversion tend to move in the same circles, kind of like two sides of the same coin.

How can we make jealousy and envy unnecessary? To answer this question I need to introduce a few spiritual precepts. These are common to many spiritual traditions and I have found them to be life changing when taken to heart and applied to real life.

Precept number 1: The outer world mirrors the inner. It is always, and I mean always, the case that whatever you choose to notice, engage with, react to, etc., reflects your beliefs, inner conflicts, and unlearned life lessons, which manifest as energy blockages and all have their life in the inner realm.

Precept number 2: Everything you believe you need is already contained within your Self, waiting to be discovered and utilized. This is based on the idea that your Self, or your energetic and spiritual being, is actually limitless, and can access all that exists in the universe, meaning all energies, information, and qualities, which is why I've capitalized it.

Precept number 3: You have an eternal Soul, or unique essence, that has chosen your relationships with intentionality, to help you return to an experience of wholeness, otherwise known as Divinity. So it makes sense that you would notice anything that contrasts with that and comprises the illusion of separation—in the form of fragmentation, neediness, and lack—within those relationships.

From these precepts it follows that whatever quality you envy in someone else is reflecting back to you a part of yourself you have denied. In psychotherapeutic circles this is often referred to as the "Shadow." If I envy someone's looks I am denying my own beauty. If I envy their possessions I'm denying my own abundance, my ability to attract or create whatever I truly desire. Many spiritual traditions speak of a "Soul"—the eternal essence of who you are. One of the ways the Soul speaks to you is by making you aware of your Shadow, thereby revealing to you a piece of the wholeness that you have yet to own or claim. Once again, your Soul is giving you the opportunity to create wholeness out of suffering. Now we can connect the dots and talk about the healing process.

Attachment and aversion are both a resistance to, and judgment of, what is. Both, in the case of jealousy and envy, feel lousy and cause untold amounts of suffering. But when the resistance is released, the suffering ends, your wholeness and all the bounty it contains is realized, and the energy required to fuel creation and attraction in any area of life, including and especially relationships, flows freely and abundantly. This feels great.

To attain this amazing shift only requires a full, unconditional acceptance of what is, right here and right now. I know you're thinking: "Only? That's easy for her to say!" But while making this shift may seem impossible, it is actually quite simple. It's a natural ability we've always had, but that has been acculturated out of us. And to experience it, here's something you can do right now: Think about something you're either holding on to or running away from. This could be an object of envy, jealousy, or some other emotion. Drop into an awareness of how that feels in your body. You are now in touch with the energetic effects of your emotion. See if you can locate the energy mass. Now imagine it to be a block of ice. If you were to bring some warm air to that block it would start to melt. Do that now with your intention; just melt enough of the block's edges to learn where the energy wants to go. All energy wants to move, and will if allowed to. Put another way, your energetic self knows how to handle energy so it doesn't remain stuck and create physical or emotional problems.

Locate the chosen direction of movement; then keep softening the block and letting it flow until it moves completely through and out of your energy field. The key is to keep your attention on the flow. Notice both the sensation of flow and how you feel overall after you have completed the process. This is the feeling of total acceptance of what is; in this moment you're experiencing wholeness. You've also just reawakened an ability you may not have used in decades (or perhaps ever).

CONTAGIOUS PRACTICE

Focus on any envy or jealousy you have been festering.
Imagine it melting away like a block of ice; its energy
being used in a better way to motivate you to succeed
in the area(s) you desire.

WHOSE LIFE IS IT ANYHOW?

LISBETH CALANDRINO

When I think of envy and jealousy I'm reminded of growing up on a lake in a small town in upstate New York. The winter people were "country people," hard working and simple. Many of them were craftsmen and earned their living doing odd jobs as handymen, house cleaners, or fishermen. The summer people were well educated and from the New York City area. Thus began the conflicts within my personality and goals. Obviously I was the country kid caught between "a rock and a hard place." Who was I and who would I become? My own values began to clash with other people whom I barely knew but who would influence me forever.

At the time I didn't realize that I was going through any conflict, I was just going through life wondering how I might acquire the things I wanted. There was no conflict in my parents' eyes: the people from the city were a way to earn a living—plain and simple. It was at this point my conflicting beliefs turned into envy. I started my never-ending quest for something I didn't have.

For the next thirty years the conflict became my focus. I thought happiness was measured by success. Could it be I was motivated by envy? I wanted what other people had. Why did I think what others had would make me happier? I don't know about you, but I never questioned my motivations. Wanting to go to college, to succeed and to start my own business didn't seem to be bad goals, but for a woman growing up in the 1940s it was somewhat different.

I loved my life and my quest for success but there was something wrong. No matter what I gained or earned I never felt satisfied or happy. It seemed like there was never enough. The harder I worked the more desperate I felt.

It has been ten years since I began to wonder about my motivations. There were times when I wouldn't finish important tasks or grew tired of things that didn't produce quick results. Success would come and go but I hadn't figured out the secret. Did I need to work harder or did I need to get smarter? I continued to go to school and to look for more opportunity. Instead of becoming more satisfied, I was becoming cynical, unsatisfied, and tired. I was worn out with my life and my choices.

By this time I was a business coach: I saw people (mostly men) having what was called a "midlife crisis." Their symptoms included leaving their families, wanting to sell their business, or not being able to sleep. After talking to hundreds of business owners I realized that these people were running away from themselves, a self they didn't know. It was a gnawing feeling, a new self that wanted to fish instead of work, a self that had fallen in love with a friend's wife. As I watched and listened I began to ask the question—why? People who were considered successful were throwing it all away; what was spurring them to their new lives? Was it a new life they wanted or to sabotage their existing lives?

I wondered how many people live by their real values, fabricated values, or a combination of both. I was beginning to doubt myself. I was suffering from the same thoughts and concerns of the business owners I had interviewed. It was becoming more evident that I was living the same conflicted life. What should I do next?

It was time to begin the search for the real me, the real me who didn't need to be jealous, and instead focus on my own skills. Could I put the same effort into finding myself as I had put into chasing success and happiness? What would happen to me if I were no longer obsessed with the old me? My health was starting to suffer and the stress was beginning to take its toll. Was I ready for this?

I was going back to my roots and began to explore my family and their values. My dad was successful with a limited education, had lots of friends, and enjoyed his life. I thought that my drive had come from the city folks I wanted to emulate. My true drive had come from my family, who wanted me to succeed and to be myself. My dad would often say, "Spend time with Stuart" (one of the city folks). I realize now he was sharing what he thought was important—new ideas, new people, and new opportunities.

As I review my life I realize how lucky I've been. I was introduced to two new worlds, worlds that I had thought were conflicting. They weren't conflicting; they shared common values. Work hard, be inquisitive, and continue to learn. I took advantage of the opportunities, went to college, and took business risks. I was making choices, my own choices.

Is success more introspective? I'm not sure, but I will do it from my safe place on a new lake. A lake that looks exactly like the one from years ago when, what I thought was envy and jealousy, was just a simple motivating force that allowed me to grow and learn.

CONTAGIOUS INSPIRATION

Allow the success of others to be your motivator. However, don't look past yourself, your family, and your peers as sources of inspiration regardless of their level of success. You don't have to be a billionaire to motivate others.

ENVY BUILDS A SWEET REALITY

PAULA SNYDER

Dreaming...

As a little girl I envied everyone. I wanted to be blonde instead of dark haired, have straight hair instead of curls, be popular and not a "geek." I wanted a beautiful smile and not the buckteeth resulting from early thumb-sucking. And I wanted to see with two eyes, not the "four eyes" of wearing thick glasses. In real life, though I loved to sing, I didn't command attention for it. I envied those who did.

Competing...

In my teenage years we could turn dreams into reality with simple cosmetic "fixes." Choosing between various procedures and enhancements, I opted for braces, hair straightening, and contact lenses. Then I was able to compete in a higher social position. Though in my mind I was still "me" when the braces came off, with my new hairdo I became someone different to those at school. Popular girls who never gave me the time of day were suddenly my friends. Boys who never had taken a second look were suddenly enamored. I forgot where I came from and fooled myself into believing I was someone else, the dream from childhood. Though I got a lot of attention, I was still envious of what others had. The changes did not get me more applause when I sang, or bring me the heart of the boy I thought I loved. Envy turned me to competition. It was still envy.

Accepting...

I thought I was very wise as a young adult. Thinking I'd begun to accept myself, I tried to turn every flaw into a positive self-promotion. My envies and jealousies were still hiding in there, but I kept an open mind. I tried to be understanding of those who made me jealous. "Why couldn't my guy love two women?" I thought during the years of "free love." I even tried to explain this once to the "other woman" (or maybe I was the "other woman"). She wanted her guy and made no bones about it. I wanted him too, but rationalized that there was room for the two of us. Who wouldn't want such an accepting, understanding woman? I was just fooling myself. Deep down, I really wanted someone to love only me and I was envious of those who had that. My envy took me on a negative and self-destructive path. I did whatever I wanted to surpass my feelings of envy and jealousy. Many a great song came out of my shenanigans, but I was still the same "geek" inside. I still envied those who had what they wanted when I couldn't find my own way.

Realizing...

Now I am all grown up. Occasionally I am struck with some envious feelings but along the way I realized something: envy and jealousy have nothing to do with anyone else. They simply stemmed from my own insecurities. I realized some things were just not meant to be. All I had wanted was to earn acceptance and to feel loved, but I had to love myself first before anything else would work out. My actions hadn't given me the self-acceptance and the love I needed. Now, when those envious feelings briefly appear, I can honestly look within myself and realize I have choices. I can choose to get better at something, or to learn something new. I can recognize and applaud others in their accomplishments instead of feeling lack in my own. I can realize who I am, count my blessings and know that I have the power to be an even better me if I so choose.

Looking in the mirror, I can see the beauty in my clear smooth skin, naturally curly brown hair, deep blue-green eyes, sultry smile, and the youth that lives in my mind. When the "envies" hit, I take a look within and feel the calm peace of a wiser age. I take my heart, write it into another song, feel the joy, and share it with others.

CONTAGIOUS ACTION

When you feel a little envy, write song lyrics listing all the things that make you "you." Start off with your name and go from there. You will be amazed at what flows!

CLARITY PAVES THE WAY

SCOTT DUNCAN

Being able to remove envy from my life was a key learning point that has helped me to continue to grow and develop. I chose to recognize that if I wanted "things," then it was up to me to get them. This did not come without challenges. In fact, one of the lowest times in my life came about by how angry and envious I felt toward a few individuals in the business world who had undercut me. They used all of their efforts for personal gain and took advantage of many people, including me, who had worked hard to climb the ladder.

One day my wife asked, "When are you going to get over it?" This question made me realize that I was engrossing myself in anger and jealousy without even knowing it. I was disappointed for being taken a loan of by past business associates while also feeling that they had gained from my efforts ("taken a loan of" is a common Scottish phrase that means "being taken advantage of"). Once I realized that I was in control of my own feelings and emotions, and that it was not the fault of others, I was able to take action toward a better future. I focused on the reasons why I wanted a better life for myself and for the people I love. This gave me clarity to move on.

Moving from a feeling of distressing envy and jealousy to a feeling of appreciation and focused direction was nothing short of transformational for me. I was able to take back control of my life and the direction of my own destiny. It was a freeing experience that you too can participate in if you choose to let go and look for the good in your life. Never give up on your hopes and dreams and, if you get angry or jealous, make an effort to make those goals clear in your mind again.

CONTAGIOUS INSIGHT

If you accept where you are in life today, and keep driving hard toward your dreams, nothing will knock you off—not even envy or jealousy.

USE IT FOR MOTIVATION

BRENDA SUTTON JONES

Sometimes life is full of surprises. Shortly after entering the workforce, I took a job with a marketing company in Raleigh, NC, expecting to get my feet wet in sales and hopefully learn a bit about marketing. Little did I know that my enthusiasm for people and my desire to help clients become successful would make me a natural sales professional, and that I would end up being a top producer in the company. What started out as a job quickly turned into a career. The company grew bigger each year and so did my compensation.

After nine successful years, suddenly the company was sold and things quickly changed. At first, the change in ownership was shocking because I had no idea that the owner I worked for had any intention of selling her thriving business. Then, there was the inevitable change of culture that resulted from a small company staffed by women being bought by a larger company, one with thirty-nine men on staff and just one female salesperson—little ol' me! But, after nine years in the business, I was confident in my skills so I figured there was little to worry about.

Within the first week of new ownership, the CEO came to visit me in our Raleigh office. He tossed me a check for $93,000 and said, "You are making a whole lot of money."

I replied, "Yes, and it's a good thing, because the more I earn, the more the company earns."

Evidently, he saw things a bit differently. I was told that I needed to give up some of my account base to the other sales reps, including one of my lucrative pharmaceutical accounts, which I had developed. Then I was told that it was unfair for me to earn so much when most of the sales guys were earning significantly less.

As you might imagine, this did not sit well with me. In all the time I worked for the company as an independent contractor, I had to earn my way into every account that I serviced. None were given to me. Nevertheless, I realized that I needed to make concessions in order to please the new boss. I acquiesced and gave up many of my accounts, including a number of profitable Fortune 500 clients, including GTE, IBM, and Alcatel. However, I refused to give up the one pharmaceutical client he requested, in particular because of how hard I worked to develop the relationship. Additionally, I knew that in handing over the account, my client would feel abandoned and the company would likely not reap the same level of loyalty or volume of business from this client.

One month later, I came to work and learned that the new company had changed the lock on my door and taken ownership of all my files—after nine years. Every current and past order was now locked away. I felt dejected for a couple of days.

On the third day after being locked out, I opened my own business. I called on every account, worked around the clock, and did everything I could to ensure that my clients had what they needed—just as I always had. Each of the suppliers I had worked with over the past nine years extended me a full line of credit, and the clients I had serviced on behalf of the company were quickly becoming my own clients.

As it turned out, the separation was just what I needed. In December 2010, my marketing company celebrated its twenty-year anniversary. From time to time I think about that CEO and how much I owe him for giving me the push I needed to start my own company. I believe that his actions were motivated primarily by jealousy and envy, which has led me to conclude the following: 1. Jealousy is a destructive emotion, particularly for those who harbor it; and 2. Envy is a natural feeling that can be positive if it's used for motivation.

CONTAGIOUS INSIGHT

Jealousy and envy are emotions of the past or present—they are powerless among people who are moving toward the future.

NV

Envy is a wicked state
To which I would
Prefer not to relate.

There is always someone
Smarter, younger, and
More appealing to the eye
Fussing over this?
Why bother to try.

All that wasted thought
On what you feel you lack
Life is far too short
For that kind of flak.

Learn to like yourself
For the imperfections
You possess
They are what make you
And a glorious part of
Life's mess!

A poem by Karen Lyons Kalmenson

CHAPTER FOUR

RELATIONSHIPS

Understand, respect, and embrace other people's uniqueness. That is the foundation of any relationship—spouses, significant others, family, friends, etc.

We are not the same and those differences are why relationships work.

Spicing up a relationship with compromise!

In divorce, share optimism with each other, children, and yourself. Divorce is not taboo and can be a manageable, and even a pleasurable experience if you let it.

So your significant other is a little disorganized and doesn't mind clutter. Meanwhile you're a neat freak and get aggravated every time you walk by his or her closet or car. But imagine a day when you are stressed out about something and your significant other reminds you that it will all work out and that you are doing everything you can. This is an example of how people can be different but also complementary.

There is an amazing balance between two people that care about each other regardless of his or her traits and habits. Of course there can be personalities that conflict but that is usually discovered early and is a main reason why people experience different relationships before settling down.

My wife, while normally a positive person as well, can sometimes get caught up in the stress of running her business. She manages a team, monitors marketing efforts, follows ever-changing compliance laws, tracks payroll, etc. This multitasking brings her stress quite often. However, I tend to point out the optimistic side of her efforts to help put things in perspective. Conversely, I sometimes have major decisions to make and tend to look beyond what's right in front of me. My wife frequently reminds me of this. As a result, I call her my "voice of reason."

There are many ways relationships can work and there are plenty of professionals, books, and other publications that address the topic. Our goal here is to present optimistic viewpoints of how two different people can get along while embracing what makes them unique from each other.

Divorce is another topic within this chapter. While divorce

can be a difficult thing for couples and their families, it can also serve as a means for making people stronger and less dependent on others. In many cases that lead up to divorce, especially with children involved, living in that environment can be unhealthy. Fighting, resentment, and negativity serve no one well. Making that divorce decision can alleviate the tension and allow people to start working on their next chapter. I was divorced, and that decision removed the tension in our relationship. It allowed us to move on with our lives while remaining friends. Prior to that decision it was a difficult environment to be in—for both of us.

The excitement of change and new beginnings can bring families together and give them a new life to look forward to. Simply look at the benefits and let them happen. No need to focus on the negative.

David

"If you want to meet 'the one,' become 'the one.' How you feel about yourself and how you allow others to treat you is the basis of all relationships in life. Value what you have to offer and realize you are special."

—Susan Young, Sayville, New York

"One day I had a huge wake-up call when one of my friends said to me, 'If you crumble so will your children.' That was all I needed to hear. From that day forward I realized that I had to take care of myself and get the support I needed in order to be the best I could for my children as well as for myself. Learning the necessary skills turned my life around, but first I had to realize that it started with me."

—Joanie Winberg, Lakeville, Massachusetts

"Divorce is an unfortunate process that many people face. Once the grieving is over and you are able to breathe again, it can be a great opportunity as well. There's a moment when you realize that you have survived, emerged intact, and have strength you didn't know you had. Don't fight it, enjoy it—there is a certain freedom that happens in the process."

—Kerry Moeykens, Covington, Kentucky

READY TO LEARN THE FIVE SECRETS OF TRUE LOVE?

JED DIAMOND

I have been counseling men and women for the last forty-four years. There are many concerns people bring but most of them relate to their desire to have a relationship where they can feel loved and where they can share their love. As someone who has been married three times (third time was definitely the charm for Carlin and me), I'm always looking for ways to improve our relationship and to share our insights with others. Here's what I'm learning these days.

Thich Nhat Hanh is a Vietnamese Zen Buddhist monk and internationally known author, poet, scholar, and peace activist who was nominated for the Nobel Peace Prize by Martin Luther King, Jr. I've always appreciated his perspectives on meditation and life. When I recently found a small volume titled *True Love: A Practice for Awakening the Heart*, I was sure I'd uncovered a gem. His words, thoughts, and feelings have enriched my understanding and practice of love. There are five simple practices that we can all put into effect if we want more love in our lives.

MAKE TIME FOR LOVE

This may seem obvious, but in our busy, fast-paced lives, love often gets shortchanged. Hanh asks us, "Do you have enough time to love? Can you make sure that in your everyday life you make the time that is needed to share your love?" We do not have much time together, he reminds us. We are too busy. In the morning while eating breakfast, we do not look at the person we love, we do not have enough time for it. We eat very quickly while thinking about other things, and sometimes we even hold a newspaper that hides the face of the person we love.

In the evening when we come home, we are too tired to be able to look at the person we love. We get lost in the TV or in other activities. We must make time for love. We must bring about a revolution, says Hanh, in our way of living our everyday lives, because our happiness, our very lives, depend upon it.

BE THERE FOR THE ONE YOU LOVE

Hanh asks us, if we are not there, how can we love? To be there for someone we love means we must first be present to ourselves. We must take a deep breath and be here in the moment. We must let our thoughts and worries of the past and the future be stilled. We breathe and we are here. Hanh suggests a simple practice of mindful breathing: "Breathing— I know that I am breathing in; breathing—I know that I am breathing out." If we do this simple practice with a little concentration, he reminds us, we can begin to still our restless minds and to be present to ourselves and the person we love.

Once we are present, we can recite a simple mantra: "Dear one, I am here for you." Try it today. You'll be surprised at how good you feel and how wonderful the person you care about will feel. "Dear one, I am here for you."

RECOGNIZE THE PRESENCE OF THE OTHER

The greatest gift we can give or receive is to totally recognize and appreciate the being of another. I remember having a friend in college. Her name was Jeannie and she had an incredible ability to make a person feel like they were special. Whenever you saw Jeannie, she always made you feel that you were wonderful. Being in her presence made you feel like you were loved, and not because you did anything. She just loved you because you were you. Hanh says to love is to be; to be loved is to be recognized by the other. If you love someone but you continue to ignore his or her presence, it is not true love.

How many times has your loved one come into the room, but you were too busy to fully acknowledge them? Hanh says, perhaps your intention is not to ignore this person, but the way you act, look, and speak does not manifest the desire to recognize the presence of the other. Appreciate the person you love several times a day. Someday they won't be there. Live every day as if you would never see the person you loved again.

Try this mantra: "Dear one, I know that you are there and it makes me very happy." Hanh reminds us, this is real meditation. In this meditation, all at once there is love, compassion, joy, and freedom—the four constituents of the true love of which the Buddha speaks. "Dear one, I know that you are there and it makes me very happy."

REACH OUT TO YOUR LOVED ONE WHEN THEY ARE SUFFERING

It is not easy being alive on the planet these days. We are living in difficult times. There is much stress and suffering. We are often tuned out to the suffering of the person we love the most. When you are living mindfully, Hanh says, you know what is happening around you. You are attuned to the suffering of your loved one in the same way a mother or father is attuned to the suffering of their child.

When you are tuned in with your partner, you know when they are in pain. You can be there for them. Your presence can mean more than any gift imaginable.

Say this mantra: "Dear one, I know that you are suffering, that is why I am here for you." When we are suffering, more than anything else, we need to feel the presence of the person we love. They don't have to do anything or fix anything. They just have to recognize our suffering and be there for us. "Dear one, I know that you are suffering and that is why I am here for you."

LET GO OF YOUR PRIDE

This is the most difficult thing to do for most of us. Often when we ourselves feel hurt, we refuse to tell the other person that we are suffering out of pride. We begin to feel cut off and alone and we become resentful that our partner doesn't see our hurt and come to our aid. Many times I have felt, "Why should I reach out for Carlin? I'm the one who is hurt. She should reach out to me." Too many times, I've gone to bed feeling lonely and sad because my pride kept me from reaching out.

Our feelings of being wronged can cause us to withdraw. Our withdrawal can be seen by our partner as an indication that we don't care about them. They then become angry or withdraw themselves. Too many times, couples begin a downward spiral of hurt and betrayal until the relationship falls apart under the weight of pain and suffering. Don't let this happen to you. Let go of your pride.

Try this mantra: "Dear one, I am suffering so much, help me please." Don't suffer in silence. Let your partner know of your pain. Reach out. This always reminds me of the lines from the song "Desperado" by the Eagles, "You better let somebody love you. You better let somebody love you. You better let somebody love you...before it's too late."

CONTAGIOUS ACTION

Five simple practices offered by Thich Nhat Hanh: Make time for love. Be there for the one you love. Recognize the presence of the other. Reach out to your loved one when they are suffering. Let go of your pride.

ACCIDENTS HAPPEN

CHARLENE WALKER

My life changed forever on November 4, 1994. As I left for work at a convenience store that morning, my husband, Paul, walked me out to the car. We were having another argument. As I got into the car Paul told me he wanted a divorce. I started the car and replied for him to go ahead. I thought the kids and I could live without him.

At six p.m. that day my mother called to tell me that Paul was in an accident on his motorcycle. She said that I needed to get to the hospital as soon as possible. When I got there my sister and her husband met me at the door. They told me it was bad and the doctor needed to see me right away. The nurse took me to the trauma room where my Paul was lying on a stretcher with tubes in him. As I walked into the room I could see blood-soaked clothes on the floor. I walked over to my husband and looked down at him. He was pale and dazed. The trauma doctor came over to talk to me. He needed me to sign papers right away so they could operate. He had lost a lot of blood and his left leg was in very bad shape. As they were wheeling Paul to the operating room he took my hand and said, "Don't let them take my leg."

The next nineteen hours were the longest in my life. The orthopedic surgeons took turns operating along with the vascular plastic surgeon. I sat in the waiting room, I walked the halls, I went outside to have a cigarette, and I went to the chapel to pray. For the two years prior, I was mad at God for the loss of my father and the heart surgery he put my son through. I got down on my knees and asked God to forgive me for blaming him. I prayed for Paul to live because I knew I loved him and now realized I couldn't live without him. Our children needed him and whatever was wrong in our life we could work out. I prayed all night long. Those prayers were met. Paul lived but knew he had a long road ahead of him.

Paul was in and out of surgeries, induced comas, and all types of procedures for four years in an attempt to save his leg. Unfortunately, by December 1998, they had to amputate. In addition, we lost our home and had to claim bankruptcy because the medical bills were over three million dollars. We rented a house with the option to buy. At the end of the lease our son gave us the money for the down payment.

Through it all, we grew stronger and closer as a family. It also made our youngest son develop an appreciation for emergency medicine (and he is now a paramedic!). As a matter of fact, during the accident the paramedics said that Paul should have died in the street but his focus on his sons kept him talking and alive.

Paul has been amputated for twelve years now. He struggles with balance. He can no longer run or ride a bike. But he tells me daily that he would not change a thing because it gave him back our family. He went through a tragedy but feels it was a blessing instead.

We have been married for thirty-four years now and I would not change a thing. We still have many things to get through, like our son in Afghanistan, but with each other and our strength in God, we will get through them.

CONTAGIOUS PRACTICE

When you look at a disagreement you have with a friend or loved one, most of the time it's over something minor. Write down what caused it and then write down what you think it will take to rectify. By the time you are done writing, you will realize how trivial it is in the grand scheme of life.

UNDERSTANDING THE ENDING OF YOUR RELATIONSHIP

LAURIE MARTIN

The ending of a relationship, whether it's a friendship or love, doesn't mean it was a mistake, doesn't mean it has to be labeled as a bad situation. Not all relationships are forever and the reason is because we come together with people to learn about ourselves. Each of us has our own experience learning about love, learning about how to express our truth, respecting ourselves, connecting deeper to who we are, learning how we give our power away, and learning what empowers us and what doesn't work for us.

We are continually fine-tuning and going into deeper parts of ourselves. When our lesson is over with a particular person, we can be grateful for the exchange, for the experience, and send them away with love and gratitude.

Many of us have a difficult time letting go of the familiar because we are afraid of the unknown and we start thinking the worst. The sooner we can switch from focusing on what we don't have anymore to what we've learned, we can walk away nurturing the beautiful lessons we had the courage to experience.

When that relationship is over, sit quietly and contemplate:

1. How did you show up in this relationship in a way that was different than in others?
2. What are you proud of about yourself?
3. What did you learn about yourself from this relationship and

the type of people you want to be around?

4. What pattern or life-changing awareness have you had about yourself through this relationship?

5. What fears were triggered?

CONTAGIOUS PRACTICE

Believe that with focused attention, strong desire, unstoppable optimism, appropriate action, and trust and faith, all that your heart desires IS there for YOU! See it, FEEL IT inside your body, and you will be led by each whisper inside your heart!

IF YOU WANT TO MEET "THE ONE," BECOME "THE ONE"

SUSAN YOUNG

Too often we believe we will never find "the one" or that no one will ever really understand us. We dream about the man or woman who will live up to our expectations only to realize it is an impossible dream. In our desire to find love, we place so many restrictions and barriers on love that it is no surprise how many people feel that no one loves or cares about them.

What I would like to explore is how to build a relationship that allows you to open your heart to another person while allowing that person to be his or her authentic self. However the person shows up, give him or her "the gift of acceptance."

There are three lessons I learned about the relationship everyone desires: love, value, special.

LESSON 1: LOVE

When I was a young girl I never felt loved. I never heard those words from my parents. They were always fighting and there was no peace or harmony. I was always being criticized for what I did wrong. It was a life sentence instead of a lesson to be learned. As a child, I hungered for love and attention. What I did not get at home I sought at school. I thought if I were perfect I would be loved. I became a "straight A" student. I was often the teacher's pet, my way of feeling a loving connection to an adult, trying to fill the void inside me.

I sacrificed my need for fun and friends to get the love and attention from my teachers. I had perfect attendance. At times,

I went to school when I was ill to satisfy my desire to be perfect at something I could control. As a child, I felt powerless over the way people treated me and how they made me feel about myself. A lesson they do not teach you in school is how to interpret the behavior of adults, who are less than perfect.

Love is the most important gift you can give another person. Learn how to make a person feel loved and cherished. You can overlook a multitude of disappointments and differences when you know you are loved. Forgiveness will build a relationship; expectations will restrict a relationship. Uncon ditional love and support make a person feel safe and secure. Give the gift of acceptance and begin to see miracles in your relationships. Give love to those who love you. Protect your heart and do not give it away to someone who does not appreciate the person you are. Everyone wants to feel loved; there is no denying it!

LESSON 2: VALUE

The feeling of being unloved often leads to over-giving. When others do not reciprocate, you feel used or taken for granted. Does any of this sound like you?

For years, one of the ways I would try to be of value was by listening to other people's problems and trying to solve them. I became a very good listener and people were only too happy to open their hearts to me. But when I needed someone to listen to me, there was no one there. I was expected to listen, yet deny my own needs. My strength for others was my façade, and the real me was struggling to feel valued for all that I gave with little in return.

Value people for who they are. Use words and actions to show people you value what they do for you. I often say, "What you appreciate, you reciprocate." It is important to give value and to be of value. Invest in those who invest in you. When you do, your worth to that person will increase as they realize that in giving, they will receive.

Do not allow anyone to take you for granted. Guard your value as a person. Choose wisely where you invest your time, money, and, most importantly, love. Everyone wants to feel valued and appreciated.

LESSON 3: SPECIAL

If you spend your life feeling you have to live up to what others expect from you, you will miss the miracle of being seen for who you are. You are special and should be your authentic self, "the real you."

When I was choosing a career, I asked my teacher what I should be. He told me to be what he was: an accountant. I did not know who I was and I believed he knew me better than I knew myself. I trusted someone else to know who I was more than I trusted myself. This was a mistake on many levels. What I realized later was that people reflect onto you who they are, and it is often not the real you.

If you were never encouraged to be yourself, you often try to blend in instead of standing out. It's a sense of "if only I was 'this,' then someone would love me." I think of all the people who went into sports to impress a woman, or the woman who starved herself to be thin enough, all in the hopes of being that special someone. Relationships come with many forms of expectations, and when you are not allowed to be yourself, you often try to be something you are not. The way to open doors to the possibilities for your life comes from feeling special. Do not allow others to place boundaries or limits on the possibilities for your life.

For years I wanted to be a writer, but I denied it because of the expectations of others. When I was sixteen, I told my boyfriend at the time I wanted to be a writer. He said, "Give up your dreams and get a job." His words had a significant role in my choosing a profession that was safe, but not me. He did not think I was special and never encouraged me to believe in myself. So, I started to doubt the inner voice that was calling me to be a writer. When I express my feelings, I feel an energy in my body that comes from a place of being myself. A writer once said, "You do not choose to be writer; it is a calling." When you have to write to feel alive, you know you are a writer.

Everybody wants to feel there is something special about him or her. Discover each person's unique gifts and talents and encourage that person to be him or herself. Do this, and you will have a friend for life. Everyone wants to feel special.

In every relationship, ask yourself three questions:

1. Do I make this person feel loved?
2. Do I make this person feel valued?
3. Do I make this person feel special?

If you want to meet "the one," become "the one." We have all heard the expression: "You have to love yourself before anyone else will." How you feel about yourself and how you allow others to treat you is the basis of all your relationships in life.

CONTAGIOUS INSIGHT

·•●•·

Give yourself the gift of love, value what you have to offer, and realize you are special. Once you do this, you will realize we are more alike than we are different.

THE IMPORTANCE OF
REVISITING THE MOMENT

ALAN MALIZIA

Before I begin, let it be known I am not married. I have never been and will likely never be married. So one may justly ask, what credentials do I possess that would qualify me to discourse on the subject? One does not need to be a horticulturalist to appreciate the various ways a rose can please the senses; nor does one need to be an expert in harmony to be enraptured by the genius of Mozart. On the other hand, it would be prudent not to climb into a lion's cage without knowing something of the nature of lions.

I am not a parent, but I am a son. I am a product of marriage. Through my experience and observation as an offspring I have come to understand the relationship shared by my parents, save the unique intimacy known only to them. Considering the joys and trials of raising three boys, I being one who contracted polio at age four, they remained consistent, predictable, and unshakeable. They were down-to-earth people who knew the value inherent to the challenging times of their youth. Whether faced with financial difficulties, providing for the needs of their children, or the merciless unpredictability of life, they were steadfast. There were no conflicts in decision making, for they respected each other's input and listened without the detrimental effect of inflated egos. No plan was put in action unless fully agreed upon. They were a formidable team. Looking back, they played well the hand life dealt them and taught me that true love does not come without its price.

The most important ingredient in marriage is love, not emotion. Love is the one thing that we all share, whether married or not, for it comes in various forms. A parent loves his or her child, a person loves his or her profession, and the expression of a special talent will exude the passion that is inherent in love. Love separates us from all other living forms that are indigenous to this world. Love is with us at birth and remains with us after death. It is the only thing we can take with us from this world. Love will be the cause of much joy and much strife.

Love is selfless, not selfish. Where there is selfishness, true love cannot exist. It is human to possess a selfish tendency. But, if viewed as a virtue it simply provides fodder for the ego that stifles love. Ego has no place in a lasting relationship. If love is as it was on the day of exchanging marriage vows, then the lover need not require the beloved to change in any way to be worthy of love. If love takes the forefront instead of emotion then change will occur without prodding and will thereby be for the better. Love does not require change; however, change requires love. Emotion ebbs and flows like the tides. Love is steadfast because it is a decision. Emotion is in the liking. Love is an act of the will. A person's special qualities and character are why we like them. But love points to no attributes for justification. It just is, by choice, "a mysterious bond between two that can't be expressed or explained" (Bishop Fulton Sheen).

Life's shortcomings can distort the views of anyone, especially the married couple, because the difficulties they face will be twofold. Since each is a unique person, so will be their perceptions of problems and events. All will be further complicated if children are involved. The husband and wife can lose their sense of oneness when the demands about them continue to mount. There are times when their life seems like a relentless juggling act. Just when one issue has been resolved or has run its course, there waiting in a seemingly endless line is another to take its place. Little, if any, time is left to rekindle love's flame.

As long as I can remember, my parents' wedding portrait hung on the wall in their bedroom at the foot of the bed. They were married in 1940 and since have gone to their rest. The image of mom so beautiful in her wedding dress with its long train, and dad as handsome as ever in his tuxedo with tails, still is displayed in our home to this day. Their love for each other radiates from the portrait as they fondly pose hand in hand. They never allowed the struggle of life to tarnish or endanger their love. At the end of each day, they needed only to gaze up from their bed to relive the most wonderful moment of their lives: when they endearingly uttered the words, "I do."

Wedding anniversaries are most important for the very reasons I have expressed in the story above. Their celebration is significantly greater than where to go for dinner or arranging a weekend getaway as grandma and grandpa babysit. Married couples should set aside the time to just look at the picture that has preserved for all time their moment, the moment when their eyes reflected two souls becoming one. And from that union emerge the words of true love: "All I am is yours." The giving of self in totality. The flame of love will never extinguish so long as we sacrifice for even a moment. The love that bonds a husband and wife can best be explained as unexplainable. I believe the lyrics of the 1931 ballad, written by Fred Ahlert and Roy Turk, depict that loving bond best: "I don't know why I love you like I do. I don't know why, I just do."

CONTAGIOUS EFFECT

View wedding photos every year on your anniversary. One in particular: the exchanging of vows. Now, close your eyes. Picture that moment as strongly as you can as if you were there. It may have been a flashback but your mind and heart will be warmed from the memory.

FIRST IMPRESSIONS

MARTIN DIANO

A majority of us wish it were possible to have a redo after meeting someone for the first time. Whether it was a job interview, lunch with a potential client, meeting new neighbors, or meeting a prospective boyfriend or girlfriend, it is in our nature to want to show the best side of ourselves. But, as real life so often demonstrates, a favorable first impression doesn't always work out as we hoped. I can certainly think back and wish for a few redos in my lifetime.

What is interesting is that if someone gives you a sour first impression, it is you who controls how that relationship progresses, according to a study on first impressions. If you are on the wrong side of a bad first impression, you have your work cut out for you. The study concludes that within just ten minutes of meeting, people decide what kind of relationship they want with a new acquaintance.

"While the power of first impressions has been well known, this research shows that the course of a relationship may be influenced much more quickly than was once believed," said Artemio Ramirez, Jr., coauthor of the study and assistant professor of communication at Ohio State University. Ramirez conducted the study with Michael Sunnafrank of the University of Minnesota, Duluth. Their findings were published in a recent issue of the *Journal of Social and Personal Relationships*.

In today's fast-paced culture, people are making immediate, on-the-spot judgments about what kind of relationship they want with the person they just met. People size up the possibilities of a relationship within minutes of meeting and that guides their future actions. This follows what researchers call "predicted outcome value theory," which states that when we initially begin communicating with another person we make predictions about relationship potential and act accordingly.

"If I think we could become friends, I'll communicate more, tell you more about myself, and do things that will help ensure a friendship. If I have a more negative prediction about a future relationship, then I will restrict communication and make it harder for a friendship to develop," said Ramirez.

People want to quickly determine if a person they just met is someone they are going to want to hang out with, date, buy from, or spend more time with in the future. We don't want to waste our time. My lifelong experience, both on a personal level and as a public relations practitioner, was filled with successes and failures in meeting people for the first time.

CONTAGIOUS INSIGHT

Lessons learned: Treat the person as you would want him or her to treat you. Ask questions about what interests the person and solicit their viewpoint. Listen. Being a good listener is critical. Above all, be genuine!

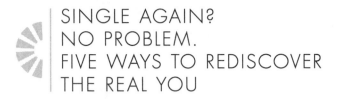

SINGLE AGAIN? NO PROBLEM. FIVE WAYS TO REDISCOVER THE REAL YOU

JOANIE WINBERG

Becoming single again is a very challenging time in a person's life. It is hard to adjust to being single, as well as living out of the habit of being married, especially if you have been married for many years.

It is suggested that you use this precious opportunity to rediscover yourself. Think of this time in your life as an adventure to explore the real you. Over the years you may have lost yourself along the way. Certainly not on purpose, but as most people try to do it all, many times we put our own wants and needs on hold to keep our families and jobs running smoothly.

Take a deep breath and start to rediscover the real you!

TREASURE YOUR GIFTS WITHIN

Realizing we are all born as "gold nuggets" is a hard concept for many people to believe about themselves. Think about how magnificent you really are! Over time, you might have forgotten your unique gifts and are only thinking of what you don't like about yourself or your life. Set a new intention, starting today, to list all of your great qualities and read that list every day.

GIVE YOURSELF A BREAK

During and after a divorce it is common to grieve, similar to the loss of someone. Many people feel the need to stay busy to keep their minds off of this stressful time, such as by working overtime or cleaning the house from top to bottom, but let this time also include pampering yourself. Barter with a friend or neighbor to watch your children or leave work a few minutes early so you can stop, for example, and sit on a park bench long enough to get that sense of the unique and special YOU. Take this time to experience life even for only ten minutes... just simply be you!

NO REGRETS! NO BITTERNESS!

Holding on to regrets and bitterness will only keep your life from moving forward. Is your inner voice working overtime with all the "what ifs" and "if onlys"? This is normal for a period of time, but ask yourself, "Are these thoughts serving me or helping me feel better? Will thinking about them over and over again change anything?" To move your life forward it is important to acknowledge your feelings and to learn from your past experiences to prepare yourself for the next exciting chapter of your life. Yes, there is life after divorce. Learn to let it go! Just let it go!

WHAT MAKES YOUR HEART SING?

What really matters to you? What do you feel is your true purpose in life? If you were asked those questions, how would you answer?

Why is it so important to be clear on what your life's purpose is? Knowing your purpose will give you a true sense of who you are and why you were put on this earth. It gives your life direction and helps you make clear and easy decisions concerning that direction. It's your compass! Without a purpose, can your life be compared to a piece of driftwood floating endlessly in whichever direction the tide decides to take it and ending up on any beach with no will of its own?

Take this time to focus on what really matters to you. Feel the true passions that exist in your heart and write them down.

BE TRUE TO YOURSELF

During and even after a divorce, we are often filled with doubts. We question ourselves about what is right, what to do, or how we feel. Should I or shouldn't I? It seems difficult to make a decision. Listen to your heart. What feels right? What doesn't feel quite right? If a situation does not feel right, honor your resistance by pausing or waiting. Sometimes waiting is the best thing to do. By waiting you may have allowed the situation to unfold more easily without having to worry! If a decision feels good or right, usually that means you are heading in the right direction. When we listen to our hearts, we are in integrity with ourselves. When we are in integrity with ourselves, we learn to say NO more easily.

Your true purpose and passions are waiting to be rediscovered within you! When you have discovered the "gold nugget" you already are, you will start to live your life with more ease and to enjoy the feeling of peace. You are truly free!

CONTAGIOUS COMMITMENT

•••• ● ●••

Honor yourself and listen to your heart. Divorce is not easy or fun but you can make it through this time of your life by realizing you will make it!

RELATIONSHIP EPIPHANIES

ELLEN KRATKA

There are many "significant others" in our lives: some show up for an instant leaving behind a memory that will last forever; others stick around for a long time, teaching us lesson after lesson—if we're ready to learn them.

Some time ago I was driving with my eighteen-year-old daughter, and she began to laugh loudly after something I said. I asked her why she was laughing. Her reply was, "I just had an epiphany." Wow! I told her I was impressed with her knowledge of that word, that she actually used it in conversation, to which she replied that I must think she's "dumb." Of course I told her, "Not true! I just think you're at a point in life when you, at times, exhibit amazing big-girl wisdom and maturity, while at other times you still revert to a little girl's type of behavior, like when you scream at me for something I've said or done." As my daughter exited the car her final words were, "That's not being a big girl and a little girl; that's being a smart girl and an angry girl."

On my way home I realized that I had just been handed another nugget of wisdom. Why isn't it OK to be both smart *and* angry? And what's wrong with being angry anyway? When my daughter expresses her anger she's letting off steam so she can be done with the related issue, unlike those "adults" among us who may not be quite so loud but who stew in it, and in some cases, hold onto a grudge for an entire lifetime. It's also her way of reminding herself that she's just given her power away and now she's taking it back. How she ultimately learns the lesson that true power can never be taken away (in other words when and why she realizes that screaming is unnecessary) is up to her.

The faster you let go of trying to prove you were right, and instead shift to "what does this have to teach me?" the more you'll gain and the quicker you'll experience emotional relief.

After I worked the experience with my daughter through to its lessons, I realized we had both had an epiphany that day.

CONTAGIOUS BY EXAMPLE

When people have a bad day or are in a bad situation, don't always feel you need to find them the answers. Sometimes they just need a compassionate sounding board. Be that sounding board and you will be amazed how quickly they find the answers themselves.

ARE YOU ESTRANGED FROM SOMEONE YOU LOVE?

CAROLYN BATES

One of life's most difficult situations is when someone you love is no longer present in your life. There are times, as a family member, a good friend, or a parent, when major disagreements occur. Frequently, this happens with life transitions and as we approach retirement with a growing concern about our health and life balance. For example, quite often children grow into adulthood and may go in a direction that parent's dislike. Or, those fifty years and older find themselves in conflict as their adult children sometimes move back home.

Are you retiring from one career and wanting to start your own business? Are your family members and friends seeing a shift in financial allocations and time? Is the focus away from them and the things "they think" should be important to you? The thought of moving away to start a new life may be a possibility or the empty nest syndrome is finally hitting home. You start thinking, "This is my life and it's time for me now."

How many times have I heard a client say, "Well, if he doesn't do this, then he can forget asking me for anything!" "If she thinks I'm going to stand for that, then she can just go her own way, make her own mistakes and live with them!" "They obviously don't appreciate all that I have done for them." "Can't they see that it's my life now and I'm going to live it, with or without them?" These are "closing" statements that usually come from fear, frustration, and anger.

Turn off your mind; get back to what's truly in your heart.

Do you want a relationship at all with this person? If so, then what do you want from the relationship? Just to be a friend? Just to make sure the door for communication is always open? Is there something you haven't said or discussed? Get your values in line with your desires then work on what you want to say. The other person only has to have the opportunity to hear it, then they get to decide what they want—a relationship with you or not and at what level. You can't put a timeframe on their response. They may reply immediately or in three years. You go into this with no expectation, just that you know where your heart is and you've said what you want to say for yourself.

CONTAGIOUS PRACTICE

Put your feelings out there to the other person. Let time, the universe, and destiny run its course. Don't overstate your feelings to other person and don't force the square peg.

I MARRIED YOU
FOR BETTER OR WORSE
BUT NOT FOR LUNCH

DEE CASCIO

Each person in a relationship needs to communicate, compromise, and cooperate. This requires a lot of understanding and empathy of each other's needs.

HOW MUCH IS TOO MUCH TOGETHERNESS?

For working people, there is little interaction during the week. Suddenly, weekends can change from time focused on individual schedules to 24/7 marathons of togetherness. And quite often, retirement throws two people together full-time. As they say, there can be too much of a good thing!

I like the saying, "I married you for better or worse, but not for lunch." This may in fact be the wife's reaction when feeling her established schedule is being encroached upon as her husband retires. Receiving this type of negative response, the husband may further feel the loss of his established work life and that he now is only a participant in his wife's world.

It's human nature to want some space for ourselves and it doesn't mean that we love our spouse any less. It just means that you need to find that healthy balance of time together and time apart. In the case of retirement, and with proper planning, these "pitfalls" can be avoided and a couple can arrive at a mutually rewarding retirement lifestyle.

FOR THE RETIRED OR RETIRING, WHY PLANNING IS SO IMPORTANT

A Cornell study done on this life stage revealed that married couples tend to experience significant conflict during the first several years after one or both spouses retire. Neither is prepared for this significant adjustment. Instead of enjoying blissful togetherness, both may struggle to understand their new lifestyle and end up feeling lost. I've heard countless stories of retirees aimlessly seeking new order in their lives; they reload the dishwasher, move furniture, and try to figure out what they are supposed to do because they have lost their old job description. Meanwhile, their spouse tries to maintain a normal schedule while worrying about their retired spouse. The burden of this responsibility can be overwhelming.

THE KEY IS IN CONNECTING

So how do you ensure you don't end up like one of these lost, frustrated couples after retirement? The key is being able to connect and communicate with each other.

Research shows that couples who reported that they were happily married were able to balance their alone time and time together in a healthy and constructive way. They respected each other's need for privacy and space. While a spouse is working in his or her career, this time is built in. In retirement, it has to be created by the couple. Pay attention to how you currently use your time and who's in charge of scheduling your time. Try not to rely on your spouse to plan your social life and take equal responsibility for some of those activities. Make sure you are developing your own activities now that you'll enjoy separately as well as those that you'll enjoy together. Make a list of activities, hobbies, and dreams and then get started pursuing them.

If you are like most married couples, you have already successfully transitioned through various stages of your life together: dating, getting married, having children, pursuing careers, among others. Hopefully, with each transition, you have found ways of learning more about each other and creating a stronger bond that has sustained you. You have learned to be more attentive to each other, respectful of differences, and patient with each other. You have developed more independence and autonomy while protecting the bond that you have.

REMEMBER THE LOVE

As couples retire and grow into the changes that are associated with this transition, they can discover a renewed love and commitment. "Successful marriage requires falling in love many times, always with the same person," says Mignon McLaughlin, famous American journalist and author of the *Neurotic's Notebook*. It is important to share your needs during retirement with one another. Find new ways of spending time together, and respect each other's need for time apart.

Remember that love is a verb. Loving your spouse requires much more of you than just feeling and emotion. It takes action, but we can sometimes lose sight of it in times of challenge. It requires more words of appreciation and spoken affirmation, and more acts of love and kindness.

When two people are willing to be vulnerable, honest, and open with each other, accepting the good along with the character defects, they will find mature love and intimacy. So love well...but have lunch out!

CONTAGIOUS COMMITMENT

You have been through other life transitions success-fully. Honor this history by communicating honestly and respectfully about your retirement dreams. Remember that you are each other's best friend and lover.

CHLOE JONPAUL

While there is no clinical definition of a toxic relationship, we are certainly aware that a toxin is a substance which, when infused, injected, or exposed, causes a destructive result. Detoxification, better known as detox, is the process that purges the toxin from the body to promote healing. I think most of us are familiar with detox programs offered for alcohol and other addictions. There are even body-cleansing regimens that people follow on a regular basis.

Sooner or later, all of us are exposed to a toxic person. That person can be a family member, a significant other, a boss, or a coworker. A toxic person exhibits mood swings, short temper, and inconsistencies as well as impulsive behavior. This type of person is very good at controlling people and situations because he or she knows how to use charm to keep the victim engaged.

It's interesting to note that even though a person is intelligent, successful, and self-sufficient in other areas of her life, she may find it nearly impossible to admit involvement in a toxic relationship. This person has a sense that something is not right, but lacks the determination to do something about it—always hoping that things will improve.

When you have come to the conclusion that the relationship you're in is toxic, there are steps you must take to overcome the abuse and pain of such a relationship. The first order of business is to stop making excuses for this type of behavior.

The second thing you must do is to confront this person in

an assertive way. Try using what is known as the "I" message. The formula is simple: When_____(describe the situation but *never* use the word "you"), I feel_____(describe the emotion—you must take ownership of how you feel) because_____(give the reason why the situation makes you feel that way). You may express your desire to repair the relationship but you must be willing to set healthier boundaries. Ask the person to think about what you have said and end with, "Can we talk about this some more now or do you need some time to think about it?"

Remember, you can be assertive without being aggressive. Keep in mind that the primary reason a toxic person is motivated to hurt others is his or her own low self-esteem and fear of exposing his or her true self to others. Without good clinical intervention, it's impossible for that person to heal.

Believe it or not, you can set limits—even with a person who ranks above you in the workplace. Your speech and body language should reflect self-confidence.

So, where do you begin in the healing process? Well, hopefully you've taken the first step: Recognize that you are in a toxic relationship. The second step: Establish and maintain a safe distance. Healing will not take place until a safe distance is reached between the source of a poison and the one being contaminated. The third step: Get help. Like a physical wound that needs to be treated and sanitized, emotional wounds need to be treated professionally as well. You really can't do this alone. Finding a good licensed therapist is essential to your recovery.

In addition to seeing a therapist, I suggest designing your own detox program; things you can do on a daily basis–but remember that consistency is the key:

1. Choose a mantra to recite throughout the day. One of my favorites is "I am strong and lovable."
2. Investigate various books and online resources such as:
www.livestrong.com
www.healthyplace.com
www.beliefnet.com
www.askmarsvenus.com

"Phylameana Desy," a holistic healing guide on the website About.com, offers two exercises you may want to check out. I especially like the Bridge Visualization exercise.

Emotional Vampires: Dealing with People Who Drain You Dry, by Albert Bernstein.

Toxic People: 10 Ways of Dealing with People Who Make Your Life Miserable, by Lillian Glass.

I Thought I Was the Crazy One: 201 Ways to Identify and Deal with Toxic People, by Amorah.

If It Hurts, It Isn't Love, by Chuck Spezzano (my favorite).

You may have been spared much more than you can possibly imagine at the moment. That person you thought you knew and loved caused you temporary misery. Trying to reclaim that love would have turned you into a victim because the pattern would likely repeat itself.

Celebration time is right around the corner so take a deep breath and get started. You're going to be just fine!

CONTAGIOUS ACTION

If you are spiritually inclined, prayer helps. Reaching for your higher power in time of need is especially helpful. One woman recently told friends, "I have learned to pray for what God thinks I need—not necessarily what I think I want."

THE DIAMOND
IN YOUR RELATIONSHIP

LYNDA SMITH

The relationship between husband and wife is one of the most important relationships that you will ever have. In her book, *Passages*, Gail Sheehy likens this significant relationship to that of a diamond.

The beginning of a marriage is a dream come true for most couples. The picture may be of sunshine, roses, and dreams of how they will live married life together. The honeymoon can last long beyond the holiday. The Bible tells us that we become "one flesh." It is easy for us to communicate and openly share our thoughts and feelings about life, challenges, and dreams with each other during this stage. This is the point at which we begin to draw our diamond—at one starting point, together.

Then, life starts to happen around us. We will most likely be building our prospective careers. The decision to have children will be on the radar. Then, your first child is born—one of the greatest blessings that any couple can experience together. Once the joy and wonder of this little miracle have passed, reality hits. We chase life, careers, goals, and friendships. Our general pace of life is fast and busy during this stage. Other children may follow. Career decisions and "climbing the corporate ladder" challenge and excite the journey. At times it may start to feel as if we are passing one another like ships in the night. This is when each partner begins to draw the opposite sides of the diamond shape.

This stage continues for as long as our children are at home.

On average, it is a period of between twenty and twenty-five years. Life is filled with family holidays, school events, and playing the happy couple in your career(s). Your most important relationship is often put on hold due to stress and preoccupation. It is critical to make special time to communicate and grow together during this stage. We need to make time for "date nights" and weekends without children, friends, or family. The woman wants to feel loved and cherished and the man needs to know that he is still the most important person in his partner's life. At this point, the opposite sides of your diamond will be at the widest distance apart unless you continue to communicate strongly and have regular time together.

The beginning of the "third age" in your life is when the children leave home. There are a lot of complex emotions going on in the minds of any couple at this stage, the most common being the empty nest syndrome. This is most likely to affect women who may not have re-entered the workforce after the birth of their children. The man may be in high-adrenaline mode and successful in his career. Or, the man may be retrenched or feel that there is no joy in the drudgery of work. It is very common for couples at this point to battle to re-engage and discuss who they are and what they need. Most individuals need to spend time alone as well as together in order to work out what all this means for the future. Sadly, at this stage, many feel it is time to part as they don't seem to have anything left in common. This is the most important part of how the diamond will regain its shape. We all have choices and can make a concerted effort to try to communicate, work out the issues and learn to fall back in love with this person you have been sharing a house and life with for the past twenty-five years.

The third age should be one of the greatest stages of your life. You are with a person who shares a history and children with you. The responsibility of parenting is over. You now have the opportunity to spend quality time together with less financial strain. You have your best friend at your side and you can travel and experience exciting things together. This part of the diamond can be fun as you discuss your dreams and challenges.

I hear many complain that these conversations don't happen. The men want to withdraw from life; women want a new career and there is no common ground. I want to challenge you that the relationship is worth fighting for. Please spend the time trying to find that love and recommit your life to one another. We are a generation that has had more divorce than any other generation. It must be so sad to part at this stage and not work at rediscovering the wonder and mystery of the person who wears your ring.

I hope this essay stimulates conversation for you as a couple and you will value the bond of your relationship. May you have a long and interesting journey back to the point of your diamond.

CONTAGIOUS ACTION

•••• ● ••••

Draw the shape of a traditional diamond and label the high and low points of your relationship based on this essay. Do this together and enjoy the communication. Agreeing on the high and low points is a high point in itself.

DON'T BE THE VICTIM IN YOUR STORY: LIFE AFTER DIVORCE

DR. BARBARA SEIFERT

If you've lost a relationship you know how much it hurts, especially if the end was not your idea. Infidelity, lying, gambling, substance abuse, or verbal and physical abuse can lead to the end. It is a divorce, no matter if you were married or not. Divorce can shake one to their core, filling them with rage and a pain they've never known before. One will go through the grieving process as they mourn the loss and the dreams that went along with it.

Sometimes the relationship dies slowly, with each partner trying to save something that isn't savable. Other times the relationship is over suddenly, with one partner wanting to leave and the other wanting to keep it no matter how bad it may be. If one partner fears being alone or for their financial future, they will fight harder. It is particularly true if children are involved. But the end happens anyway, leaving the other partner hurt, angry, or with a host of other feelings.

In her book, *Coming Apart,* Daphne Rose Kingma relates that the person who leaves goes through pain prior to leaving, but getting to the point of no tolerance is what prompts them to cheat or to end the relationship. This person is called the "Dumper." The person that is left, the "Dumpee," is aware that their partner is pulling away but chooses to ignore the signs. When they are left, they go through a second grieving when their reality is ripped open. Both go through the same emotions but at different times.

Recognize that you will go through the five stages of grief, as developed by Elisabeth Kubler-Ross, which are denial, bargaining, anger, depression, and acceptance. No one will go through these stages linearly or the same. Grief is an individual process and its progression is dictated by one's willingness to face the feelings and to do the work that is required. Denial is a coping skill that protects our psyche and gives us time to face our hurts and fears. But, as time goes on, these feelings get put aside and the hurts go deeper into our unconscious. However, if not dealt with, they will come out eventually in ways that are not healthy, such as through anger, anxiety, or depression. We can get "stuck" in one phase if not worked through. You have to go through each phase in order to get acceptance.

After a divorce, particularly if it ended badly, one can hold on to the "wrongs" that were done to them. "He cheated on me," "She took everything I had and didn't care about me," "It was as if my feelings didn't exist," "He/she hasn't seen their children or given me any support to help me take care of them." These are all products of divorce that can leave a void and prevent one from moving forward to creating a new life. Often, low self-esteem causes the "Dumpee" to stay in a bad relationship and to rue the end of one. Being left hurts and can send out the message of "I'm not good enough." They take it personally as opposed to seeing the faults of the person that left. Perhaps the "Dumper" felt insecure and needed to feel better by yelling and calling the "Dumpee" names, maybe they couldn't cope with having a bad job or financial concerns so they turned to drinking or pornography. Perhaps they were not getting what they needed in the relationship but did not know how to ask for it, so they sought it through someone else.

However your relationship ended, it is important that you

do the work necessary to help you get through the plethora of emotions so you can move on with your life. There are two ways that can help: One: Get angry. Depression is anger turned inward so find the ways to release the anger—find a punching bag or beat the pillow, go in a field and scream, exercise, or journal your feelings. Do something to release the negativity, which will allow you to let goodness in. Two: Don't be the victim in your story. It is easy during divorce to place blame for the wrongs that were done to us. How we perceive these wrongs dictates the level of hurt we feel. If your spouse left you for someone else, it is easy to tell others how rotten they are and how you gave them everything. We often don't want to see how we may have played a part in the story.

Marriage takes two; it is not one person's fault for the demise of the relationship. Perhaps you were "too busy" with your job, perhaps you aren't one to express your feelings so you hold onto anger and let it out all at once (such as yelling or withholding your affections). Perhaps you saw the signs but purposely chose to not confront them. The point is that you had a part. *Taking ownership will help you to realize the situation for what it is and will help you in the story you tell.* Somehow, it helps to lift one's esteem and to move on faster. Not playing the part of the victim will help you to move on and find life after divorce.

CONTAGIOUS INSIGHT

Review any hurts you've undergone and determine if you are the victim or the cause—or both. You will realize that it really does take two 99 percent of the time. No one person is at fault. Then, own your part and let go so you can move on.

CAN RELATIONSHIPS SURVIVE REALITY? YES!

LISBETH CALANDRINO

As a child I didn't think much about my parent's relationship. They argued at times and they made each other laugh and cry. My mother used to say that relationships were almost impossible because they consisted of two different people with two different agendas.

Every so often my parents appear on my horizon. It's usually when I'm having a meltdown with my significant other. I don't understand why he is doing that thing—the thing I've asked him so many times *not* to do. Doesn't he get it, doesn't he know?

My parents seemed conflicted about many things but they also shared many things. One thing I remember, I always thought they would stay together and that having loud conversations didn't seem to matter. As I go through life, I'm convinced that Italians are loud and expressive. Shouting doesn't seem to be a problem except for those non-Italians within earshot. Like all of us, they were a product of their upbringing and their parents.

By any standards, my parents were both beautiful people. The butcher and the milkman both flirted with my mother; her smile was enough to cause a flirting epidemic. My father loved it; he had won the girl of his dreams. Women flirted with my dad; his smile also caused a flirting epidemic. Unfortunately mom didn't find this an attractive component of his personality and I believe this eventually caused their breakup when they were in their seventies. They lived apart and they lived together but they never got divorced.

Our most powerful role models are our parents. Sure we watch our friends and their imperfect loves, we read books about relationships, and try to uncover our own secrets. We know when our friends have picked the wrong mates; it's so clear, don't they see it?

I didn't know what my parents thought or how they felt; it was never discussed. How did they work out their demons of poverty being second-generation immigrants? What were their struggles with money? All I remember is there was never enough and I vowed when I grew up there would be. The missing component for me was the discussion. I knew the boundaries, but what I didn't understand was how to navigate them. What I didn't realize was my "never enough model" applied to everything and would be in my psyche forever. It passed for ambition, focus, and hard work.

All of us start with a working relationship model, a fragile one at best, but it's ours. It just happens. We meet our prince or our princess, complete with their own model. It is rare that the models are discussed or that we ask our new love to try on our life model. We judge everything in life by our own standards. We share life, feel pain, and meld excitement as a couple but rarely do we share our "relationship model."

It's no wonder many of our sentences start with, "Why doesn't he (or she) understand?" "Why doesn't he (or she) know what I need?" Our model is one destined for disaster.

A suggestion: instead of building those first dates around "Do you like football?" how about a conversation that starts with, "What was it like to grow up in your house?" "What were your parents and siblings like?" Too personal you say? The prince or princess doesn't want to talk about it? Up goes the crimson flag! What better time to be personal before you get personal.

Remember the model for your relationship has already

been determined. Only you and your partner have the power to bring it to reality.

CONTAGIOUS EFFECT

·•● ● ●•·

Listen with an open heart and an open mind. Ask the hard questions before you're caught up in a fantasy relationship and have too much invested. Ask before you're singing, "It's better to have loved and lost than never to have loved at all."

COMPLEMENTARY ATTRACTION

NANCY FERRARI

If I were to assess the beginning of a relationship, the word "dream" comes to mind. I think of a young woman and her time spent daydreaming of meeting her future husband. Everything is just so dreamy in the beginning. This is a euphoric feeling, however, the problem is that reality has a way of setting in quickly as the dream-state (aka the honeymoon) fades and the business of the relationship begins. "Opposites attract" is an interesting concept as I find it adverse to the Law of Attraction. Are we truly attracted to the opposite of us, or to someone who complements who we are? I'd say "complementary attraction" should be the term because when someone complements who you are, they bring out the best in you.

When I interview psychologists, therapists, and relationship experts, the common thread found in their advice for a successful relationship is communication. Once those walls of communication break down or walls of distance and resistance build up, the relationship becomes strained. Misunderstandings, assumptions, presumptions, and loneliness become the reality. In essence, there is no perfect relationship, however; in order to live in harmony with your mate, it takes work. The word "work" implies a hardship and this is not what I am referring to. Working on a marriage or relationship requires attentiveness, as well as respect, trust, and honesty. If any aspect of that relationship is compromised or unattended to, it's out of balance and needs to be put back into alignment.

If a relationship truly has a strong foundation, it can be built up again. I place a high premium on qualified marriage counseling and therapy. The objective is to provoke deep thought and insight along with guidance to renew a healthy and loving relationship. With love and light.

CONTAGIOUS INSIGHT

According to many sources, it only takes six seconds upon meeting someone to make a lasting impression. Think back to those six seconds when you met your soulmate. Now, all of a sudden, it doesn't seem like work as that memory starts to fill your heart.

I FOUND MY FAMILY

BECKY WOODBRIDGE

The 1970's television show, *Eight Is Enough,* wasn't based on my family, but we certainly could have supplied its writers with a few storylines. Our own family of eight included my parents, five daughters, and one son—and, yes, my brother was the spoiled one of the bunch. I was number four from the top. Essentially I was the middle child.

No two siblings were alike and each brought a strong personality to the dinner table. It was a lively household, but it also was a close-knit one. We were the family that played together—no group in the neighborhood could get a baseball game going quicker than ours.

That's not to say that we didn't have our share of fights. But when push came to shove we always stuck up for one another. One memory stands out—and to this day warms my heart. My brother and I got off the school bus one afternoon and started walking home. We weren't speaking that week for some reason. But when one of the neighborhood kids began picking on me, my brother didn't hesitate. He rushed to my defense. He was mad at me, but he was still my protector.

As we grew up we gradually drifted apart. We were adults leading our respective lives. What didn't register was the anger that seemed to intensify over the years. Our little childhood fights didn't compare to the arguments we had as adults. We could not sit together at a family function without one sibling yelling at the other. Each year, the divide seemed to grow greater and greater. We were lost as a family. As time went on, I began filling that void with friends—people I could choose to become my "new" family.

One day my parents said to me, "Our only wish is for you kids to get along." The words weighed on my heart. How could we have become so angry and distant when we had so much fun as children?

My friend Cyndee recommended that I attend a workshop in Louisiana called Education for Living. I went not only to learn about myself but also to find out how to bridge the gap that had left our family estranged. As the workshop unfolded I began to learn about the breakdown in our family. It started with me.

I was judging the members of my family. Worse, I couldn't see past those judgments—as if they were cast in stone. My journey of self-discovery led to some new and deeply profound truths. I had to not only change the way that I viewed my family but I also had to look at my own public identity. I had to shed my judgmental skin. Slowly, I began to open my mind—and my heart. I stopped walking into a room with expectations of what my family should and shouldn't do. I became more accepting.

I always had thought that my intentions were pure—that I was "helping them" by offering my rather pointed opinions. But actually, it was driving wedges between us. No one wants to be judged all the time. My siblings never felt like I accepted them for who they were; it's no wonder they turned sour when I was around.

It didn't take long for my brother and sisters to notice the new me. Better still, they began to act differently around me. There was less fighting and more communication. We began to spend more time together. For the first time in years, it felt like we were a family again.

People who judge think they are superior to those they are judging. I learned this the hard way. I'm now a recovering, judgmental person—"recovering," because it's easy to fall off the wagon and start judging again. I have to remind myself that it's just my opinion, and not the truth.

I love and accept my family, and I want them to be who they are. I never realized how cool my family is because I was spending so much time trying to make them what I thought they should be. I'm proud of my family and I am glad I found them again. I can't imagine the journey of life without them.

CONTAGIOUS PRACTICE

When you find yourself judging others that don't fit your ideal of who or what they should be, stop yourself. Immediately contemplate all the things about you that you feel are less than perfect. Combine your "human-ness" with their "human-ness" and, guess what? You will realize that we are all just human and our flaws are as beautiful as our talents.

HITTING THE "SUPER GROW" BUTTON

FAYE LEVOW

There is nothing like a relationship to hit the "super grow" button in your life, if you allow it. Consider this: Two distinct individuals with different upbringings, viewpoints, interests (even if some are similar), strengths, problems, and values, come together to build a life. Talk about challenging! It's a wonder that anyone stays in a relationship for very long at all!

So it's no surprise that relationship challenges are a fact of life. Do you want to go through the challenges with this person or that person? No matter whom you choose, in order to make it work, you need good communication; you need to allow for differences, be respectful, and be willing to grow. If you resist the growth part, you're going to have a very difficult time indeed!

Most of us have a "fairy tale" idea regarding relationships. We've been taught that after the wedding, life is "happily ever after." Television and movies only show us snippets of relationships yet give us this crazy idea of what our lives are supposed to be like. Life happens 24/7; it's not scripted and it doesn't neatly fit into thirty, sixty, or ninety-minute segments laden with ten-minute commercial breaks.

The key to a good relationship is good communication, where you talk about issues, work them out, and tell the truth. It's not always easy. Your feelings and emotions may be completely different from your partner's for the very same issue or event. (Remember—different points of view).

It is important to *allow* each person to have their feelings and their perspectives. Those feelings are completely legitimate for that person, even if you see things differently. It helps if you try to see the other person's perspective, much of which comes from their upbringing and their life experiences. Put yourself in their shoes as best you can and see if you begin to understand where they're coming from. Some people are better at expressing their feelings than others. Be patient—patient with yourself and patient with the other person.

Open yourself to discovering who you are with your partner. This may be different from who you would be with someone else. Do you like who you are with that person? Why?

In a relationship, you have a grand opportunity to learn from each other. Grow together as you support each other in achieving your dreams. No matter how long you have been together, you are always growing and changing, so there's always something new to discover.

When you are committed to being together and creating a life, you have the freedom to make mistakes and deal with challenges because you have the framework of your relationship to fall back on. Life is like a trampoline, no matter how high you bounce, you will still land on the trampoline. However, what you want at one stage of your life may change in the future. Do your best to shift the expression of your love and friendship, rather than throwing it away.

This was the case with me many years ago. I was with the father of my children for twenty-two years. But what I wanted in my twenties was very different from what I wanted in my forties. I felt stagnant and unhappy. It was no one's "fault." We were growing in different directions and were no longer able to meet each other's needs. I am very grateful for our years together and he has been a great dad to our daughters.

Everyone has their own path to walk and when you regard

everything that happens as an opportunity for growth, there is no blame and no victim. Satisfaction comes from being genuine and knowing that you have fully engaged in the relationship.

CONTAGIOUS PRACTICE

Tips for when things are rocky: Don't assume. Ask for clarity: "What do you mean by that?" Focus on your own feelings rather than pointing fingers: "I feel uncomfortable/sad/confused/trapped/hurt/etc. when..." Shift the attitude with, "This is what I love about you..." Take a walk together. State that you need some alone time to think about things. Go to the beach together. Being out in nature does wonders for shifting attitudes. Hug. Don't answer back; just listen. Then ask, "Is there anything else you want to tell me right now?" and then just listen some more. (Rinse and repeat...as many times as necessary!) Offer to give your partner a massage.

CHRIS AND STANLEY

MICHAEL BRAGA

"Pick up the phone Stanley. Just answer the phone. I need you to answer!"

I made a deal with Stanley. My commitment was that I would call him every morning at 9 a.m. Calling Stanley was my first thought when I opened my eyes each and every morning for three months, until one morning Stanley didn't pick up.

I should call him Dad like most sons do, not Stanley. Dad was his name for the first decade of my life. Somewhere along the way our family roles were reversed and he became Stanley. Without Chris (my younger brother) and Stanley, I was the lone male left in my immediate family. I felt stripped of my roles as a brother, a son, and even as a father. This was rock bottom, but life wasn't always like this.

Stanley was a great father in his own way. He hugged us at every greeting and goodbye. He was also a good disciplinarian making sure we studied, practiced sports, and respected others. His father and uncles were good disciplinarians as well. The "Braga Bridge" in Rhode Island was named after my great uncle that had died in Pearl Harbor (whenever I go over that bridge, I think of how our family tree has weathered the seasons, lost some leaves, and sprouted new growth). I admired Stanley's love for us despite the issues he attempted to work through, including an injury that put him on permanent disability from his job at the shipyard. In permanent pain, he became dependent on alcohol and drugs.

Our mother worked full time as a RN. She was strong on education and hard work, which I came to appreciate years later. She had a rough life and dealt with it in her own way—not by becoming an alcoholic but a workaholic. Our parents eventually divorced, which resulted in absentee parenting, forcing Chris and me to live independently at an early age.

Both of us boys had too much freedom, but we had each other. As the big brother I was responsible for Chris. I cooked breakfast, got us off to school, helped with homework, and brought Chris with me everywhere I went. But I was a kid too, and this was more responsibility than should be placed on the shoulders of a child. In our teenage years, partying took priority in Chris's life. It overshadowed education, sports, and music.

Chris eventually got married, but he never gave up partying even after he had a baby girl. Eventually his wife demanded a divorce when alcohol and drugs took complete control of his life and therapies and interventions were out of reach. The "straw that broke the camel's back" was Chris's actions during my wedding weekend. He could not wake up for their flight back to Rhode Island. His wife left him passed out in the hotel and returned home to get the ball rolling on the divorce.

Chris returned to Rhode Island and moved in with Stanley. Stanley was on Percocet for pain from his disability and was still drinking. The combination of the two was wearing him down. For three years I made it home quite often to deal with the repercussions of both their addictions.

I knew things were bad when Chris contacted me and requested five hundred dollars to bail Stanley out of jail. I wired the money immediately and purchased tickets to fly up days later. In the interim, I called the prison and to my surprise found out that Stanley was still there. What did Chris do with the money? My first thought was that he used it for drugs so

I called my friend Dennis and asked him to check on Chris. Dennis went over to my father's house and found Chris dead on the couch. He had overdosed.

I now had the horrible job of telling my mother and father (who was still in jail) that Chris was dead. The good news, that probably softened the impact, was that we found out that day that my wife was pregnant with our daughter. My mother still broke down, but her wonderful boyfriend of many years has been a rock in her life and I can't thank him enough for helping her through this. Stanley, on the other hand, threatened suicide and was under heavy observation. We had to leave him in jail for a few more days for his own protection. Eventually I took him home and stayed with him until he demonstrated that he had accepted Chris's death as best he could. This is when Stanley and I made the deal: I return home and promise to call him every morning. He promises to stay alive.

Three months passed since Chris's death and my life was just getting back to normal. I made my daily call to Stanley's house but one day Stanley didn't pick up. Instead, a sergeant answered and told me that Stanley Braga was found dead. He was very callous and told me to come to the morgue. Before I had a chance to explain who I was or where I was, he hung up. Another family member gone and another hole in my life.

Life has not been easy over the past six years with the deaths of Chris and Stanley. While Chris's death was an unfortunate episode in our lives, I obtained a heightened respect for my role as a father and husband. Chris was not there for his daughter any longer due to a sad and unnecessary chain of events. I never want that to happen with my family. I love my life and have learned to savor it. I also appreciate the love, respect, and compassion my wife has exhibited all these years.

My life lesson from the death of Stanley is this: No parent is perfect but I learned to respect the love a parent has for a child regardless of where they strayed. Unfortunately most people don't realize it until that parent is gone. My father's life and death was an unfortunate waste of a smart person who could have been an asset to society. His love for family overshadowed his flaws.

"A single beam cannot support a great house."
—Chinese Proverb

CONTAGIOUS PRACTICE

Consider this exercise from The Gratitude Power Workbook by Nina Lesowitz and Mary Beth Sammons. They suggest that we list the following with regard to our loved ones that have passed on: 1. What did this person mean to you? 2. What are the memories you wish to treasure? 3. How did this person bring you joy and meaning? 4. What is your gratitude toward this person?

EMBRACE

Will you walk in my garden
Our hands to hold?
Will we never be parting
If we ever grow old?

Will you stay with me
As bad arises?
Life writes its own rules
Some with nasty surprises.

When the sun no longer
Smiles on my face
Will your love be stronger
As I dream in your Embrace?

A poem by Karen Lyons Kalmenson

CHAPTER FIVE

BUSINESS AND CAREERS

Jobs can be a stepping-stone and a destination at the same time.

Adapting, learning, and making new contacts during a troubled time.

Jobs we don't want can lead to jobs we do want. Job hunting and accepting lower pay may be the remedies for the past and the start of a new future.

Don't be afraid of entrepreneurship if that's your dream.

It's easier than you think and the tools are right in front of you.

Get a taste—"baby step" your way in.

Current financial troubles can yield future prosperity. We need market corrections in order to have cycles as well as buyers, sellers, and prosperity. We need market corrections to educate younger people on the dangers of greed and speculative bubbles.

You can't defy gravity.

I have endured both hard times and prosperity in my life. I have grown businesses and hired people who came to depend on the pay and benefits our company provided. I have let people go and made difficult cutbacks that not only affected my family but also our employees and contractors. One thing that always reigns certain for me is keeping a smile and finding that silver lining in every roadblock and tough decision. Stock market collapses, real estate collapses, industry collapses, and even fraud have all rung our doorbell over the years. What is the by-product of all these experiences? Opportunity!

Opportunity appears in every cycle. If you lost a job but always dreamed of something else, maybe it's time to make the jump. If your investments took a hit, maybe there are buying opportunities. No matter what the specifics are, train yourself to be a contrarian (definition: "a person who takes a contrary position or attitude," *Merriam Webster's Dictionary*, 2010 ed.). For example, two brothers I know are retired pilots. Their pensions took a setback over the past few years. Instead of sitting back and doing nothing, they took a significant portion of their remaining pension dollars and started buying rental properties in southeastern Florida at rock bottom prices post-real estate bubble. They filled these properties with tenants and not only preserved their principal but also created an income stream. They will most likely see asset appreciation as well, due to their low-cost basis.

Many people have obligations that range from feeding a family to paying a mortgage. I understand and believe that diligence, along with a positive attitude, will prevail. If you blame outside factors as the cause of your troubles, then I can assure you that they will take longer to rectify.

When the tech bubble burst and many of our clients and vendors went belly-up, we were facing a difficult situation. My company, Goliath Technology, was a data center procurement and integration company. We specialized in the management of information technology products and services for clients around the world. Being passive about the tech bubble was not an option if we wanted to survive. We took the opportunity to offer credit memos for free equipment and services to large blue-chip organizations and educational institutions. In essence, while we were down we were giving money away. The result? Instant growth with a new, stronger client base. When we were victims of a multimillion-dollar international fraud, which stung many companies in our industry, we took the opportunity to develop our security, disaster recovery, and redundancy business. This ultimately grew a new segment of our company that didn't exist before.

For many of you searching for a job don't be afraid of uncharted territories and emerging markets. Your talents may fit in a whole new industry. Ex-Wall Streeters can be the perfect fit in finance for assisted living facilities or green technology firms. Assembly line workers, or mechanics from defunct car dealerships, are the perfect fit for battery companies, electric car component manufacturers, and even foreign car companies with factories in the U.S. If you're a union member, you will find that more and more unions now understand the need to diversify their employer base across a variety of industries. If you are non-union, there are many options if you follow technology and emerging markets. Head back to your college, technical school, or trade school. Most, if not all, offer lifetime career services for alumni.

Attention Entrepreneurs, *it's time to launch that dream.*

You can baby-step your way in without taking 100 percent of the risk on day one. Start drafting a basic business plan that analyzes the market(s) you wish to enter. Once you see a dream on paper you are further along than you think. Launch the business and sacrifice some free time now to test the waters—nights, weekends, etc. According to a great book called *Getting Real...* by 37signals (Jason Fried, David Heinemeier Hansson, and Matthew Linderman), you do not need to launch a website with all the aspects in place. Get the underlying service out there and let market demand dictate what it needs to grow. The same applies to any entrepreneurial endeavor on and off the web. Make one widget and sell it. Make two widgets and sell them. Baby steps.

For those of you sickened by the collapse of your investments, please smile. Regardless of your age you have now learned to diversify. You have now learned the value of balanced portfolios and short- and long-term strategies. What's better is that you now have "kid in a candy store" choices of affordable investments in stocks, bonds, funds, and even real estate. Buying after a collapse dramatically improves your upside potential in addition to any ongoing income from dividends or rents. In recent security-related corrections we have seen a shakeout of poorly managed (and often fraudulent) firms. Thanks to these shakeouts it is much easier today to find quality investment professionals for any size budget.

David

"My career made a dramatic leap forward when I decided to apply for an internship three years ago. I had just graduated college and there were no entry-level marketing jobs available. I knew the pay was low but I figured it was something, and the experience would be crucial. Now I am in a full-time role with the same organization with great pay and responsibility. I took a chance that many family and friends thought I was crazy for taking, considering the amount of money and time I had spent on my education. I went with my gut and didn't look back."

—Maria Rosado, Indiantown, Florida

"Convert the shame of financial disaster into your new start! Take the disgrace you feel out of consumer debt, by not looking back at the financial mistakes but instead look at the new beginnings and education that the experience offered you."

—Amy Beller, Southold, New York

AUDI OF AMERICA: WINNING THE RACE TO BRAND REVIVAL

DALE BUSS

When Scott Keogh ascended to the position of president and chief executive officer of Audi of America in mid-2012, it marked yet another significant moment in the spectacular rise of the German luxury brand in the U.S. automotive market. Keogh not only had been chief marketing officer of the American arm of Audi, as the brand and sales ascended during the previous few years, he also had played a key role in the company's American product strategy as well.

By elevating one of his key lieutenants when Johan de Nysschen suddenly departed to run the Infiniti brand worldwide, thereby ensuring a relatively seamless transition, the company sent a clear signal to the world that Audi of America not only was on the right road—but it also wasn't going to let up on the gas. The optimism among Audi executives and dealers that had turned around the company has become essential to the corporate DNA of Audi of America.

Indeed, the turnaround in Audi's brand reputation and sales in the United States over the last several years has been remarkable. Sales plummeted to just twelve thousand vehicles in 1991, from seventy-four thousand six years earlier, after Audi suffered a series of recalls because of sudden unintended acceleration in its Audi 5000 models, which were linked to six deaths and seven hundred accidents. The brand essentially lost fifteen years of progress in America to this debacle.

But over the last five years, Audi finally has come of age in the U.S. market, thanks to a long-term turnaround strategy that has begun clicking on all cylinders. Audi continues to significantly outgrow its primary U.S. competitors, BMW and Mercedes-Benz, in percentages of sales increase. Brand leaders now consider Audi likely to reach its goal of 1.5 million sales in America before their earlier-established deadline of 2015, and rather abruptly Audi of America has become a key player in the German parent company's goal of overtaking BMW in global premium-segment sales.

Perhaps more impressively, Audi's greatest gains lately have come in the most rigorous part of the U.S. premium market—the upper segment, where Audi recently introduced overhauls of its A6 and flagship A8 models as well as the new A7, and then sport-performance versions of each.

Meanwhile, Audi dealers continue to spend record amounts on their facilities and personnel to make sure they can keep pace with—and continue to augment—Audi's rise. Bobby Baillargeon, for instance, bought his second Dallas-area Audi outlet in 2007 and is glad he did. "I'm not exaggerating—probably three to five times a month I have someone who is a serious contender in auto retailing contact me and want to buy one of my Audi dealerships," he said. "And we're not just talking about brokers here but about powerful dealers with big names."

The Audi transformation in the United States didn't come easily, however. De Nysschen, a long-time Audi executive and most recently head of Audi of Japan; Keogh, a high-ranking marketing executive at Mercedes who defected to Audi in 2006; and Chief Operating Officer Mark Del Rosso, who was sales chief in the northwest region for Lexus, had to dig deep into the existing Audi culture. They had to transform a relationship with U.S. dealers that long had been soured by the parent company's unwillingness to broaden the product line for the American market and by U.S. management's previous insistence on using incentives and cheap leases to "move the metal" and meet volume goals, despite huge damage to the brand and Audi's long-term prospects.

Del Rosso also quarterbacked an internal transformation at Audi, emphasizing trust as the currency of relationships within the company as well as between Audi and its dealers. He made Stephen Covey's book, *The Speed of Trust*, required reading and preached the imperative of commitment, honesty, and transparency. Del Rosso knew that embracing Covey's credo also would result in the kind of integral positive thinking that would be required to make Audi's turnaround substantial and long-lasting.

As with most fundamental reorderings of corporate culture, things started out rocky. "In January, 2008, it was insanity," Del Rosso recalled. "I would ask some of my key people, 'I'll see you tomorrow, right?' But once the new culture becomes strong enough, people who don't get it will sit on the side, then they'll either leave, or you help them leave. And once you work on trust, it's amazing what can be done. As soon as you start getting results, the results will set you free."

To be sure, Audi still faces a number of issues as it seeks to build on its accomplishments. Some, for instance, have challenged its decision to build its first North American plant in Mexico, where Audi plans to begin producing the Q5 crossover vehicle in a couple of years. But Audi of America has given all of its constituencies, internal and external, plenty of "reason to believe" with its performance over the last several years.

So when, in early 2011, Audi of America celebrated breaking through the one-hundred-thousand-a-year sales level the year before, "it was a monumental occasion for the company," recalled Matt Carpenter, Audi of America General Manager of Vehicle Sales and another important component of the turnaround team. It was time to celebrate the transformation of optimism into achievement. "We needed to have a milestone. And it started making everyone in the company believe."

CONTAGIOUS EFFECT

One doesn't need to rewrite their business plan nor reinvent the wheel. Simply take an inventory of the market, your competition, and take a bird's eye view of your place in it. Just by initiating an analysis of your organization, you are already taking a step in the right direction toward success.

"B"ING THE BEST

RICKY WADE

Growing up in Jamaica I was no stranger to poverty. I was directly exposed to it but knew that hard work and positive energy would yield success. I also knew that giving was just as important—no matter what life handed me. Giving was actually a lifestyle for our family. You may think you are lacking but there is always someone who is worse off than you. By giving back you are not only giving others a chance, you are demonstrating your appreciation for what you have and the opportunities that were presented to you. Ray Kroc, founder of McDonald's, said it the best, "You have to give back to the community that supports you."

This book discusses "positive forward thinking," the practice of recognizing a positive future and using that to endure the difficulties of today. I always believed that working hard would yield a great future for me, hence my positive forward thinking. For example, my first job was working in a clothing factory as a young child and I never looked back!

My ultimate goal was to be a commercial pilot and I started a career in aviation. I dreamed of being a captain that took people all over the world. I was on course for this dream but my life took a sharp turn when my father died in a plane crash. It forced me to readjust but I believe a key part of life is being able to readjust when necessary. Don't be scared to alter a long-term plan when things don't work out. A key trait that I believe all humans have is their resiliency. I found mine and it led me to a mentorship program in the largest food service chain in the world—McDonald's.

I came to the United States as an immigrant. I felt that this McDonald's opportunity was my segue to the American dream. At the time, my uncle gave me a piece of advice that was one of the most valuable assets I took with me. He said, "Be true to yourself, be disciplined, and stay focused. You will go through challenging moments but never take your eyes off the vision of where you want to go." That advice led me to an assistant manager position in Miami, Florida, and then I worked my way up through McDonald's corporate over twenty years.

In April of 2001 I achieved the unimaginable for a McDonald's corporate employee—I purchased seven stores and became a franchisee in Palm Beach County, Florida. The risk and expense was not without stress but I believe in passion, patience, and perseverance. Together with my wife Lissette, we then grew to eleven stores and a staff of five hundred people. Today my goal is to achieve twenty-five stores within the next ten years. I think goals should be challenging and this is a challenging goal! I chose the corporate name of "B"ing the Best because this name reflects the philosophy my wife and I instill in our McDonald's team, our family, and the community.

My life's lessons of hard work, achievement, and giving back are the cornerstones of my community involvement. Our family takes great pride in helping inner city kids focus on the positive and molding them into good citizens. Making a difference may be a lifelong journey but providing opportunities for low-income youth yields a positive environment and a brighter future for everyone.

CONTAGIOUS INSIGHT

An altruistic value system is defined by two key principles that can be applied to any corner of the world: 1) Creating independent young adults is far more productive than fostering an environment of dependency; and 2) If you are doing business in a community, you should be involved in the community as well and help shape its future.

NO WRONG TURNS

SUSAN ORTEZ

I could not remember if my bank appointment was on Third Street or Second Street so I decided to walk down Second. As I walked down the street I realized I was in the wrong place so I turned around to head back to Third. At that moment I was looking at the front door of a law firm. I was drawn to their front door for some reason but wasn't sure why. I ignored this feeling in order to get to my appointment.

I finally arrived at the bank and met with a loan officer. I was applying for a loan so my daughter could attend college that following September. This had been a difficult task as I recently lost my job. Unfortunately, I was advised that my credit displayed a large debt balance. The combination of having debt and being unemployed made me ineligible for the loan. I was advised to reapply when I secured a stable job. My daughter could have applied for a student loan but I didn't want her to start her future laden with debt.

As I walked out of the bank I remembered the front door of that law firm I saw earlier and decided to head back. I walked in without a resume. It was noon and there were two well-dressed men standing at the reception desk. It turned out that these men were partners in the firm and were just leaving for lunch.

Mustering up as much confidence as possible, but still nervous inside, I asked the two gentlemen if the firm was hiring. I explained that I was an administrator for another firm that had closed their doors during the financial crisis. At that moment one of the partners invited me back to his office and quickly interviewed me on the spot. He said I got the job on the premise that I would send him my resume within twenty-four hours and it matched the experience I had explained. I could not believe it! They were about to advertise the opening—my timing was perfect.

Needless to say I got the job and the loan. My daughter is now entering her second semester of college. The wrong street was the right street!

CONTAGIOUS ACTION

It's easy to dream about success and where we want to be in the future. It's easy to visualize and hope that it materializes. But the reality is that optimism, hope, and materialization require one thing—EFFORT. When you find yourself daydreaming about where you want to be, also try to visualize the effort required to get to that point. The combination of these items, along with optimism and confidence, is what comprises our reality. They are mutually inclusive.

DEAD BROKE IS NOT DEAD

KAREN WRIGHT

I was dead broke. I'd heard others say this, but I'd never personally been that far out on a flimsy limb before. And the wind was picking up. My consulting business had experienced rains and droughts over the last nine years, but this time no rain was in sight.

Fear and panic overcame my pride as I stood before my church congregation and I finally admitted the truth out loud. I needed work, any work. Housecleaning, car washing, weed pulling—anything. Tears watered my plea for help. Afterward, a gentleman told me the state park needed an aid for the six weeks remaining of summer. As park ranger, he guaranteed that if I applied I would get the job. It paid $9.05/hour. I tried not to think of the $250/hour my consulting clients used to pay. It would take me three and a half days of park work to earn a single hour of consulting. But, consulting clients didn't exist so I took the job.

I arrived 7 a.m. on my first day. The sky was a glorious blue and I thought, "It's going to be great working outside for a change." My coworkers showed me the ropes. First task every day was to clean the park's four large bathrooms. Scrub toilets, clean sinks, mop floors, empty trash. I wore a baseball cap that first day to keep the sun out of my eyes, but that cap quickly became my shield from the public. I felt shame in having to do such menial work. My cap, pulled low, hid my embarrassment from anyone who might look my way. The rest of that day was spent picking up trash and weeding parking lot medians beneath the hot summer sun. I went home physically dirty, exhausted, and emotionally wrung-out. I hated my situation! I wanted my old life—clean and respectful. Six more weeks of this just made me want to cry. Why was I being punished?

After my emotional tantrum, I soberly faced my options: Quit and find something else. But, in my little remote town, there wasn't anything else. Bite the bitter bullet and just persevere. But this daily ego-raping was torture. Stay and find the gift in this unwanted turn of events. This seemed my only real option.

So, I had a long talk with myself—and my ego. I knew that with my harsh judgments about my job came a deep-seated belief that I was better than those who accepted such subservient work. I didn't much like myself for that. Slowly my humiliation turned into a realization that I was now one of those I had so cruelly judged. Yet, I was still the same person I used to call "consultant." Did my job dictate my value?

I decided that cleaning toilets did not define me and went to work the following morning with my baseball cap raised, a smile on my face, and friendly words for those I engaged in conversation—even while picking up trash. I was in the customer service business, I told myself. My job was to make sure that our guests had the best vacation ever. So, I took pride in how clean and litter-free I kept my park. The meaning of service slowly emerged. And, although the word may share a root with subservient, being of service is anything but debasing.

For the next week or so I had fun. I managed my own time and tasks, I performed superbly. Then, one day, a few hours into pulling yet more weeds, I realized my body was working on autopilot—no thinking. Believing that my thoughts create my future, I chastised myself for wasting this opportunity to visualize possibilities. Here I was not thinking, not creating—I was just pulling weeds. But, try as I might, focus kept escaping me and I'd wake up an hour later to realize I'd checked out again. My enjoyment of the park turned into exasperation. One night, on a call to my friend Marcia, I lamented my inability to focus. She asked me if a Tapping Session (Emotional Freedom Technique) would help. Unfamiliar with Tapping, Marcia explained that I might find out what was going on with me. EFT is about returning the mind, body, and feelings to a state of balance and harmony so you are not limited by negative emotions. It is conducted through your fingers with acupressure points and tapping.

She asked what was bothering me most about my situation. I said, "I feel I'm wasting my life sitting here in the middle of nowhere pulling weeds." Over the next hour we took my initial complaint through a series of physical and emotional shifts. Repeating the phrase, "I'm just sitting here in the middle of nowhere pulling weeds," began to sound so ridiculously comical. First because it was angering me so much, and, then, because it was actually true. This is what my life had become, not at all like my hopes and dreams. Sadness became acceptance and acceptance became peace. Even though this was not my life's plan, I was still who I was and my potential hadn't changed at all. There was a sense of serenity in body and mind. Not acquiescence, not submission. But a sense of surrender to the reality that I was not, and never would be, defined by my circumstances.

My friend commented, "Don't you find it fascinating that in this job that's caused you so much anxiety, you found yourself meditating for hours on end?" I hadn't looked at my weed-pulling unconsciousness as meditation before. I laughed at my blindness. She offered, "I'd say that you weren't sitting in the middle of nowhere pulling weeds, but that you were sitting in the middle of NOW HERE pulling weeds." Now here...

present. It doesn't take a rocket scientist to see the symbolism. I was cleansing—right there on warm summer days breathing clean fresh air. Learning to be present with life.

After six weeks I found a job waiting tables at a local restaurant, another job in service, another chance to strip away a bit more of my sniping ego. I can't say that I walked in free of embarrassment. At the park I was around tourists all day, pretty easy to be anonymous. But people I knew came to the restaurant and were surprised to see me waiting on them. So I got to take my ego in hand again and remember the truth of who I was.

The past two years have not been what I would have wanted. My hopes were loftier, my desires more abundant. But, I've never learned as much about myself, truly, as in this two-year journey. I used to consider those who settled for low-paying jobs as lazy and ignorant. How hardhearted and arrogant I'd been—not anymore. I often say, and believe, that great work comes to those who do small work with dignity and pride. We are given to in proportion to our ability to accept gratefully and responsibly. Looking back at ten years of self-employment, I realize that I'd been constantly afraid. My thoughts were all about me—my finances, my success, my reputation. I sincerely believe that the past two years have been the crucifixion of my ego. Being placed in positions of no authority and little public respect, I was being asked to consider who I was, not just what I was doing. And whether as a waitress or consultant—I was not my job. It did not give me my worth. Those who serve the welfare of others focus upon the act of giving. I'd always focused on what I'd get in return.

This time of tribulation is not about failure. It's about being purified in the furnace of truth and from that I've learned:

Success is not tied to a financial worth.

I can contribute greatly from seemingly humble places.

I won't be abandoned for telling the truth.

I'm much stronger than my ego.

My mind can be my friend or foe and that I either command it or it entraps me.

Sometimes you must leave all you know to find what is worth knowing.

Only those who serve will ever lead.

There is joy in doing whatever I'm doing with the highest honor and commitment.

I never know enough to judge anyone or anything rightly.

Finally, I learned that life is a process of becoming. Today is tomorrow's stepping-stone. Yet today is a gift of great value not to be squandered or trivialized. I do not know what comes next in my life. But I do know that my apparent setback has blessed me with the strength to accept the humble or exalted path with equal gratitude. There is no menial work. There is only the magnificence of who we are shining through all that we do.

CONTAGIOUS INSIGHT

When you find yourself in a job that is not where you expected to be, just remember Gandhi's famous saying: "The best way to find yourself is to lose yourself in the service of others." That lesson will help you get through today en route to tomorrow.

TAKE CHARGE OF
YOUR FINANCIAL FUTURE

MICHAEL POLLOCK

When I was about twenty-two years old, I made a stupid decision about how to invest a few thousand dollars that had been given to me by my father. I bought shares of a foreign company without really understanding its business prospects or the amount of risk posed by putting all of this money into a single stock. Years afterward, I can't remember my reasoning, but I vividly recall that the company soon failed and my investment became worthless.

Determined not to make the same mistake again, my next investment was in municipal bonds. This seemed entirely safe— but, in fact, they weren't. Although government-issued bonds rarely ever fail to repay investors on maturity, they can lose value in the marketplace before they mature when interest rates rise.

Rates did start to rise, and my investment began to erode. I panicked and decided to cut my losses by selling my holdings and putting the remainder of the money into a bank savings account, where I kept it for several years. It was bad enough that I made such mistakes. But then I compounded my errors by switching to what amounted to no investment strategy at all. I was clueless about what to do, and thus, I did nothing.

In some respects, these experiences mirror developments in the U.S. financial markets, including the financial crisis, which erupted in 2007. During the crisis, many people watched in horror as the value of their investment accounts plummeted.

The Standard and Poor's 500 Index, a broad gauge of stock market performance, fell by nearly 40 percent in 2008. Unusually, many seemingly safer investments, such as bonds issued by state and local governments, were also hit hard. What's worse, just as markets were about to hit bottom, many folks pulled their money out and put it into bank deposit accounts and money market instruments. By doing so, they locked in large losses in stocks and other securities.

Despite some notable hiccups, financial markets were healing by 2011. Broad stock market indexes had recovered nearly half of the losses suffered in 2008 and many types of bonds also rallied strongly from their lows during the crisis. Some forecasters believe that the ensuing years could bring a significant recovery in the nation's economy, even as unemployment remains high by historic standards. But even if that happens, it may pose different risks. For example, if inflation rises, that will erode returns from bank deposits and money market instruments. If interest rates rise, some types of bonds, such as those sold by the U.S. Treasury, may actually lose value.

Yet many investors still remain paralyzed about what to do next with their money, an executive of a large financial advisory firm told me recently. Some are keeping funds in low-yielding bank or money market accounts, and others remain in bonds. Many are avoiding stocks altogether.

This isn't a pitch for investing in stocks. Rather, it's a reminder that it's important to be proactive in managing your assets. Diversification has never been more important. It's also easier than ever before, even if you aren't wealthy and can't afford to pay a professional advisor to manage your money. For example, there are mutual funds that invest in a mix of stocks, bonds, and other assets all at once. Thus, by owning the shares of one fund, you can spread your risk around widely and reduce the chances of being in the wrong place at the wrong time.

If you aren't sure how to diversify your portfolio, it may make sense to hire an investment advisor at a respected financial institution or brokerage firm. Some big mutual fund companies also offer guidance to individual investors on how to manage their money, and they charge somewhat lower fees for their services than advisors.

The most recent bout of economic and market turbulence is now behind us as I write this, but most likely we will see more turbulence in the years ahead. By taking charge of your financial situation you may be able to reduce the risks of getting hurt the next time around. It's not a matter of making all the right choices, but, rather, of making some of the best choices.

CONTAGIOUS COMMITMENT

It's easy to tell yourself that today's losses prepared you for the future. But it's not easy to look at your statement knowing it had a few more zeros. Get over it, have confidence that it could have been worse, and use the fundamentals for future investing even if you're starting with just one dollar.

ELEMENTS OF SUCCESS

LEONARD VELASQUEZ
My career has had a multitude of turns with upside opportunities. The first two elements of my success have been attitude and desire. Starting at an entry-level position with only a high school education, I climbed the corporate ladder in banking to middle management. With a positive attitude and desire I have achieved both financial and career growth in spite of a litany of changes encompassing our company's mergers and acquisitions, operational and political re-organizations, company layoffs, and process and system changes. Maintaining a positive attitude and a desire to accept changes in our lives provides the avenue for evolving in an ever-demanding society driven by the need to compete and deliver.

Another key element for job success is networking. I have learned through the years that I don't need to know everything about everything. I simply need to focus my energy on my area of expertise and reach out to others who are more knowledgeable in their areas of expertise. It's amazing how much success you can have if you just know the right people to contact. Networking can be a real asset in getting results as you continue your career journey.

A fourth element of my success was achieved via hands-on practical experience. Twice, in my forty years of service, I took lateral positions without any salary increase in order to develop my technical and business skills. In both cases I reaped what I sowed. There is nothing that can take the place of real life exposure in a working environment. It allows you to get a real understanding of the milestones that need to be reached in order to attain the goals through both individual or team efforts.

The fifth and last element is listening. I have found that listening can be far more powerful than most people credit it. The art of listening can lead to achieving the milestones of success. If you listen attentively and then restate the high points of an important dialogue, it will validate the effectiveness of those communications.

CONTAGIOUS PRACTICE

Attitude, desire, networking, hands-on practical experience, and listening are critical components of success regardless of the industry, regardless of the location, and regardless of your demographics. So be positive, crave the goal, don't be too proud to look to others for guidance, and shut your mouth until it's absolutely necessary!

FORGING A PATH
BETWEEN HOPE AND FEAR

SAM LIEBERMAN

I have come to the conclusion that the whole idea in life is to make life simple versus easy. And believe me, there is a major difference. Through the years I have been constantly bombarded by clients worrying about different issues that have come up either in their business or personal lives. More often than not, when the conversation begins, their thought process shifts from one item to the next, and then again to another, and another. The net result is that they are overwhelmed and unable to think clearly about the important issues.

Throughout our lives we each have been in this situation. The best way to resolve this dilemma is to write each issue (problem) on a pad of paper. Now you can visualize the scope of each problem. Then prioritize the list into groups of immediate, near term, or long term. Then attack these issues one at a time, crossing each off the list as it is accomplished. Along the way you will find new obstacles present themselves (some in ways that you had not even considered). Rather than becoming more frustrated and upset, try to view this as a new piece of the puzzle. I like to remind myself of something that I told my daughter when she was young and would constantly ask, "But what if?" In my infinite wisdom I stated, "You can't slay the dragon till the dragon raises its head." There will always be dragons in your life and business, but if you approach each systematically you will be able to conquer the issue and put it behind you.

During the past few years we have all lived through turbulent times and witnessed events that were unimaginable, even unfathomable, to most. The net result was that most of us withdrew from the game plan that we may have had in place prior to the events—very understandable. I have long had the approach toward my trading that "when in doubt—do nothing." We always want to be in control of our destiny, but during this trying period we were frozen with fear. But...as the dust settled, we had a choice: either remain frozen, or create a new game plan that encompassed the existing circumstances.

If we break the events into their most simplistic form, we come to the conclusion that the government is forcing us to take risk (by creating a near-zero interest rate) though that is not where your mindset is. After many hours of thought, I came to the following conclusion and set a process in motion to help achieve my customer's goal: namely, try to get a decent yield on their money while simultaneously reducing the risk of loss of principal. By doing nothing we eventually realize that our money is not working for us and after inflation we are losing money. By chasing yield, we are scared to death (and rightly so) that when interest rates do rise we will have major losses in our portfolio. But with sensible thought and diligence, we found a way to lock in a strong yield while giving ourselves downside protection.

After many years of trial and error, and living through numerous crises, I have come to the conclusion that one must set attainable goals and have a process in place to achieve them. There is nothing unique about this thought, but the main thing to keep in focus is where you want to get to, constantly review the goals and the process being used, and most importantly, stay within your comfort zone.

CONTAGIOUS PRACTICE

If the reasons for making your initial decision have not changed, there should be no reason to change your process. But, if the reason for making your decision has changed, don't be afraid to react. You do not have to dance every dance.

BE LIKE GUMBY!

BARBARA WULF

It's a tough job market out there, no question about that, but this downturn will pass. When? How? I don't know, but tough times call for a tough, flexible attitude. There isn't time for self-pity or feeling like a victim. Remember Gumby, that pliable green guy made of clay? Just the thought of Gumby makes me smile.

I encourage you to find the emotional support you need to keep you from spiraling downward. These are trying times, but remember, this is not all about you; it's about the economy, the global economy. Take charge of yourself! You can't change the economy, but you can change your attitude. You can work on bending, swaying, and learning to be flexible—and adaptable.

Here are some ideas to consider:

Self-Preservation—Walk, read, go to the library, go to the park, go to the workforce centers, go fishing, plant a garden (seeds are cheap), go to church, call a friend, go to a work support group...just go. Refuse to get stuck, rigid, breakable, and fragile. That sense of desperation will not fuel your ongoing job search. When you get to an interview, you will have a better "state of mind."

Volunteer—It is often true that we get more than we give. Now you might have the gift of time of your hands. Look around. Where could you use some of your talents to assist others? Maybe it's a week working on a Habitat for Humanity building project, serving a meal for the homeless, tutoring a student, or helping an elderly neighbor. Volunteering can help us stay connected.

Work Smart, Not Just Hard—Make sure you are working your job search in the most efficient way. I encourage all of you to "think outside the box." Write an *impact* letter not merely a flat, traditional cover letter. Add interest, appeal, and a "hook" to your letter. Be genuine and engaging.

Informal Networking—In the meantime, you might connect with a temporary employment agency, become a coffee barista, or work retail. When you are around customers, there is a chance to talk with people you don't know and to expand your circle of contacts. These kinds of jobs expand your casual networking and can lead to an informational/referral meeting to increase your work and training options.

Your Sense of Humor—Laughter can lower your blood pressure and kick in natural endorphins. You need several laughs a day and most of us don't get that. We all need to lighten up to help cope with stress.

Retrain or Diversify—Be realistic. Are your skills "cutting edge?" Are you in a saturated field? Has your job been outsourced? Is it time to get reinvested? Learn how you can transfer or expand your skills with an informational meeting with another professional or schedule a visit with a college advisor or career center.

CONTAGIOUS EFFECT

Blessed are the flexible for they shall not get bent out of shape!

CONVERGING CORE VALUES WITH PASSION

JOSEPH CARBONE

In 1996 I became president and CEO of The WorkPlace, Inc., a Connecticut-based nonprofit. The organization primarily administered government-financed workforce programs. Throughout its history, The WorkPlace struggled to find ways to distinguish its work from other organizations that offered similar programs.

Fairfield County business leaders led the Board of Directors of our organization. They wanted the business principles of free enterprise to be applied to this nonprofit, which was 100 percent reliant on government funds.

Like The WorkPlace, I too was struggling when I arrived. I had worked for several years for a conglomerate with major interests in manufacturing defense vehicles. I did well, spent much of my time in D.C., and made more money than I ever did before. It seemed good for a while but something changed inside of me. One day in 1994 I closed the biggest deal for the company. The senior folks called me into the executive conference room to celebrate my success. A big bonus would definitely be coming but I just couldn't enjoy the celebration. I felt this incredible void, almost shame. I recall telling my wife that night that I felt like I needed to shower ten times that day.

My mom was always my hero. She raised me and my four brothers. My dad had died when I was young, so Mom's influence was a force, a wholesome and noble force. She taught us that searching and seizing opportunities to do good for others was the greatest joy on earth. No coincidence that all five sons were in public service at one point.

Although I was an economics major in college, my experience was in human services until I took the job with the defense company. I never made much money but I was happy and at peace with myself. I would rush to get home from work so that I could hold my children and tell them something that I did that day that made a difference to someone in need. Their affection and approval were priceless.

The WorkPlace, Inc. was struggling to redefine itself. I was struggling to honor my core values. Our missions were seemingly miles apart. But missions don't need commonality to converge. They need driven individuals with a passion and determination to achieve. It's the perfect match for sure.

CONTAGIOUS INSIGHT

There will be opportunities along the way that disguise themselves as inopportune. Ignore the disguise. Each opportunity, whether appealing or not, has its purpose. Let it be another rung in your ladder. So here's the message: Trouble finding your career? Search your soul and follow it.

I DIDN'T WANT TO CUT
MY HAIR, SO I QUIT!

JOEL HELLER

Each day we make choices in our personal and professional life and sometimes those choices lead to life-changing events. Life is all about making choices and finding happiness. Would you quit a six-figure job on account of a haircut? I did! It's a little more involved than a haircut, but the decision turned out to be one of the catalysts of a life-changing event for me. The decision helped me to decide what I want out of life.

I spent twenty-plus years working in the insurance industry and making my way up the corporate ladder. By all external viewpoints I was doing quite well. I managed the largest region in the division and was well respected within the company. I had the plaques, budget, and salary to show how successful I had become. All of that, however, did not provide happiness. That type of success can come at a very high cost. I was working eighty hours a week, spending my waking hours tied to a Blackberry, and traveling enough to know the gate layouts of most airports. My professional life had overrun my personal life and I was losing touch.

I found myself missing birthday parties, family dinners, and other important life events. I would find time to make a congratulatory phone call, send a card and a check, but in the end I knew something was missing. My wife and I had become comfortable roommates. She supported each step up the rung. She moved from state to state with me as I made each career-enhancing move. She found a new job in each new town, never complained, and turned out to be the greatest cheerleader I know.

One of the things I would do to unwind was to go camping in remote sections of northern New England. I enjoy tent camping where there is no cell service. I can commune with nature and be free from the tethers of modern life. One night while sitting around the campfire I saw my future: a radical change in life and significant paradigm shift. Life is not what you do, but who you are. I envisioned a life free from the Blackberry, airports, and eighty-hour workweeks. I also envisioned a life free from haircuts!

On one of my last junkets to meet with my boss I was advised that I should get a haircut. I was reminded that I would be meeting with the Board of Directors later that day and a haircut was strongly urged. I promptly responded, "My mom used to tell me that," and walked out of the office. The revolution had begun. Heading back on the airplane I couldn't get the campfire vision out of my head. I sat back in my seat and planned my future.

Back in the small New Hampshire town I call home, I sat down with my wife and discussed all the thoughts that had been running through my head. I had a clear vision of a store we could open in a nearby town; it would be a small retail clothing and jewelry store selling fair trade clothing, jewelry, and crafts from local artisans. I would utilize my business skills to create something from scratch and put the airports, Blackberry, and haircuts behind me. I set out to build the store we had always wanted to shop in.

Why would I give up all that I had achieved and leave a successful career behind? I had come to the realization that achievement and success aren't based on money, titles, or plaques. True success is based on happiness of the heart.

In short order I resigned my position, started writing a business plan, and fulfilled the vision. The action was empowering, terrifying, and enlightening all at once. There was no steady income to fall back on, no corporate structure to rely on, and no boss to tell me what to do. Quickly, however, I found what I had been looking for in life. I was empowered to build my life by my rules and my moral compass. I also found that life is filled with wonder and beauty when you decide to take the path less traveled and to enjoy the walk. The support I received from family and friends fills my heart with joy. My wife and I have rekindled our relationship and we feel like newlyweds again. I've made time to reconnect with old friends, attend family events, and wake up to the life I always wanted.

Time will tell if the business holds up or not, but if that is the question you ask, you are missing the point. The question is, "Have I found happiness?" The answer to that question is "Yes."

CONTAGIOUS PRACTICE

•••○•••

1. Success is defined by your personal happiness. 2. Don't let the fear of failure inhibit your quest for success. 3. Embrace your passion (it makes it fun to get out of bed in the morning). 4. Don't worry about the Joneses because no one knows who they really are. 5. Large salaries, fancy cars, and big houses don't define success. 6. Embrace change. 7. Be the person you want to be. 8. Family and friends are more important than money and titles. 9. You control your happiness and attitude. 10. Be suspicious of any job that wants you to get a haircut.

THE DAYLIGHT OF HOPE

ELISA HAM

The perfect order of the changing seasons, the ebb and flow of the tides, and the darkness that leads to the light of day suggests that there is a mysterious intelligence at work in the natural world. Although I cannot comprehend the essence of this power, the sense of awe that I've experienced, while witnessing the intricate detail of a snowflake or the brilliance of the autumn leaves, assures me that it exists. I believe this same force orders our lives as well, establishing a design that can only be understood when we look back and realize how circumstances mysteriously fit together, creating patterns of sadness and joy, darkness and light. I discovered this design at work when the doors to my lifelong dream of teaching elementary school never opened but a different path presented itself, one that would bring me more inner fulfillment than I had anticipated or imagined.

It's 6:00 a.m. I hear the phone ringing, but I do not want to answer it. I know who it is—a secretary from one of the local elementary schools calling to ask if I am available to substitute. The thought of it makes me cringe. Here I am, a Magna Cum Laude college graduate with a B.A. in English and a Teacher's Certification, and all I've been doing is filling in for someone else. I've had enough of trying to control giddy children excited about having a day off while their teacher is away. I'm tired of distributing someone else's lessons to a class that is not mine.

I had started substitute teaching with the hope that it would lead to a full-time opportunity. Unfortunately, no such opportunities presented themselves, even despite my reluctance to never refuse a job and my diligence at being as conscientious as possible. Instead, I was filled with a growing sense of frustration and despair, especially when almost three years had passed and I still was not teaching.

The sense of confusion and disillusionment I felt overwhelmed me. One day I fell to my knees and prayed that I'd find my niche in life, where I could utilize my skills and education and contribute to the well-being of others. Not sure what step to take next, I picked up the phone and dialed the number of a local community college, hoping that someone there could give me some guidance.

A week later, I was sitting in Mary Christian's office as she looked over my resume. I told her of discouragement at not being able to find a full-time teaching position and asked if she had any suggestions as to how I could utilize my education. She asked, "Would you like to help adults learn to read or write?" She then offered to introduce me to someone who could tell me more about it.

Judy Beech's warm smile and bright eyes welcomed me when I met her. Judy was the coordinator of the campus Writing Lab, where students met with tutors to get one-on-one help with their writing. Judy read my resume and asked me a few questions about my philosophy on teaching writing. She seemed pleased with my answers and asked if I'd be interested in working a few hours in the lab. I was shocked that this meeting would lead to a job offer. I said "Yes," but I had doubts; it was a step away from my ideal of teaching. Instead of nurturing my own class of young, receptive minds, I'd be meeting for only thirty-minute intervals with mature students who'd be more set in their beliefs and perhaps resistant to my guidance.

A couple of weeks later, I cautiously walked into the Writing Lab with the feeling that I was just settling for this type of work. I did not realize that I was at the start of an enlightening profession. I'd soon discover that working with community college students would bring its own fascination, especially when I'd work with students like Randi.

When I first tutored Randi she was unwilling to even talk to me. I asked her questions about what she was working on, and if she would share it with me by reading it out loud. Her eyes would not meet mine as she curtly replied, in a stuttering voice, "No, I don't want to, but I will if I have to." Sensing her resistance, I tried to embrace Randi; I told her I was looking forward to hearing her read her paper and that I knew she had some interesting ideas to share.

With a monotone voice, Randi raced through reading her paper about her high school counselor. When she was done, she mumbled, "I hate writing," and looked away. Even though the essay was a mix of jumbled ideas, I was determined to find something in the writing that Randi did well. I reread the paper and showed her the details she used to convey her feelings about Miss Burkely. I told her how her love for Miss Burkely resonated through her words and reminded me of how much I admired my own eighth grade history teacher. I explained that she had a skill that she should use more throughout the paper. When I was done speaking, Randi looked at me in disbelief and said, "You like the details?"

After showing Randi something that she could do well, she sensed that I was listening to her with an attitude of acceptance, not criticism, and a breakthrough occurred. Her stuttering waned. She now felt comfortable to share her ideas and give her best effort. She told me about how she would not have made it through her four years of high school without Miss Burkely's support and guidance. She further explained that she plans on becoming a counselor someday to help students just as Miss Burkely helped her. The conversation that ensued led to the ideas for her thesis statement, as Randi discovered the meaning she wanted to get across. Randi beamed with pride as she experienced a success.

Students' eyes fill with wonder when they assert themselves and succeed, even in something as small as writing a grammatically correct sentence or an organized paragraph. They gain faith in themselves and their ability to pursue and realize their dreams. Often, during an appointment, I'll hear affirmations such as, "In ten years, I'll have my own business." "I'm going to be a police officer." "After I graduate, I'm going to be an RN." The positive attitude and hope I witness every day from the students confirms the power of the mysterious intelligence working in the natural world and within each of us. I have found working with community college students to be even more inspiring than the wonderment of the child's mind that I had hoped to nurture.

Almost seventeen years have passed since I began those few hours which Judy offered me. These hours led to increased opportunities as I completed my master's degree and my thesis project with a curriculum for teaching writing one-on-one. I've also been teaching writing courses at the college and plan to pursue a second master's in English. When I think back to the closed doors which led to my frustration of not being able to realize my dream, I knew that a force was leading me on another path which I did not plan, but which has been even more fulfilling.

The peaks of joy and the valleys of disappointment in our lives can be brighter when we have hope. Once we are aware that the awe-inspiring force that manifests its power in the natural world is operating in our lives, our faith develops. We can then hope and look forward to our future with expectation, knowing that this same force is behind the design of our lives, mysteriously turning the darkness of closed doors into the daylight of success.

CONTAGIOUS INSPIRATION

Do not despair when your lifelong dream is crushed by the darkness of doors that bang shut on it. Face the future with hope that the intelligence that orders our lives will lead you on another path that will open to the daylight of success!

EXPAND THE VISION OF YOUR FUTURE

MARY ANN DAVIS

As I talk with people who are considering a career change, many people say something like, "Well, I have been a teacher all my life, so I guess I could look for another teaching job." Or, "All I know is accounting." When I encounter that sort of thinking, I remind them that no matter what kind of work they have been doing, they have some transferable skills—skills that are used in many occupations with just a little adjustment.

Inevitably, by taking into consideration the transferable skills they possess, they have more career options to consider. Additionally, if they identify a potential occupation in which they have interest and it fits with their personality and values, but they don't currently possess the primary skills required, I encourage them to consider how they could acquire the skills needed to do the work. Sometimes that means finding volunteer work. For others it means continuing their education or finding a training course. Look for a way that you could develop the skills you need to do the kind of work you desire.

If you are considering making some type of change in your work, I encourage you to expand your vision of your future and don't just consider the same kind of work you have been doing. Do some self-assessments or work with a professional to assist you in identifying your particular factors to keep in mind in considering other occupations. At some point, you will want to get those thoughts written down. The more details you can include, the better. Begin in front of your computer or with a blank sheet of paper. Write down the following: What, Where, With Whom, and How as beginning topics. Then start to fill in those details:

WHAT—What kind of work do you see yourself doing? Will you work directly with people, things, or information?

WHERE—Will you work in a service organization, a business, or perhaps in government? Small, medium-sized, or large? In your community or elsewhere?

WITH WHOM—Regardless of what type of work you will be doing, you will most likely have some interaction with people. Will those people be medical or legal professionals, laborers, upscale customers, the homeless, etc?

HOW—Think about how you will accomplish your work. Will you oversee the work of others; will you be part of a team or an individual contributor? Will you walk door-to-door, sit at a desk, stand behind a counter, climb a telephone pole, etc?

Put down what you can then set it aside. Go back to it after a day or two and add anything else that has occurred to you. This applies to individuals currently in the workforce as well as to those who are looking at returning to the world of work.

CONTAGIOUS ACTION

When considering a new career direction, the decision should not be based solely on the job titles you have held. You are encouraged to not only evaluate your current skills but also your interests, personality, values, and other factors pertinent to your situation.

WHAT ABOUT YOU?

LISBETH CALANDRINO

We worry so much about our business and product branding we forget about our personal branding. What is it that successful companies have figured out, companies such as McDonald's, Starbucks, and Dunkin Donuts? Your first answer might be good marketing but more specifically it's about their brand. Branding used to be just for products but not anymore. Branding is a combination of tangible and intangible characteristics that sets you apart from others. Whether you define it or not, you have a brand. Branding is your reputation; it's what sets you apart and the value you bring to the situation. As my mom said, all you have is your reputation. You're not defined by your job title or your job description; you are defined by the value of your reputation.

What have you invested in your reputation to increase your value?

As the CEO of your own company, what you stand for is as important as what you sell. When there is a "disconnect" between who you say you are and what you do, it makes people lack trust in you. One of the best examples of this disconnect is Tiger Woods. Over the years, his agency has worked hard to portray him as a serious, focused golfer and family man. Although this may be true, incidents in his life make us question his previous branding. It can take many years to repair your brand once your reputation is questioned. To stand the test of time, a brand must be built from the inside out, not the outside in. If your brand is performance-based like Tiger's, you're only as good as your last performance.

We all have a brand. Paris Hilton's brand is one of a beautiful, wealthy young woman living her life. If her "fun loving" gets out of hand it changes the nature of how she is viewed, especially when it is revealed via the tabloids.

I don't think many of us think too much about our brands but we should. This is why your social media profile and behavior should reflect who you are. It is foolish to post anything that is not flattering to you on your social media platform.

Here are some things to consider while building your brand:

First is clarity. Who are you, what do you do, and why does it matter? As you think about yourself, consider what makes you different and is this difference important to the customer you're trying to reach? The answers to these questions will help you determine your market strategy. If things aren't going right you may have the wrong strategy or the wrong customers. Remember your business can have lots of customers; you just can't have all of them. If you're clear on who you are you will get your share.

Second is consistency. Can you be counted on to act the same way no matter what the situation? I once had a boss who was fine until about the third week of every month when the inventory was due. She became nasty, angry, and just awful to be around. When the monthly figures were unveiled, her job was on the line.

The last is your character. Character is what makes you *you*. This is your personality, your sense of humor, or as the French put it, your "joie de vivre" or love for life. Your love for life is what makes people want to connect and get to know you. This is your gift and your "personal flair." I know people say, "Lisbeth, you move so fast, you have so much energy and enthusiasm." I consider these my gifts. On the other side is the Lisbeth who gets bored easily, burnt out, and occasionally short-tempered.

The better you know yourself the better you will be at connecting to your "special customers and friends."

CONTAGIOUS COMMITMENT

Build the brand that makes you, you. Stay true to that and your brand will be something that people can count on—associates, family, friends, etc.

CONCERNED ABOUT A DELAYED RETIREMENT?

DEE CASCIO

Many of us have been astonished at the unprecedented losses in the stock market, the uncertainty of the real estate market, and the extremely shaky economy. Are you thinking that the solution to this economic downturn is to postpone your retirement for another five, ten, and even fifteen years? Wrong! The assumption that you need to totally postpone your plans is based on a faulty premise that retirement is primarily "financially based." You might be thinking if you had enough money, you could have a successful retirement, but without all of the money you had originally planned for, there is no way that you can retire. This belief is not only faulty, it ignores the fact that more and more people want to continue working after they retire, and not just because of economic reasons. Many people, including Boomers, are setting a new precedent by making work, on their own terms, a part of their retirement portfolio.

LESS MONEY IS NOT THE PROBLEM; MORE MONEY IS NOT THE SOLUTION

Financial security is only one aspect of successful retirement. So much emphasis has been placed on money that many people retiring have adequate financial resources but no direction, no plan, no purpose or meaning to their lives. Each day looks just like the last. I have observed this, read about it, and heard people share their stories about this phenomenon. Many adverse situations that begin as serious problems can actually create new opportunities in life. Why not turn a negative into a positive, by using the economic downturn as an opportunity to reconsider what you had always planned for in your retirement years? Is moving to another location what is really best for you? Is stopping work completely your ultimate objective?

Maybe you could retire when you originally planned by thinking outside the box. When you created your original retirement plan, did you really know what you wanted? How many of us have made important decisions in the excitement of the moment, only to reflect back on them at a later time with regrets?

In Marc Freedman's book *Encore*, he describes a number of people whose lives were destined for a traditional retirement; however, through unexpected life circumstances, a downturn in the economy, or injustices they experienced in their work environment, everything changed. These individuals used the gift of this extra time and adversity to create opportunities that made a significant difference in their world. They experienced a more successful retirement than they had ever envisioned. It took stopping, reevaluating, and changing direction to make this happen. After they examined their changed circumstances, they were determined not to use the next thirty years of their lives playing golf and getting lost in a leisurely life. They decided to make a difference on their own terms.

If you haven't carefully considered the non-economic aspects of this important life transition, then maybe this is an opportune time to stop and reconsider your future. This effort could lead to an improvement of your original plan as it morphs into a whole new vision. The old adage from the 1960s—"Failing to plan is planning to fail"—is as alive and well today as it was then.

CONTAGIOUS INSIGHT

•••●○●•••

Many are working in retirement but doing it in a different way and doing something that they truly love and enjoy. What have you always wanted to do but didn't have the time or money to do? Is there a cause out there that could bring you some income but not tie you down and rob you of hard-earned free time? What was a dream that you had when you were younger that you would like to pursue in retirement? These are the kinds of questions that could lead you down the path of self-discovery.

POSITIVE ASPECTS OF
A MARKET CORRECTION

DAVID MARTIN

In 1994 I started my career in financial services, working as my father's assistant at PaineWebber in Stamford, CT. My father was a Senior VP and one of the big cheeses of the branch. He had many clients who were wealthy and loved their Connecticut tax-free insured municipal bonds. I came along fresh out of San Diego State University, School of Finance.

Bring on tech stocks… It was 1994 and everyone was using computers with Intel's microprocessor and Microsoft software, two stocks which became a "must own." What came next in 1995 was the beginning of the world's information highway: the Internet.

The Internet was so revolutionary and innovative that it caused a stock market bubble, termed "the Internet bubble," which is how history will classify the crash of 2000. This crash is considered the biggest drop since the Great Depression of 1929 (seventy-one years without a good crash).

WHAT THE "MARKET CORRECTION" OF 2000–02 DID TO BENEFIT MY CAREER FOR THE SUSTAINABLE FUTURE

Prior to March 2000, and only for a few weeks thereafter, my clients and I were so caught up in technology that at times our portfolios were 100 percent tech stocks without a single "blue chip" holding. We ignored dividend stocks and other safer investments so we could focus 100 percent of our attention on new emerging technologies that were part of the "new economy."

From 1995 until 2000 we made millions of dollars in profit by investing in tech stocks with funds borrowed against the value of our holdings. The process of borrowing in this capacity is called "Margin" and it is very dangerous, especially in an exuberant market.

Next came the oceanfront condo and high-performance yacht. Oh yeah, how can I forget the second brand new car, a BMW M-series convertible. I became a capitalist monster. What happened to David Martin?

REALITY CHECK: WHAT GOES UP MUST COME DOWN

While we were making money overnight, my mother kept trying to remind me about gravity; what goes up must come down. Then in March of 2000, just two months after my mother died from pancreatic cancer, the market came down from its unjustified levels. My mother was right.

THE NASDAQ INDEX

The Index, which reflects the hundred biggest tech stocks, went up 400 percent in less than ten years, the unhealthiest period in its history. When a bullish cycle is happening it creates an uncomfortable feeling as an investor. You are making money in your previous investments and at the same time fearful of making new investments. In this case stocks were getting expensive but we kept buying, worried that stocks would keep going higher and we would miss the boat. For example, if you go shopping and see shoes you like for $100 and then next week you see them again for $120, you feel that you're not getting the same value you would have gotten two weeks ago when they cost $100. In stock vernacular, I refer to that cycle as "chasing" the stocks higher.

This real life example is why corrections bring so much health to the marketplace. Prices drop dramatically in a market correction. You just have to have investment discipline to "buy low, sell high."

During 2007, symbol SPY (the Standard and Poor's Exchange Traded Fund, which reflects the stocks of five hundred large publicly held companies that trade on either of the two largest American stock market exchanges) traded over $150 per share and was the most popular Exchange Traded Fund (ETF) in the world. Less than two years later, in March of 2009, SPY traded below $70. This was an amazing deal if you were buying instead of selling in March 2009, typical of a bona fide contrarian.

Following market corrections, as intense fear subsides, new capital tends to flow into the markets creating improved balanced and stability. It's the periods of fear and greed that make market conditions unhealthy, going up too much or down too much. The periods following these market corrections were the healthiest periods I have experienced in my sixteen years of investing.

So, when companies like Google trade at $700 per share, true investors should not be comfortable paying that much. It's like the old saying, "Last one in is a rotten egg." True investors should make new investments after market corrections when the probability of loss is much less.

CONTAGIOUS EFFECT

•••●**◯**●•••

During periods of fear and uncertainty, the stock market will drop and go through a correction phase thus creating favorable circumstances for new investments and future profits. Use that to your benefit instead of dwelling on past losses.

TRUE RICHES COME FROM WITHIN, NOT FROM A WALLET

HARVEY REPHEN, ESQ.

As I reflect on my personal life experiences, I find myself viewing a common theme in reference to universal survival and self-preservation. I know that this has many different connotations for each individual. As a child, I witnessed many of life's hardships suffered by the people around me. Helplessly I watched them endure unjust pain and torture because there was no one around to protect and guide them. At a very early age, I knew that I would one day dedicate my life to being of service. What really resonates for me is a combination of helping people find their inner strength and helping to relieve their burdens as they figure out how to rebuild their lives. One day, clarity came to me. The best way I could be of service is as a consumer debt advocate. One of many profound lessons that have come out of my past is that there is no shame in financial difficulty. What makes a person rich is not the size of their wallet, but rather the size of their heart and principles.

In today's atmosphere of financial distress and economic uncertainty, there is a new type of threat to consumers—a type of debt collection called "Vampirism," which basically is the process of draining the last drop of financial wealth from consumers who are unable to pay their bills. This mentality poses a severe threat to those attempting to recover from financial devastation. However, Congress created the FDCPA (the Fair Debt Collection Practices Act) to regulate practices such as these.

The FDCPA protects the consumers' rights by limiting the who, what, where, when, and how of debt collection. The primary power of the FDCPA is that it gives you, the consumer, the right to sue any debt collector violating your rights. Plus, the debt collector has to pay you up to a thousand dollars and your attorney's fees, making it a fairly easy, free, and effective method for you to be protected from by abusive debt collectors.

The two most common violations of the FDCPA are:

1) The failure of debt collectors to identify themselves as a debt collector attempting to collect a debt (and that any information would be used for that purpose). In every conversation this warning is necessary.
2) A message is left on an answering machine and someone other than the consumer it is intended for hears it (a very common circumstance). This is called "third party disclosure." So almost any message left on an answering machine today is potentially a violation of your rights.

It is a little known fact that the FDCPA can be used as an offensive weapon in helping consumers eliminate debt and clean up their credit reports. Often when a debt is legitimate, and there has been an annotation of such a debt on a credit report, it is almost impossible to have it removed. Furthermore, instead of receiving the thousand dollars, you can negotiate to have the original debt dissolved, thereby eliminating the debt and cleaning up the credit report at the same time.

It is extremely important that all physical evidence be saved, such as messages left on your answering machine, letters received, and a written call log containing the date, time, and content of any conversation with any debt collector. Following these simple procedures will ensure that you have a strong and easily proven case. The FDCPA can stop the harassment and abuse and even take you from despair and financial devastation to hope and freedom.

Even though we as a country are facing hard economic times, there is a stronger awareness as to what is really important in our lives. A person's true wealth is based on something even more valuable than money; it's based on the integrity of the person and how they choose to live their life.

CONTAGIOUS ACTION

The Top Five Signs of a Brave Person:

1) *It takes a strong person to admit they need help. So whenever somebody comes to me asking for help, I am honored to have the responsibility of helping, protecting, and strengthening this person.*
2) *Knowing who to ask for help. Seek competent counsel; you cannot be as effective as a professional. Good counsel can get the harassment to stop.*
3) *Maintaining a strong positive attitude combined with affirmative action is the key. In this case, form a plan of action to create mental relief from the pressure.*
4) *Moving forward even when you don't feel strong enough. Think of those around you that are important and how giving up on yourself would devastate them.*
5) *No matter how competent the counsel is, or good the advice given, it cannot be carried out without your willingness to take an active role. Balance between having trust in good counsel, letting them do their job, and knowing when to make your own decisions.*

REINVIGORATING
ENTREPRENEURIALISM

RICHARD ANTHONY

The jobless economic recovery has created a national mania for entrepreneurialism. Given the dearth of good paying jobs, people of all ages are being encouraged to consider self-employment. Companies too are being exhorted to rekindle the spirit of entrepreneurialism that gave birth to them.

Derived from the late nineteenth-century French word *entreprendre*, the word *entrepreneur* means simply "to undertake." In the U.S., entrepreneurs were folk heroes, perceived as young, undisciplined eccentrics who thrived on risk, developed infallible instincts, made A.D.D. (Attention Deficit Disorder) a virtue, and were either lucky or unlucky nonconformists.

Paradoxically, "entrepreneurial attitude" is often used by hiring managers to describe ideal candidates who have a demonstrated ability to "think out of the box," "push the envelope," and infuse the organization with "breakthrough thinking." Once wooed and hired, however, they too usually enter a culture that is antithetical to risk-taking. Worse, it punishes movement outside of the bounds of the tried and true.

Having consulted with companies of all sizes and across major industries, I have often wondered why entrepreneurialism is seen as something outside of the mainstream of corporate America. In most cases, payroll employees are not treated like risk-takers and are generally constrained by their job descriptions. On the other hand, when they take calculated risks, implement a plan, and accept the risk of failure, employees are therefore, by definition, entrepreneurs. It's a pity their employers don't see it that way.

Ordinary people are capable of doing extraordinary things when the goals and objectives are clear, they have a personal stake in the outcome, and risk-taking is rewarded. Company executives sometimes need a little prodding to see the merits of changing their ways and establishing an entrepreneurial culture. Most organizations go through periods of slow growth and unrealized potential—ideal circumstances for internal entrepreneurs to blast through barriers. Becoming an entrepreneurial organization begins with liberating people from their job descriptions and adopting a partnership approach to management/employee relations. Every organization has the potential to reinvigorate the entrepreneurial spirit that initially propelled them beyond the gravitational pull of failure.

CONTAGIOUS PRACTICE

Sometimes it's best to throw away the rules that most organizations tend to operate by today. Instead, get back to the raw energy that spawned the venture and energized it in the early years.

RIGHT A WRONG,
IT MAY BE LIFE-CHANGING

BARBARA RADY KAZDAN

Some people can't rest until a wrong is righted or a hardship relieved. Others see the bigger picture: What is causing that injustice or hardship? How can we interrupt the chain of cause and effect?

For years I worked to alleviate poverty in the workplace and in the volunteer arena. As a forty-five-year-old homemaker, I discovered my vocation had a name. I'm a "Social Entrepreneur," someone who seeks new ways to solve old problems like homelessness and hunger. Social Entrepreneurs try to find and fix the root cause of the problem. My cause was adult literacy. I knew that when people reach adulthood without basic reading and math skills it's often because they weren't well served by the public education system. Some never went to school or couldn't finish because they had to work to help their family. Regardless of the reason, they need a second chance.

Drawing on professional and volunteer leadership experience, I founded an organization that offered low-literate adults a path to high school equivalency diplomas, living-wage jobs, and college. It took two years to get the public support I needed to make it happen. Then I reentered the workforce as founding executive director of an urban literacy coalition. When I was young, there was no name for people who create a better way to address a social issue. Those pursuits weren't listed in the dictionary of occupations. So people like me followed conventional paths until something spurred them to act. Then they taught themselves how to lead a social movement or start an organization. They didn't know that there were others like them from whom they could learn and with whom they could share. When they encountered challenges they had no colleagues to guide their way.

Now Social Entrepreneurs are recognized as pioneers in a burgeoning field. They gather at conferences to exchange ideas. They collaborate on exciting initiatives. Their successes change the status quo, bringing hope to seemingly hopeless causes. They come from many backgrounds and generations but share certain traits. They are pragmatic idealists: people who know how to develop an idea into a practical reality. Like business entrepreneurs, they set out to build a better mouse-trap. But their goal is not to achieve personal wealth; it's to change the world.

Just as businesses create and test a franchise in one locale with a view toward replication, social innovators launch pilot projects designed to be copied. Their dreams are contagious, so they quickly attract colleagues and supporters. They may be precocious or late bloomers but once they get that bee in their bonnet to fix an entrenched social pattern that is holding people back or creating more harm than good (think nursing homes), they reinvent themselves. They pursue their new passion wholeheartedly, full speed ahead.

Is there a social injustice that you cannot stop thinking about? Do you see people suffering but feel powerless to change it? In the social change arena you could join or start an organization that addresses the problem. Choose an organization that is forward-looking, dynamic, and bold. Find a volunteer or staff role that fits, and discover why so many people work in the nonprofit sector, where compensation includes intangible rewards.

Your efforts can change lives, including your own. Everyone

flourishes in workplaces where ideas matter, values count, and teamwork trumps seniority. The compensation includes benefits that transcend conventional offerings. And who knows, maybe when you get involved in someone else's passion, yours will be awakened. There might be an idea percolating in you that you will be ready to try. You may be surprised to find that you're a Social Entrepreneur!

CONTAGIOUS BY EXAMPLE

If you're between jobs or happily employed, consider a role in the nonprofit sector. It may offer fertile soil for your personal and professional growth. Investing your skills and experience in service to a cause has a lasting impact on the well-being of others. Check out local community events to find active nonprofits in your area. Also contact the local Kiwanis Club, Rotary Club, Lion's Club, and even the Chamber of Commerce for listings.

FINE-ANCES

We have entered an age
Of financial downtrend
But this is not the beginning
Of the end.

It is the start of
Some challenges new
Career change possibilities
A fresh point of view.

And every day you remain
Above ground
Your world is still out there
Opportunities abound.

A poem by Karen Lyons Kalmenson

CHAPTER SIX

MATURING AND STAYING YOUNG—HEALTH, FITNESS, AND RELAXATION

Stop worrying!

We often forget the good parts of our lives because we worry too much about the negative, the future, and even the past. Why? Your family and friends don't benefit, your career doesn't benefit, and, most of all, you don't benefit.

You have nothing to lose by being positive versus the stress you will definitely gain by being negative.

This chapter discusses health, outlook, hobbies, wellness, and the importance of relaxation.

"You might feel impatient when things are not as final as you hoped...Let go of the fear that you won't have enough and the world comes to you."

—Dear Abby

"Maturing and Staying Young," I like this title because it conveys exactly what people can do, concurrently, if they keep a positive attitude and live a healthy, fulfilling life. The expression that "age is only a number" is very accurate when you think about the advances in medicine and the revolution in wellness, exercise, and sports.

Exercise in some form is vital not only for your physical being but also for your mind. It stimulates many aspects of a person and it directly affects their confidence, relationships, outlook, and even their work performance. For myself, I find that some form of exercise every morning is critical as it carries me throughout the day. My outlook remains positive, my performance is efficient, and my energy stays strong. The days that I miss morning exercise will usually start to drag by the early afternoon. In terms of physical benefits, I am able to keep excess weight off and still maintain the fair appetite of diverse foods and beverages I enjoy.

Many professionals that had been stimulating their minds through their occupation have found it difficult to retire. Those professions can include lawyers, doctors, architects, engineers, writers, accountants, chemists, biologists, and various skilled tradespeople. All those years of stimulus have most likely put their minds into a cycle. A "cold turkey" shutoff can unbalance the mind and potentially age a person rapidly. Time and time again we see retirees take on consulting jobs, part-time teaching careers, and mentorship outreach. I believe this is something many retirees should consider regardless of their financial position. It is a form of exercise that the body and mind crave. We consider this a wellness that keeps the mature young.

Wellness has taken on a wider meaning today and encompasses topics such as yoga, chiropractics, meditation, vitamin supplements, mind exercise, and many aspects of Eastern and Western medicine. It is a diverse multibillion-dollar industry that is growing and becoming widely accepted among Generations X, Y, Baby Boomers, and more. In terms of relaxation, imagine having that metaphorical weight on your shoulder. Perhaps it's a speaking engagement, an interview, a major bill coming due, an upcoming surgery, or maybe that first date with someone special. Imagine the feeling of elation when that weight is lifted, just seconds after the episode is over. It is a wonderful feeling. Unfortunately, most people don't look at the moment that follows the completion of the event; they only see the event itself and are terrified.

When viewing an obligation with some sense of anxiety, you are causing yourself unnecessary stress. I can tell you from many years of obligations that it is easy to change this habit. First, feeling prepared for the obligation is an important step. You immediately remove the question, "Am I prepared?" Second, focus on the end result of the obligation, not the obligation itself. For example, by speaking at the lecture, you will potentially land ten to fifteen new clients and gain additional notoriety. Or, once you pay that loan, you will be back in good standing with the bank and on the path to improved credit. Third, if the obligation is something that makes your heart race (such as public speaking), focus on something that is unrelated just prior to the event. For example, in your mind, focus on the emblem in the center of a spinning car wheel or the blades of a ceiling fan. The idea of focusing on something unrelated, but simple and consistent, will distract the fear and allow you to perform.

These things may sound odd but they have worked for me and many others. You and I both know that whatever it is we are stressing about will eventually be over. Hence, something we can look forward to. That "looking forward" is the key to making the looming event or obligation go smoothly and the basis of "positive forward thinking" which is the underlying theme of this book.

"You have nothing to lose by being positive versus the stress you will definitely gain by being negative." This is a phrase I coined and have been saying for years. Say it to yourself a few times and really let it sink in.

David

"Peter Walliman, a Swiss scientist, has an interesting and profound view on beauty. Here is a part of it that moves me, 'The whole is inherently beautiful. In the seed of a plant slumbers the Beauty of the meadow. A single drop of water holds the Beauty of the ocean. The laughter of a child reveals the Beauty of humanity. Beauty fills the whole of being: from grain of sand to universe. Beauty lies in the first cry of the newborn, and Beauty lies in the last breath of one dying. Beauty is omnipresent.'"

—Tom Loosmore, Hampton, New Hampshire

"Approaching life is like docking a boat. Approach the dock slowly; if you approach too quickly you will hit hard. Your smooth landing not only yields confidence but it also keeps the boat in good shape. Your life is the same. Take it slow, relax, and allow things to work out for the best. This mentality will give you, your body, and your mind a lifetime of faithful performance."

—Rebecca Rescigno, Seattle, Washington

"I met an interesting woman the other day in her sixties. She was carrying a bag that had a logo on it from a local art studio. It turns out that she took classes and taught there as well. In learning more about her painting, which had turned into a lucrative new career, I was amazed to find out that she had only recently taken up painting after humoring her friend to take a class with her. This woman related how she found peace, creativity, and passion for art and painting. And she discovered a hidden talent that she might never have uncovered otherwise. How many of us have the same story—or want to? No matter how old you are, it is never too late to chase your dreams and uncover your passion."

—Dr. Barbara Seifert, Orlando, Florida

TIME HEALS; TESTS REVEAL

DR. ANDREW FAGELMAN

Each year there are over 40 million visits to health care providers in the U.S. for the routine common cold. That is a huge number considering there are only 307 million people in the U.S. (as of July 2010). That means 13 percent of the overall population visits a doctor, or clinic, for a cold. In many cases we find that a majority of these people do not necessarily have to run to the doctor at all.

The human body is an amazing thing that naturally adapts to fight ailments, such as the common cold, which is predominantly viral in origin. Just give your body time, it will fight and most likely win. So next time you're feeling sick with the common cold, relax, rest, and your body will do its thing. Sure, the cold may knock you down a few days but it is building up your immune system in the process. The immune system is essentially a memory that will not allow the body to get sick from that virus again.

Recovery from a cold can also be affected by the mind as well. According to a recent article in the *Wall Street Journal* by Jennifer Corbett Dooren, "A study (by researchers at the University of Wisconsin, Madison) of more than 700 patients found cold suffers who get a pill, regardless of what it contains, have less severe symptoms and recover a bit sooner than patients who don't take pills....Researchers concluded that there can be a placebo effect with the common cold."

So far everything I have mentioned is not only cost-effective for the patient, it is less taxing on the health care system as a whole. Plus, taking these natural steps is making you stronger and more resilient against future ailments. This common cold example is only one ailment and it is easily self-treatable for many people. However, if you have a high fever or prolonged symptoms you should see a doctor.

Another health and wellness topic of importance is vitamin D. Vitamin D deficiency is the most common nutritional deficiency worldwide. Why does this occur? This occurs because we aren't out in the sun as much as our ancestors. Plus, we are using sunblock in massive volume, which blocks the natural absorption of vitamin D from the sun.

Protecting your skin with sunblock is important, and for many people it is critical. However, taking a vitamin D supplement each day can easily make up for what is being lost by not having direct exposure to the sun. Unfortunately, many people underestimate the importance of vitamin D and its deficiency not only increases the risk of certain skeletal issues, it is now recognized as a deficiency that increases the risk of many chronic diseases including cancer, autoimmune disease, Type II diabetes, heart disease, hypertension, infectious disease, osteoarthritis, and depression. We strongly urge patients to be tested for their vitamin D levels, and 75 percent of the time their levels are deficient.

CONTAGIOUS ACTION

·•○●○•·

Letting a cold run its course and adding a vitamin D supplement to your day, if permitted by your doctor, have profound effects and lead to a longer, healthier life.

HEALING AND CURING

TERRI SCHANKS

The word *heal* is a verb…active, moving, fluid, full of life. *Cure* is a noun…a person, place, or thing, but more importantly, the passive recipient and observer of the actions or movement of another. Cure is also a reference to salting the flavor and life out of something for the sake of saving it. Such is the difference between healing and curing. If necessity is the mother of all invention, then the need for a cure is probably the mother of all healing.

Cures are about surviving while healing is about thriving. Cures are about what the experts think they know regarding you, or a disease, and then restoring physical function to the body. Healing, on the other hand, is about what you come to know and believe about yourself.

Before I moved into a private practice dedicated to healing I worked in hospice for several years. During that time I had the opportunity to be around hundreds of people while they were dying, and at the time of their death.

While working with adults, a common theme was the desire to be healed, and we would often discuss the differences between healing and curing. The truth is that I haven't seen a lot of cures in my life, although I have seen some. In my work, I've seen what would be considered miracle cures by the medical establishment: tumors evaporated from scans, bones and ligaments inexplicably knitted back together, addictions removed as if by magic, hearts and organs mysteriously restored as if brand new. But the truth is that most people I worked with in hospice still died from their illness—they were not cured. Yet scores of them were healed in a deeper sense as their relationships to self, wholeness, family, friends, and God were restored.

I have worked in healthcare (alternative and Western medicine) for years. I have come to believe that you can be healed and not cured, just as you can be cured and not healed. Sometimes grace filters in like spiritual penicillin and we experience both. Healing can take place at many levels, many of which may not be recognized by a scan or a doctor or anyone else. Nonetheless healing can take place in invisible yet profoundly tangible ways. Life traps can be worked through and new insights can be gained. Broken relationships and past hurts can be repaired while a new sense of peace can be found through the healing balms of forgiveness and acceptance. All of this can happen without any outward physical changes that would be marked as a cure, yet there is no doubt healing has taken place.

Curing is about not wanting to carry the pain, but healing can be about letting the pain carry you. Curing asks, "What needs to be fixed?" while healing asks, "How can I grow? What can I learn?" Thomas Merton said, "The more we try to avoid suffering, the more we suffer." Zen teaches that the obstacle is also the path and without pain there is often no compassion.

Healing is about living life to the fullest and not getting too worried about what the experts say because what is deemed healthy today may not be considered healthy tomorrow. Healing is about remembering that laughter can be the best medicine. Doug Larson, the famous runner and 1924 Olympic gold medal winner, said it best, "Life expectancy would grow by leaps and bounds if green vegetables smelled as good as bacon." To your good health!

CONTAGIOUS COMMITMENT

On the path to wholeness and healing it's important to remember that if you refuse to give up some bad habits, you might not actually live longer but it might just seem longer. So start making those improvements today and live a longer, better-quality life.

A SILVER ELEPHANT

JACQUELYN SAAD

I remember the day well, November 9, 2005. I was scheduled for surgery following a diagnosis of breast cancer. I got out of bed, having slept little, and dressed to go to the hospital. I was scared for myself and for my family. My son was only fourteen and he hadn't taken my diagnosis well. My husband was supportive and strong, but he looked like a deer in the headlights. My sisters were trying hard to hide their distress, but I was not fooled.

It was a long day but the surgery went well. The doctor was confident that the cancer had been removed and that it had not spread to my lymph nodes. All that would be required would be a few rounds of radiation and I would be done. I went home and spent a couple of days reading and watching TV and then went back to work feeling good and optimistic.

Unfortunately, the pathology results revealed that the cancer had indeed spread to my lymph nodes. More surgery would be required followed by months of chemotherapy and then a course of daily radiation. The day I got that news was followed by the longest, darkest night of my life. If I didn't make it, I figured, my handsome husband would find a new partner and I was okay with that, but my son would be motherless all of his life. I could barely stand to think of it. And then there was treatment. I didn't want to go through the pain. Didn't want to be sick. Didn't want to be weak. Didn't want to be bald. At some point in the night my husband and I realized neither of us was asleep. I told him how scared I was. He held me close and let me cry.

Eventually the sun rose and so did I. Life went on and there was still work to do. I still had to go to the office. Still had to take my son to school. Still had to get dinner on the table that night. I went through the motions of daily life still fretting about how I would get through the long course of treatment ahead. At some point that day I decided that getting through cancer treatment is like eating an elephant. It is possible to eat an elephant. You just have to eat it one bite at a time. With my limited artistic skills I drew an elephant and put it on my desk. After each treatment I erased a little piece. By July 21, 2006, it had vanished. I had eaten the elephant.

The second surgery I had revealed no further evidence of cancer. In the world of cancer talk, statistics are normally quoted for the five-year survival rate. I more than survived; I thrived. As I write this I am five years cancer-free. Tonight I will celebrate with dinner in the company of those I love and a couple of glasses of really good champagne.

And I will wear the gift I bought for myself to mark this milestone—a silver Pandora bracelet. Hanging from its center is a shiny silver elephant.

CONTAGIOUS ACTION

•••●•••

When faced with a problem that looks too daunting to get through, try to remember you don't have to do it all at once. Create a calendar or timeline and cross off the milestones as you progress toward your goal.

LIFE BEGINS AT SIXTY-FIVE

ROSEMARY H.

Life begins at sixty-five. Well, that's what I'm counting on anyway. I've decided that I am ready for a "new" life, another honeymoon with my honey. We've been through a lot lately, being pulled different directions, and we did it together—George, me, and God.

I have always been a planner. I planned my whole life out since I was a child and it turned out perfectly...a good paying job right out of high school, my own apartment with two of my dearest friends, lots of fun times, and the support of a wonderful, loving family. Then I met George. I knew he was the one the moment I met him. We were married six months after we met. He far surpassed all the husband requirements that I had imagined since childhood. We had three beautiful children, two boys and a girl. We've had a "can't ask for any more" kind of life. It was prosperous, fun, and exciting. We went, went, went and did, did, did. But then God decided to show me who was in control and decided to rearrange our charmed life. What an awakening!

Things all began to change about five years ago. Our children were happily married with lives of their own. We were so proud and looking forward to living in paradise forever. Our oldest son Daniel traveled "home" from where they lived in Georgia to join my husband and our other son and son-in-law to fish in a tournament in the Bahamas. At the dinner table the night before Daniel began to have a lot of pain. I rushed him to the hospital.

By the time we got there he was gray. The doctor called for us to come back to the room where Daniel was. The doctor said, "Stand here where Daniel can see you. He is having a heart attack and we're preparing him for surgery." What did I just hear? He's only thirty-six! Needless to say they didn't get to the Bahamas. There is a good ending to the story. Daniel has made some necessary changes in his lifestyle and continues to monitor his medical condition. They have a precious son and daughter now. Life is good again. The Lord works in strange ways.

At about that same time our other son, Jeremy, began to have his own set of problems. Before we knew it he was divorced and living with us again at the age of thirty-four. I knew it was temporary. He met a woman right away and they were secretly married. About a month later they told us and proceeded to move her in too. I still knew it was temporary! Shortly after, they were involved in a car accident that left them both disabled. Fast forward four years and they are still here, unemployed and unhappy. The pain clinics have done their evil on them and us. I won't go into details but there seems to be no light at the end of the tunnel. We pray every day that God will take them in His loving hands and heal them and us. They are still here for a reason.

In recent years our sweet daughter, Cybil, had her own dilemmas. She had severe pain for several years and was certain she was being misdiagnosed. As a result, she finally went to see an in vitro specialist. He found other complications, which could lead to a hysterectomy in the near future but he wanted to give her a "window" to see if she could conceive a child. Not easy to hear at age thirty-two. On top of that, she endured another setback, which came in the form of a fall that broke her pelvis in several places. So, after a long recovery, her young body is repaired and back to normal. God for sure has a plan for her.

If all this wasn't enough, my dear eighty-four-year-old mother, while traveling, had a stroke which led to several more strokes shortly after. She also lost her rental property to foreclosure, which was her primary income. Since then I have taken on a lot of responsibilities to help make her life easier. No, I'm not having a pity party. There is a point to all of this.

The biggest story to come down the pike was a surprise visit from the brain tumor fairy. My fun-loving, smart, and energetic husband was told he had an inoperable brain tumor and had six months to live. He had just retired. What about all the traveling we were going to do? What was I going to do without him? He is my rock. What about my family who depended on me so much? Would I be able to carry on? So here's the rest of the story…Most of you know the drill for the "big C" so I won't go into detail, but after a year and a half of radiation and chemo, George is tumor-free. The team of doctors at Duke University, and those here at home in South Florida, have been wonderful.

So, here is where God's love really shines: my husband, who never was a God-fearing man, has found that faith in God and man can make miracles happen. We now attend church regularly and try to put our trust in God on a daily basis.

There are many other people out there with stories that are much more challenging and difficult. This story's mine. These days I continue to keep very busy with my family. I ponder my life of the last four years thinking, I have become so much stronger and blessed because of all the changes. So as I approach this milestone birthday, I need to retain my trust in God because He holds all the plans.

CONTAGIOUS EFFECT

It's easy to count your problems. Going forward, every time you mention a problem, also mention a blessing in your life. Just doing that will add light to your troubles and hopefully make them less of a burden.

LITTLE KNOWN SECRETS OF MOVEMENT

ELLEN KRATKA

One of the best ways I have found to stay young is to keep moving, and that means every part of you: your breath, your body, your emotions, and your ideas. To back this up I'd like to share a story. Some years ago a group of scientists did an experiment. They put knotted chains on vibrating platforms. The chains were all different gauges (thicknesses) and had different numbers of knots in them. The platforms were all the same. The result of the experiment was that every single chain unknotted itself subject to enough vibration. For some chains it was only a few minutes; for others, much more time was required.

So how does this relate to you and your health? Well, it turns out that the proteins in our bodies have a chain structure, and they too can get knotted, especially when subjected to the stresses that life throws at us. To unknot your proteins—and feel limber, strong, and energized as well as more relaxed and peaceful, which is the only state that supports health—all you need do is give your body enough movement to accomplish it.

I've heard many people say, "I tried exercise, but it didn't really help me." I now believe that many of those people stopped a week or a day or even a moment before the unknotting process could complete and they could feel the benefits.

So what kind of exercise works, you ask? Here's the best part of the story! ANY kind, from disciplined aerobics to jumping up and down and shaking to music, will give you the results in increased well-being you desire. In fact, the more fun you have the better, because then you're likely to stick with it. And it's not necessary to overly stress yourself. One to two minutes of vigorous movement followed by a minute or two of rest, repeated several times, is actually the best type of workout for your heart, lungs, metabolism, and immune system because it follows the natural waveform of energy.

Don't forget to breathe deeply while you're moving. The thorough circulation of oxygen exponentially increases the benefits of exercise by feeding, cleansing, and revitalizing all of your cells. Breathing out on the contraction (in strength training) or on a stretch, and breathing in on the relaxation phase will quickly oxygenate your entire body. Breathing fully also gets you into the habit of allowing yourself to receive— new information, helpful energies (like sunshine and vibrations from the Earth), love, abundance, etc.—and allowing yourself to let go—of toxins, outdated beliefs, old traumas, emotions (energy in motion), other people's stuff, etc. These are important habits to instill and ones that too few people have taken the time to master.

To boost the benefits of movement even more, think happy thoughts or send out some love while you're doing it, perhaps to the accompaniment of inspirational music. Your energy field has no boundaries and no limits. As you feed energy into it, it will naturally grow and touch more and more people, whether they're aware of it or not. So be sure to fill your field with good. If you're able to do some of your movement outdoors, you'll feel a natural connection with nature and all (human and animal) that pass by. But you can create this same feeling indoors, too, if necessary.

Your bonus will be the sensations that indicate well-being. You'll soon understand why many people say exercise is addictive. Don't be surprised if you start using words like "bliss" and finding yourself smiling more often, in addition to experiencing more productive days and a longer, healthier life.

CONTAGIOUS ACTION

Plan on thirty to forty minutes each day for exercise. Any type of exercise you like. Stick to that schedule even if it's raining, even if you're traveling, etc. Make sure you don't skip a day. If you do, you need to make it up by adding an extra session the next day.

CARTOONS, ICE CREAM, AND THE GRATEFUL DEAD

JOEL HELLER

Cartoons, ice cream, and the Grateful Dead are a few of my favorite things. I like these things so much that I have incorporated them into my daily life. I have crafted my personal outlook on life around the wisdom I discovered in cartoons, ice cream, and the Grateful Dead. It may sound silly, but we can find inspiration for life in some strange places if we look close enough.

Many years ago I came across a *Peanuts* cartoon that changed my outlook on life. I don't recall the first two cells of the cartoon, but I'll never forget the last cell. The cartoon ended with Lucy telling Charlie Brown, "Worrying is simply a waste of time." As I got older and took on more responsibility in my personal and professional life I found myself thinking about the cartoon more and more. Lucy had bestowed on me words of wisdom that would change my life.

We face many challenges and stresses in our life. Oftentimes, the pressures of life lead to fear and worry. Lucy taught me, through a single sentence, how to approach the day. I could either spend my days worrying about outcomes or I could spend my days thinking about solutions. Energy spent on worrying takes away from energy we can use to find solutions.

I really enjoy ice cream, and Ben & Jerry's ice cream is my favorite brand. I am fortunate enough to live within driving distance of where they make the ice cream so I have been to the complex a number of times. On one visit I came across a

T-shirt that said, "If it's not fun, why do it?" I have tried to incorporate this idea into my daily life. Don't take this to mean that I avoid life's challenges or difficult tasks. What I have tried to do is to incorporate fun into my daily life. I try to keep a positive attitude, laugh, and take time to enjoy the fun that can be found in everyday life. I attempt to find the fun in rising to the challenges of life. Learning new things can be fun, and conquering difficult problems can be fun, if we approach them as mechanisms to grow as individuals.

The Grateful Dead has taught me to stretch myself beyond my limits and to do so without fear of failure. Whether or not you like their music is irrelevant to the lessons I have learned. For thirty years they performed concerts without a predetermined set list. At each concert they attempted to create a new musical experience. They challenged themselves and the audience to think and listen beyond what had come before. Sometimes this resulted in awe-inspiring concerts, and other days this resulted in performances that were less than memorable. No matter how the concert turned out, I appreciated the fact that each day they performed, they were challenging themselves to improve, try something new, and do so without fear.

My favorite things in life have taught me to approach each day with a positive outlook. I try not to worry about what may go wrong, but spend my energy focused on how to be successful. I have learned to view each day as an opportunity to improve by challenging myself to try something new. You'll never know what you are capable of if you do the same thing each day. I don't let worry or fear of failure hinder what may be possible. If we do this, and never forget to have fun along the way, we will find our lives enriched in ways we never imagined.

CONTAGIOUS PRACTICE

Consider a change in your routine once in a while. A different breakfast, saying hello to people at work you normally don't connect with, meeting an old friend for lunch, exercise (or a new form of exercise), going to a local museum or park you never visit, etc. All these things add new dimensions and aspects to your life. Enjoy them with a spouse or significant other if you can.

THE GIFT OF TIME

MICHELE NUZZO

What are you doing with the rest of your life? If you're a Boomer approaching retirement, you could be retired for as long as you were employed. The recreation model of retirement worked when retirement lasted for only a few years. It does not work for Baby Boomers who now have a third of their lives still ahead of them. Imagine what it would feel like with nothing to do for the next thirty years.

Like all transitions, retirement is both an end and a beginning. When you retire you give up not only financial compensation, but also part of your identity, your relationships, and a structured way to spend your time. It is only natural to feel a sense of loss and fear about the unknown. If you take time to discover who you are now, retirement can become the beginning of an exciting new chapter in your life.

One size does not fit all. Whether you cross things off a "bucket list" or embark on a new career, retirement can be an exciting time to follow your passions and live your dreams.

FOCUS ON THE FUTURE

Maybe you have failed to plan for retirement because you fear looking into the future. We're afraid that nothing exciting will ever happen to us again. The good news is that you have the power to change that. Whether you call it your next phase, the second stage of life, or your third act, you can look forward to endless possibilities. You have the power to reinvent yourself, to form strong social connections, and to make the world a better place. One of the best ways to look forward to your retirement years is to create a vision of your dream life then to create a plan to get there. Picture yourself in perfect health, surrounded by people who love and inspire you. Imagine waking each day to a life full of purpose and passion.

In the past, planning for retirement focused exclusively on financial planning. Today we are fortunate to have resources that focus on planning our retirement lifestyle. In his book, *The New Retirement*, Dr. Richard P. Johnson describes factors that contribute to retirement success. These factors include attitudes about work reorientation, perceptions about health and aging, and projections about satisfaction with future life stages.

FOLLOW YOUR PASSION

It can be difficult to follow your passion when you're not even sure if you have one. What gets you out of bed in the morning? Who do you admire? Think of characters in books or films, whose lives you would like to have. To fan your creative spark into a bonfire, read *On Becoming an Artist: Reinventing Yourself through Mindful Creativity* by Ellen J. Langer or *The Writer Within You* by Charles Jacobs.

If you have no idea what you want to do, start by searching online or browse catalogs from community colleges or adult schools. You don't need to rush into a new role; you can work with a coach or take a self-guided tour. Meditate, walk, write, paint, garden, and get out of your head. What would you do if you had unlimited resources? What would you do if you knew you couldn't fail?

LEAVE A LEGACY

As we plan for retirement, we focus time and energy on our financial portfolio, but we usually neglect our psychological portfolio. Nancy K. Schlossberg, Ed.D., suggests ways to assess and reshape your identity, your relationships, and your purpose. In her book, *Revitalizing Retirement*, she examines mattering as a universal need and a critical component of a fulfilled lifestyle.

During your retirement years, use the gift of time to create precious memories and leave behind your legacy. Capture your memoirs in a journal or DVD. Engage the services of a personal historian to document your legacy. Yours may be entirely one of introspection, or you may choose to leave a legacy in a more public way. In *The Ultimate Gift* by Jim Stovall, a wealthy patriarch leaves a legacy in the form of a special gift for his great nephew. The young man is required to perform a series of tests in pursuit of his treasure. The tests and life lessons resemble a fictionalized account of an ethical will. An ethical will is not a legal document. It is a way to leave a legacy, share life's lessons, and pass on your values. In many cultures, ethical wills were originally passed down as part of an oral tradition. Later they became written or videotaped.

BECOME THE SOLUTION

Money is not the only reason many retirees reenter the work-force. Some seniors miss the challenge, the camaraderie, and the opportunity to contribute. Boomers are in a position to solve some of the most pressing problems facing society today. For inspiration, check out *Encore: Finding Work that Matters in the Second Half of Life* by Marc Freedman, founder of Encore.org, formerly Civic Ventures. *Encore* is not a manual on how to find work after fifty. It is about reinventing retirement as a time to find meaning, make connections, learn new skills, and leave a legacy. Your second half of life is the time to discover a "new dream" to replace the traditional idea of retirement.

DO YOUR PART

You don't need deep pockets to touch lives. If you don't have the resources to establish a foundation, do what you can. Maybe suggest that friends and family pool their resources by donating to one of your favorite causes. Do your kids a favor; clean out your garage and closets now. Donate the goods to a local charity and spare your offspring the burden of sorting through mountains of stuff later.

When you make a difference in a more personal way by volunteering, you can change many lives, including your own. It is also a path to new friendships and a chance to use your skills and wisdom. Search online for organizations such as Volunteermatch.org to find opportunities that match your interests. Volunteering as little as two hours per week has been shown to have positive effects on both physical and mental health.

JOURNEY ON

Like Dolly Levi in Jerry Herman's masterful musical *Hello Dolly!*, you may decide to get some life back into your life "Before the Parade Passes By." Travel provides adventure and opportunities for personal growth. Whether you are searching for spiritual enlightenment or the perfect éclair, go for the gusto! You don't need to travel around the world to rediscover your sense of wonder. Environmental groups such as the Sierra Club offer local trips and tours. If health permits, travel can give you a new perspective about the world and a deeper understanding about yourself.

Retirement does not mean the end of your life. It is the beginning of an exciting new phase of personal growth. How do you want to grow? What visions and dreams are germinating inside you? In the words of author George Eliot, "It's never too late to be what you might have been."

CONTAGIOUS ACTION

Step away from that couch and become your own action hero! Put down the remote control and write a daring script for the final act of your remarkable life.

THE REFUGE AND
RELEASE OF HOBBIES

LEE SHILO

I was one of those kids that pissed off, annoyed, or otherwise made people very angry for no apparent reason. So it was no shock finding out that my mother thought I was going to be a midget ("little person" as they are called now). I was so small that one Halloween my older sister dressed me up in her doll clothes. It was embarrassing and humiliating until I found that I was making out like a bandit in the candy department.

My first taste of death and tragedy came at an early age when I witnessed my older brother drown right in front of me. I had lost my best friend and protector, and began to face life alone. Without my brother I always got picked on, teased, and beat up by the local bullies. I swear, getting beat up all the time made my body's recuperative powers triple in recovery time.

An adult friend of the family took me down to the local boxing club one time, intent on teaching me how to defend myself. I let him know that I was getting beat up enough on the streets and did not need more pummeling inside a boxing ring! That, however, was the beginning of something that would remain with me for the rest of my life. Knowing that I could actually learn how to defend myself was liberating.

We eventually moved to the big city, which was good for me because of the variety that city life offered. I began investigating the many self-defense schools in the area. There was karate, judo, kung-fu, taekwondo, and something called "aikido." I pestered my poor mother for months to pay for lessons on self-defense, but with the little pay she earned it was not enough for her to even entertain the thought.

To my surprise and delight, a neighborhood friend of the family happened to be present at one of my pleadings and offered to pay for three months of training plus my martial arts uniform. He promised that if I attended the school without missing a session, and really tried to learn, he would consider paying for another three months of training. There was, as usual, only one catch: he would choose which martial arts school I would attend.

It all started off simple enough, with respectful bowing and common courtesies. The first thing we were taught was how to land properly once thrown to the ground. We were taught things like rollouts, arm-slaps to the ground, and how to scream really loud before we landed. It was all very exciting except for one thing: no one told me that I would suffer from bad headaches for the first week. Being tossed to the ground repeatedly creates trauma to the brain, similar to shake-trauma in infants. Eventually my body learned how to handle it and I gleefully continued on, learning throws and ground holds.

I did not let my benefactor down, and did not miss a single lesson. He ended up funding me for the whole year until my mother saved up enough to take over the payments. After some time I landed myself a newspaper route and proudly began paying for my own lessons. Bullies soon learned to become intimate with the ground when they tried tangling with me. Getting beat up all of the time soon became a thing of the past.

As the years passed, I became interested in learning more about other martial arts styles, and this soon became my life-time hobby. Shotokan karate was my second choice, and was with me during the next awkward stage of my life.

The transition from school to the workforce was not a problem. The stress actually began when I struck out on my own. Rent, groceries, and bills were a nightmare. I do not fault my mother though; she was busy enough with two jobs trying to put food on the table and never did get around to teaching me the finer points in life. So for goodness sake, parents, please take the time to show your children how to budget.

As time went by, I became fully initiated into a self-reliant lifestyle. Many of my friends were also proficient in one martial art or another. That is when I decided on my next martial art style, kung-fu. I went on to learn that kung-fu was not a style, but a system of many styles, and would take an infinitely longer time to learn. Kung-fu began with ten to twelve styles and has now risen to over one hundred and fifty.

Now, after more than thirty years of learning and teaching kung-fu as a hobby, I have developed my own small style of kung-fu called Jing-Tao ("Quiet Way"). Through all of the trials, tribulations, and changes in my life, this hobby has remained constant. It has been my lifeline to sanity when tragedy and doubt have struck. It has been my comforter when solace was needed, my friend through thick and thin, and grief and happiness. My hobby has allowed me to be free from bullies, kept me physically fit, introduced me to my present wife, and has allowed me to even write about it.

CONTAGIOUS COMMITMENT

Without hobbies you have no refuge or release from harmful negative energies. Find one that you like and it will serve you well throughout life.

THE BEST DOCTOR
FOR YOU IS YOU

DR. CARLOS GONZALEZ

What happens to a car that sits in the driveway for a long time? The battery goes dead. So you jump-start it and then you drive it around the block once or twice. The battery will go dead again because you did not drive it long enough. Pretty soon that battery is not going to jump-start anymore and you're going to need a new one. Many people get up in the morning with a dead battery even after sleeping all night. They might not have had a good restful sleep because they ate a heavy meal late in the evening. Stress and worry will also interfere with getting a good night's sleep.

Many times people don't realize just how poor their health is, and they neglect taking care of it. They get up in the morning and reluctantly go to work. They get through the morning with caffeine and donuts. They overeat at lunch. They get home after work exhausted and then plop on the sofa to watch TV for hours as well as eat another low-fiber, high-fat dinner. The most exercise many people get is walking to the mailbox. It's sad to see so many of my patients who are in their fifties and sixties who have been on all kinds of prescription drugs for years but still suffer with the same symptoms.

Some people have learned to live with their health problems. They are used to the usual headaches, sinus problems, allergies, acid reflux, asthma, anxiety, and migraines. It's amazing how many people believe that these symptoms are normal. These symptoms plus high cholesterol, high blood pressure, diabetes, and cardiovascular problems are the result of poor lifestyle choices. Eventually their health problems get to be too much and they go to the doctor for the never-ending prescription-drug roller coaster. Others self-medicate because so many drugs are now available without a prescription.

When was the last time you felt good without taking any drugs, alcohol, or caffeine? Maybe it's been a while. The good news is that you can change all that. It is unfortunate that sometimes it takes a good scare like a heart attack before one makes the commitment to a much-needed change of lifestyle. For some people it's a divorce, and for others it's a doctor telling you that if you don't stop drinking you will die from liver failure. But whatever it takes, JUST DO IT. You have so much to gain. Do it for a loved one; do it for yourself.

Too many people think that since they do not feel horrible that they are okay. But the absence of pain does not mean you are OK. Other warning signs are headaches, high blood pressure, constipation, allergies, and numbness in the extremities.

Decide now to make the necessary lifestyle changes to improve your health. If not now, when? It's too easy to put it off until tomorrow. Write something as simple as, "I will start taking better care of myself." Or, "I will go walking thirty minutes every day." Start making one simple change at a time. As the weeks go by add to your goals. Once you get started you will gain momentum. Recruit—when you support each other and hold each other accountable there is less room for failure.

It is wonderful to be able to wake up without needing an alarm clock and all those toxic jump starters to get the day going. Many people get up an extra hour earlier and go to a gym or simply go for their morning walk. It takes only thirty to forty minutes of moderate exercise to feel really good and energized all day. Equally important is to feed your body nutritional foods. Many people think that since they exercise they can eat whatever they want. If you exercise it is extremely important that you eat healthy too. Remember that the key to success is consistency and moderation.

The more natural your diet of raw fruits and vegetables, whole grains, purified water, less meat, etc., the better. Stay away from fast foods and packaged foods with added synthetic chemicals whose names you cannot pronounce. If you eat wholesome foods you don't have to overeat to satisfy your hunger. Eat to nourish your body, not to feel full or stuffed. Supplement your diet with good-quality vitamins and minerals. Get off the couch and away from the TV and do a little exercise four to five times a week. If you just can't get away from the TV, put an exercise bike in front of it.

There are many excellent chiropractic, naturopathic, homeopathic, and medical doctors who can help you. There are also some very good massage therapists, acupuncturists, and personal trainers who can all become part of your health-care team. You're not alone.

To those of you that have made the commitment to a healthier, happier, and longer life, congratulations! You are on your way to feeling so much better and preventing years of pain and suffering. Be patient, change takes time. Healing takes time. Remember, the best doctor for you is YOU! Your health and quality of life depend on it.

CONTAGIOUS PRACTICE

Scientists say that it takes twenty-one days to form a new habit. But that can be changed and replaced with a better habit. Got any old habits that you need to get rid of? Do it now. Repetition, repetition, repetition.

THE POWER OF MIND, BODY, AND SPIRIT

DR. BRIAN DENHOFFER

Within the next few paragraphs, you will be presented with some ideas to use so you can create your world filled with contentment, deep relaxation, and enthusiasm in all that you do. First, I will share a little of my background to give you a better understanding of my perspective and the source from which these ideas were born.

Since childhood, I have been the person who cared, the person who engaged children or adults who were alone at social gatherings and appeared to be tense. When I sensed this, instinctively, I took on the role of healer and began helping people with a perspective shift. I acknowledged to them what I sensed and encouraged them through gentle words and kind behavior to enjoy the moment and have fun. I shared with them that they were loved, and deserved to be loved in mind, body, and spirit. It is from my intuition and all my interactions with people that I learned what made others feel safe and relaxed.

Through my education, I came to a better understanding of how the body and mind work in a deep and profound way. And from my postgraduate work studying conscious language, body dynamics, and addiction, I learned how words, feelings, body movements, and mind chemistry affect our emotions and health. The synthesis of all of this work has given me great understanding of how to help people heal and relax. Now let's get started.

THE POWER OF WORDS AND EMOTIONS

One way to help people heal and relax is by encouraging them to be aware of the power of their words and emotions. Our words and emotions used in concert with each other have an ability to create our reality. When a person says, "I can't relax," their brain says, "Okay, I cannot relax" and it finds ways and means for this to be true. For example, circumstances will manifest to create the feeling of tension; the person becomes frustrated by another person or event thus making this statement true. My invitation to you is this: Be willing to transform these types of destructive statements by saying with deep emotion something opposite and constructive like, "I feel completely and fully relaxed, here and now and continuously." In choosing your words with purpose, feeling, and strong awareness, you will more healthfully create the world that you choose to live in.

THE POWER OF KINDNESS

Another way to create your relaxed world is through your profound power of utilizing kindness in your daily life. Being kind to ourselves and others creates a huge opportunity for a relaxed, peaceful feeling for you and for all involved. Remember, whatever we focus on, expands. So the more we pay attention to being kind and focusing on a kind energy within, the greater the chance we will respond with kindness to people in consideration to however they act, and then we may alter the manner in which they choose to respond to us.

THE POWER OF PHYSICAL ALIGNMENT

You can feel more relaxed as you understand your own power in your own healing. Our bodies are designed to be self-healing and have an innate intelligence that leans in the direction of wellness. Realize your body and mind together (also known as our nervous system) controls and coordinates every function in our body. Our skull and spinal bones protect our precious nervous system, so if there is any misalignment of our spine, our body chemistry is also out of balance. This affects all levels of function and performance in one's life including walking, weight management, energy level, mood, digestion, perception, and social behavior. A chiropractor gently helps your spine and body to be in alignment. In alignment, your chemistry is in balance and every level of function and performance in your body and mind is optimized. Everyone, from pregnant moms to newborns to mature adults, deserve to have their bodies gently aligned by a chiropractor on a regular basis and thus maximize their ability to enjoy a spectacular quality of life!

THE POWER OF OBSERVING THOUGHTS

Another way to have a more relaxed and peaceful life is to "watch" your thoughts. What I mean by this is, when any thoughts, emotions, or actions that you express are harmful, I invite you to become a powerful compassionate. A compassionate observer is one who can quiet their mental activity and create a distance in their mind and body from internal and external stimulation. When this is done, it is as if they are watching their lives on a movie screen. Compassionate observers are involved with what is happening and have perspective to healthfully respond to all situations. So, as you develop this skill to step outside or float above the issue at hand and stay fully aware of any of these harmful, dysfunctional ways, your brain will automatically transform them into healthy expressions. You may be surprised by the levels of enthusiasm, ease, and connection you gain as you utilize your power of the compassionate observer.

THE POWER OF BREATH

Being connected to wellness is the power of breath. Give your power of conscious breathing a go, because as you breathe more fully, inhalation and exhalation, the calmer and more relaxed you become. As your breath is, so follows your mind and body. Shallow breathing creates tension and deep breathing creates relaxation.

THE POWER OF PRESENCE

You can give yourself one of the greatest gifts. This powerful gift is your presence in relationship with yourself and others. The power of presence means relaxed and fully receptive listening and heart-centered sharing in all your interactions. To help strengthen your presence, bring yoga into your world. Yoga connects you to paths that include your mind and heart, the practice of breathing and meditation, awareness, and courage. So give yourself and others the gift of your presence today!

It has been my pleasure to share some of my ideas to increase the power you have within you and to feel relaxed. You deserve to be, do, and have all you choose.

CONTAGIOUS BY EXAMPLE

••• • ••

Seek out and create wellness partnerships with individuals who can inspire you, guide you, and attend to you as the unique individual you are. These partnerships will help you discover your specific mind and body needs.

THE ANTIDOTE FOR STRESS

ELLEN KRATKA

I have been studying stress for several years now: what it is, why it arises, and how to conquer it. I've read articles and books from neuroscientists to mystics. I've come to the conclusion that the only real antidote for stress is love, and, at its root, that's what all the other remedies and antidotes are based on and require as well.

Does this surprise you? If so, perhaps it's because we tend to think of love as something soft, vague, and largely irrelevant to the "serious" parts of our lives. But the truth is that it's highly practical, and the most successful people have a lot of it—for others *and* for themselves.

Here is a quiz to help you understand how you manage stress:

What would a person who has mastered stress do in these scenarios?

Person 1: a) Blame others for a bad situation? b) Assume responsibility for their own decisions, learn from what went wrong, and find a way to correct the mistakes?

Person 2: a) Work harder when the pressure increases? b) Take ample time to refresh and regroup so that the work could be accomplished more effectively?

Person 3: a) Beat themselves up mentally after receiving criticism from a boss or client? b) Realize that everyone is entitled to their own opinion and the only one that really counts is their own, based on an honest self-evaluation of their motives?

Person 4: a) Refuse to take on a project that is unfamiliar or out-of-the-box? b) Utilize passion and self-confidence to see the project bear fruit and generate the strength needed to accomplish it?

Person 5: a) Isolate themselves to protect their own feelings? b) Stand up for their own truth and radiate to others the empathy that comes from understanding that they must have their own reasons for saying or doing what they do?

Notice that each of the "a" responses implies a belief:

Person 1 believes others cause him or her problems.

Person 2 believes he or she has to work harder and harder (probably to please others).

Person 3 believes on a deep level that he or she is not smart enough (or is a "screwup").

Person 4 believes he or she is not capable of taking on a challenge.

Person 5 believes other people, either as individuals or in groups, are not safe.

Of course the answers are all "b," but the interesting question is, "What do all the 'b' people have in common?" The answer is that they value themselves enough to not get swept up in stressful situations or relationship dynamics. They remain the calm thinking, resilient center in the storm. And this capacity can only come from self-love, which means they know without any doubt that they have a permanent lifeline to all the wisdom, qualities, and resources they'll ever need.

There are books that have been written about "cut-off valves," meaning all the mechanisms that have operated so automatically and dependably up to now to keep you from feeling the love that came with you into this life. So how do you become the individual who loves him- or herself completely? Simply by unblocking the cut-off valves.

All these beliefs imply that love (and whatever else the

believer desires) has been limited or cut off by someone or something. Conversely, self-love erases all these negative beliefs and, instead, yields absolute knowledge that you are an amazing, magnificent, capable, and deserving human being who has come here to learn, create, and enjoy the process. No one can take that away from you. If you really allow the love in, you will discover that stress cannot withstand its presence.

CONTAGIOUS EFFECT

Consider the scenarios above and divulge to yourself realistically which category you fall into today: a or b. After taking the quiz, strive to be the "b" person and don't accept anything less for yourself in the future.

LIVING FOR TODAY

CAROLYN BATES

Is "living for today" the answer to dealing with stress, with tragedy, with divorce, with illness, with retirement transition, with the empty nest syndrome, etc.? Living for today seems to be the cure for just about everything! Why is this so hard to do? Why is this something that is so hard to put into reality?

Are you a person with a lot of energy or are you a struggler? People who naturally have energy to spare are also people who put effort into each day. They are accomplishing something all the time, completing tasks, following passions and interests, staying active, staying connected to themselves, their families, their friends; they are typically moving forward. They're busy and for the most part, they're not easily frustrated or overwhelmed.

A struggler, on the other hand, is someone who is constantly running and adding things to their to-do list, the piles building around them; they are rarely able to feel that they are organized and settled. Some believe this is a deep-seated anxiety caused by abandonment or low self-esteem; that the "struggler" is looking for validation, acceptance, maybe even a false sense of a higher social standing. Their schedules are always jammed; they are frustrated because they don't feel like they can get everything done or anything completed. They overpromise and underperform. They are always expending massive amounts of effort that usually attracts emotional chaos and confusion. The concept of just saying "no" isn't possible. They are distracted most of the time, as they are always dealing with the crisis of the moment. At the end of the day, they are depleted of all their energy, are usually mentally and physically exhausted, eat unhealthily, sometimes drink too much, have trouble sleeping, and haven't really allowed themselves to feel the joy in what they're doing.

Look at your days, look at your agenda. Just working harder only will decrease your productivity and alienate you from the things that really count. Being organized and consistent will produce more positive results. "Living for today" is only possible when you decide to believe this is what you want.

CONTAGIOUS ACTION

You have to make YOU the priority. Once you have done this, then you will be able to make the changes and decisions necessary to accomplish "living for today."

HOW TO GET MORE "ME" TIME

DR. BARBARA SEIFERT

Life seems to be flying by these days. We fill our daily lives with so many activities that we don't have enough time to just relax and enjoy. We become expandable, giving to our jobs, our families, our pets, the community, or any other number of activities. While some of these activities are not a choice, such as our families, there are other areas where we overcommit ourselves, leaving us feeling tired, both physically and emotionally. Even our families can exhaust us with their daily demands. Without good boundaries, we will continue to commit and start feeling resentful of these demands. We will lose sight of ourselves and forget how to get "me" time.

Self-care is one of the most important and basic activities that one can do. It is vital to our self-esteem and our confidence, giving us the ability to focus on areas that are important to us. Self-care is critical to our physical and emotional well-being. When we give more of ourselves to others, it says that we are not as important; over time it can lead to resentment and frustration. If not addressed, emotional problems can develop such as anger, anxiety, or depression. Health problems can also occur. If self-care is so critical, why is it so difficult to do? Why are some people unable to say "no" and set good personal boundaries for themselves?

A lot depends on our emotional type and the coping skills that have been imprinted on us.

"Emoters" are those who feel every emotion and have

empathy for others. They are the helpers but often forget to help themselves.

"Guilt Riddens" want to make up for a wrong they believe has occurred, regardless of whether they caused the wrong or not. They often overcompensate.

"Saviors" feel they need to save others from adverse situations. They want to prevent others from "walking through the trenches" and feel it is their obligation to do so.

"Good Ones" have been put on their perches by others who feel they are the stars of the family. This causes them to feel they must do more which becomes exhausting.

"Insecures" don't highly value themselves so it feels easier for them to focus on others to avoid facing or placing importance inside.

All of these emotional types have one thing in common: they expend and focus externally but cannot focus internally.

But, there is good news. It is possible to work with your emotional type to be more effective in your life. By doing so, you can set boundaries that release you from your guilt and set you free. The following steps can help you get more "me time":

1. Be aware of your feelings—frustrations, stresses, anger, sadness, etc.; self-awareness is the key to changing behavior. Take up journaling to capture these emotions.
2. Challenge the thoughts you identify. Thoughts are not real but the perceptions we make of them, either big or small, can be let go.
3. Vow to resolve your past. If you feel guilt, review the incidents of an event to see if you really were responsible and if there was any other outcome possible.
4. Practice forgiveness, which is not forgetting or saying you are "okay" with what another person did; it is about releasing the negative feelings of what happened.

Now that you have started to resolve your past, it is time to focus on your present. This will set the path for your future:

5. Make a list of the areas in your life on separate pieces of paper: husband, wife, kids, home, work, friends, church, etc. You can't fix what you don't know.

6. Prioritize them into levels of importance to see what is crucial and what can be let go. This is the time to learn the art of delegation.

7. Make a list of all activities that you like and which ones give you a sense of relaxation, peace, or energy. Examples include: exercise, yoga, meditation, reading, prayer, singing, dancing, or gardening; perhaps you've wanted to learn photography or cooking.

8. Use the power of visualization to help you develop the life you want. While the kids or your significant other are occupied doing something else, take five minutes to picture the life you want, and enjoy it.

9. Learn to say "no." Set personal boundaries to avoid feeling overwhelmed and prevent resentments that can build when you overextend yourself.

10. Practice, practice, practice! Changing behavior takes awareness, clarity, and consistency so keep at it. Recognize and hold on to the benefits you are receiving.

CONTAGIOUS PRACTICE

It may seem hard at first but the more you practice these steps above, the easier it will be to live an emotionally free life—more aware, more secure, and more confident. "Me" time will become a habit, not a luxury!

THE ALI KNOCKOUT

INEZ BRACY

"Little by little the bird makes its nest."

—*Haitian proverb*

I was never a boxing fan until Muhammad Ali came into the ring. I was fascinated with his motto, "Float like a butterfly, sting like a bee." It was a thrill to watch him stroll into the ring, bounce around on his toes, and before you knew it, his opponent was flat out on the mat.

Ali spent numerous hours preparing, practicing, and working toward his dream. He knew exactly what he wanted. Even with all of his preparation, Ali took time off to relax and have fun.

I too knew what I wanted. My dream was to have a thriving speaking and coaching business. I'd spent many hours studying and preparing; now I was ready. I decided to go fulfill my dream! Each day I'd be somewhere, attending live and virtual networking events, attending teleseminars. I was in constant motion, floating like a butterfly. I didn't have time to take off, relax, and play.

Then, I started feeling a slight soreness in my throat; I didn't recognize the precursor to what was to come. Being off guard and not paying attention, I kept up my frenetic pace until I was flat on my back. I couldn't talk, my body ached, and I could barely get out of bed. I'd suffered the Ali punch, the famous Ali knockout!

Suffering the Ali punch allowed me to finally take stock of what I had been doing. When I was slightly better, I started questioning what I'd been doing. I asked myself, "Is this a valid dream? Is this the way to achieving it? How will I know if I'm on the right path? Please send me a sign!"

It's amazing how God responds when I'm truly at my lowest point, when I'm not sure of what to do. Once I felt better, I was finally able to check my emails and to my surprise, my answer came. No, the emails were not from God, but sent by friends and clients.

The information in the emails gave me the answer: yes, I can have my dream but do it differently! I put my guidance into action and created SPICE: Sassy-Phenomenal-Inspired-Conscious-Empowered woman—a vehicle to help women unleash their femininity, maintain healthy self-esteem, and develop confidence while living a joyous life.

Through creating SPICE I've become conscious and aware of the time I spend working and always allow time for relaxing and playing. I've learned to slow my pace so that I don't have to be everywhere all the time. In the process I take care of myself with physical and mental exercise to avoid the Ali knockout.

Changing your life can be as easy as making a decision and moving into action. The choice is yours. Little by little you can design the life of your dreams.

CONTAGIOUS COMMITMENT

A few simple steps to embrace the change you desire:

Set aside five to fifteen minutes each day just for you.

Use your special time for meditating, reflecting, or simply sitting quietly.

Write a list of the goals you'd like to achieve. This list of goals helps keep you on track for creating the change you desire.

Celebrate at least one thing every day. A celebration is anything you want it to be. You can celebrate getting up in the morning, a smile from a loved one, or watching the sun rise or set. Celebrate the simplicity of life.

Love unconditionally. Give and receive love NOW. Loving unconditionally is not based on "you do this and I'll love you." Love simply because you can.

Laugh at yourself. Laughing at yourself ensures that you don't take yourself too seriously.

TAI CHI

SCOTT DUNCAN

In my early twenties, I started to learn Tai Chi (Chi Kung) to help me relax. I felt as though I was generally angry, tense for no particular reason, and that this may be a good way to change my approach to life. I was a young adult at the time, and the practice was often seen in the Western world as being something for older adults. As a result, I was mocked for trying something different but I was glad in the end that I stuck with it. I ended up training as an instructor at a foundation level.

As I started to practice Tai Chi and other relaxation techniques, more often I found that my ability to concentrate, see things through to completion, and control my reaction to external factors was greatly enhanced, thus giving me more energy and confidence. I found that simple breathing exercises helped me center, bringing me into the moment, and reducing the inner voices that were causing a lot of mayhem.

Bring awareness to your breathing a few times a day, while in a safe place (not while driving or operating machinery). Take a few deep breaths in through your nose and out through your mouth. Imagine the most relaxed feeling you can and begin to imagine moving that feeling up to your head and down to your toes. If you can add in a feeling of happiness, places and people you love dearly, take notice of how that feels. As you continue to breathe, spread that feeling around your body.

Susan Jeffers, Ph.D., the famous author that has helped millions of people overcome fear, said it best: "90 percent of what we worry about never happens." There are more constructive ways to deal with your emotions throughout the day: simply find space to clear your head, go for a walk or cycle, try something fun and new, or simply smile a little more at the things that normally faze you. It is amazing how simple things can alter your state and help you feel more alive, especially if you begin to love the things, people, and situations around you a little more than you did in the past.

Try relaxing music and remove stimulants from your diet if you can. The mind and body can relax much more if you have a little more balance. Often when you speak with someone who is experiencing a lot of stress, you will find that they are submerged in one area of their life—the "wheel of life" is buckled slightly and cannot turn effectively.

Be aware of how you describe your life—do you say things like: "It is getting me down," "I just can't get out of this situation," "I feel suffocated by debt." If you listen to how you talk about the stresses in your own life, you can simply flip the statements into a positive to help you feel better and more relaxed.

You can play a game with your mind by creating a story to replace whatever it is that is getting you down. Imagine you are freeing yourself from the situation, bounding, skipping, and jumping out through the issue. Shrink the negative idea, image, or sound until it is a wee tiny grain of dust that you can wipe away with your finger.

No matter what your life situation is right now, simply breathing more deeply, paying attention to what is happening around you, and spreading feelings of happiness, laughter, and joy will help change your outlook on life. Before you change the world around you, have a good look inside, relax, and free up that tension.

CONTAGIOUS INSIGHT

We often need to stop for a moment to relax, concentrate on our breathing, and chill out. You can only achieve great things if you learn to relax at times.

THE CALMING NATURE OF KINDNESS AND GRATITUDE

DR. COLLEEN GEORGES

"When you are kind to others, it not only changes you, it changes the world."

—Harold Kushner

IT FEELS GOOD TO BE KIND

When someone does something that bothers us, it is often easy to draw that person's attention to it. But how often do we remember to tell people when they have done something that we appreciate? It's just as important for people to know when they have done something special, as when they have done something that could use improvement. People certainly need to learn from their mistakes in order to grow and develop. However, people should also be afforded the pleasure of acknowledgment when they do something well. Compliments feel good to those both giving and receiving them. It's nice to know that your kind words are the reason for someone else's smile.

Sometimes when we notice the strengths of others, we hold back on letting them know what we observed. We do this for a number of reasons. Sometimes we think that the person must already be aware of his or her abilities, so there is no need for us to say anything. Sometimes we think we will have another opportunity to acknowledge the person. Or, maybe, others' strengths make us feel a little inadequate and we don't want to call attention to it. It is ok to feel a little insecure at times and, believe it or not, a compliment can help raise our own self-esteem. Rather than letting an opportunity to make someone feel good slip by, we should take advantage of it! It is natural to occasionally envy others' abilities. We need to accept envy within ourselves and try to turn it into admiration. Admiration can inspire us to achieve great things.

We frequently call attention to others when they disappoint us or fail to keep a promise. However, we do not as often remember to say "thank you" to others for their kind deeds. Saying "thank you" may seem like such a simple task, but think of how good it can make you feel to hear it. And it can feel good to say it too. The more we say thank you to others for their kindness, the more appreciative we become as individuals. It reinforces a feeling of being fortunate, even if just for the small things. And feeling fortunate helps us live more satisfying, healthy lives.

In our busy lives, we sometimes look past the people we encounter or forget that they are people too. At some point, you may have noticed a person in front of you in line in the supermarket treating the cashier rudely because he or she is moving too slowly. However, had this person considered that the cashier was just another human being with a life and a job, maybe he or she would have acted differently. Although we may never really be able to see into the worlds of every person we encounter, we can be assured that they have problems and rough days just like we do. It is better to treat every person you encounter as if they are having "one of those days" than to assume they should always be on top of their game.

BE THANKFUL

We often find ourselves complaining or venting to others about our problems. We all need to voice our frustrations once in a while. However, for all the venting we do, how often do we acknowledge all of the good in our lives? Even during the roughest times, we generally have something to be thankful for—be it shelter, health, friends, etc. It actually feels really good to remind ourselves of the things we do have. When we first start to think about it, our list may be small. But the more we consider it, the more we realize how much we have to feel good about. It's empowering!

CONTAGIOUS BY EXAMPLE

Don't frustrate yourself by focusing on others' inconsideration or by what you feel you're missing in life. Make it a habit to acknowledge the positives in others and the many gifts you do have.

BEAUTY IS

Beauty is as one perceives it
If you see it in yourself
Others will believe it.

Do not refer to me
As a woman of a certain age
I am just a woman
Who will not be
Chronologically caged.

A poem by Karen Lyons Kalmenson

CHAPTER SEVEN

NEED HELP GETTING SOMEWHERE?

Mastermind group—your own personal board of advisors.

Ask for help and you will receive it.

Serving as someone else's mentor.

Napoleon Hill said it best: "A group of brains coordinated or connected in a spirit of harmony will provide more thought energy than a single brain…. When a group of individual brains are coordinated and function in harmony, the increased energy created through that alliance becomes available to every individual brain in the group" (Napoleon Hill, *Think and Grow Rich*, 151). While this may have been an idea from early last century it is incredibly timeless. No matter your age, economic status, or career, we can all learn from someone else. Different personalities, outlooks, philosophies, and experiences are all there for us to observe and to potentially help us on our journey.

A Mastermind group is an alliance of two or more people dedicated to a specific goal. For some, this can consist of legends long gone. For example, in business, we read about Ray Kroc, Conrad Hilton, Dave Thomas, Andrew Carnegie, John D. Rockefeller, etc. In optimism, we read about Norman Vincent Peale, Dale Carnegie, Helen Keller, etc. In religion and literature the list is endless. All of the people listed above are deceased but I value their stories as if they were here today. That is the beauty of publications and information available to us at any time via the Internet.

A Mastermind can include living role models as well. Whether it is someone you can speak with, or an icon whose story is available through a variety of resources, you should reach out and learn from their experiences. Learn from those who appeal to you and take advantage of their knowledge. Why make things more difficult when many of your answers are right in front of you from people that already did the work?

Remember, the light bulb still has its foundation in Humphry Davy and Thomas Edison.

Now let's switch gears and talk about mentoring others.

Serving as a mentor not only exposes you to altruism and goodwill, it can also dramatically improve the life of someone else. Your experience and guidance is invaluable. If everything you learned at this point was put away into a box, what good is it?

Legacies do not have to be millions of dollars, buildings, or parks; they can just be your time and advice. Fairfield University, my alma mater, has a great phrase that describes how alumni can help the school: "time, talent, or treasure." In other words, an alumnus can offer any one (or all) of these items to the school as part of their alumni giving.

At this point in my life I have taken my knowledge and experience of building powerful internship programs and have offered it to countless organizations. This goodwill has driven these organizations to new heights while saving them money in the process. More importantly, we have created thousands of jobs for students worldwide and shaped their long-term career paths along with boosting their confidence and generating income.

Today I continue to launch internship programs for every entity I am involved with and every board I sit on. I make sure that students and recent graduates receive the knowledge and experience they need to move forward in their academics and in their careers. Everyone benefits including the schools and the community as a whole.

One of my favorite quotes on this topic is from Dale Carnegie: "The man who forgot himself in service to others would find the joy of living" (Dale Carnegie, *How to Stop Worrying and Start Living*, 184).

David

"When I think about the importance of reaching out to mentors, I think of the popular Zen story: A professor once visited a Japanese master to inquire about Zen. The master served tea. When the visitor's cup was full, the master kept pouring. Tea spilled out of the cup and over the table. 'The cup is full!' said the professor. 'No more will go in!' 'Like this cup,' said the master, 'You are full of your own opinions and speculations. How can I show you Zen unless you first empty your cup?' People that come to learn a subject many times have ideas and preconceived notions of their own. They need to open their mind and learn from the wise."

—Hideaki Nishimura, Osaka, Japan

"Looking to others for guidance is important. Following their footsteps is a great opportunity to take advantage of something that has worked in the past. I remind my students of that often. However, there is also some inner searching that needs to happen as well. Be a leader and not a follower all the time, be an innovator."

—Victoria Smithe, Sag Harbor, New York

WHAT WILL YOU MASTER THIS YEAR?

SUSAN ROSS

"Many business failures are due to a lack of organization and harmony."

—*Unknown*

THE MASTERMIND PRINCIPLE

A Mastermind is largely a dialogue, a free flow of ideas and energy, uninterrupted by ego, assumptions, and judgments. It's built upon the open-mindedness of the members to new, controversial, and even "crazy" ideas. In a Mastermind group, the harmonious energy of the individuals connect, creating a powerful synergy (the "Master Mind") used to brainstorm, problem-solve, and create powerful solutions that can only come from collaboration. In other words, the sum of the power of the group is greater than that of its individual members. It is truly a meeting of minds in pursuit of common goals, which might seem unreachable on your own. The synergy created is palpable. Two horses create enough strength to pull two-and-a-half times their weight—the synergy of Mastermind brains creates a similar strength of energy and ideas.

A MASTERMIND GROUP CAN MAKE THE DIFFERENCE

I am so passionate about the power of the Mastermind because I have witnessed firsthand the miracles produced by the power of many minds converging through harmonious dialogue in a well-facilitated group to fulfill the members' common goals. Joining a Mastermind group is a commitment to mastering your possibilities. Your facilitator and peers will challenge you to reach deep, tap your talent, and accomplish far more than you may ever do alone. I am excited to share this amazing process in my quest to lead a World Mastermind Tribe in which we ask ourselves constantly as individuals and as a group: "What will I master today? This week? This year?"

In his epoch 1923 book, *Think and Grow Rich*, Napoleon Hill defined the Mastermind process as, "An alliance of two or more minds blended in a spirit of perfect harmony, cooperating for the attainment of a definite purpose." Many icons of the twentieth-century, including Andrew Carnegie, Henry Ford, and Thomas Edison, as well as a host of presidents and statesmen, credit the Mastermind process for some of their collective success. Yet we find it is a vastly underused business and life-building tool today.

THE WHY OF THE BUSINESS MASTERMIND

According to a Dun & Bradstreet and *Inc. Magazine* study:

33 percent of new businesses fail within 3 months,

50 percent fail within 2 years,

Over 60 percent of new businesses fail within 3 years,

Of the 40 percent remaining, only 40 percent are profitable at 5 years or 16 percent (the "Sweet 16," as I call it),

Only 5 percent ever reach $1 million in annual sales,

Only 5 percent of those reach $5 million in annual sales,

Of those who reach $5 million, only 2 percent get to $10 million.

Would it therefore make sense to do everything in your power to study, research, plan, and carefully orchestrate your business development process in line with established successful entrepreneurs? The proven path to success includes collaborating with others who have what you want and can help you get it. It's working "on your own" but not alone without reinventing the wheel. Rather, it's utilizing the strengths and experience of others.

MORE TECHNOLOGY ANYONE? IT IS LONELY AT THE TOP!

A study published in the *American Sociological Review* found the number of entrepreneurs who felt they had *nobody* with whom to discuss business matters, more than doubled to about 25 percent recently. Clearly, there is a growing thirst for connections, accountability, and collaboration, even in this world of social connectivity.

WHO JOINS A MASTERMIND GROUP?

There are many types of Mastermind groups, including same-company or same-industry, women, mixed business, virtual, and more. You could form a weight-loss Mastermind group, a parents group, or any group wherein members seek similar goals and are willing to participate in a positive and harmonious dialogue, followed by tough questions and strong commitments to accountability and results.

WHAT IS THE PURPOSE AND ROLE OF THE FACILITATOR?

The facilitator's role essentially is to keep the team accountable. This may include duties outlined by the International Association of Facilitators, such as:

Create and sustain a participatory environment,
Honor and recognize diversity, ensuring inclusiveness,
Manage conflict and evoke creativity,
Guide the group to consensus and desired outcomes.

WHAT HAPPENS DURING A MASTERMIND?

The beauty of a Mastermind is that you can make your own

rules to suit the group. After years of fine-tuning, I have a formula that works beautifully. Members appreciate the organization and our specific process is designed to bring out each person's strengths.

For example, the "Hot Seat" portion is the highlight of all my groups. Each member's current challenge is queried, clarified, and "Masterminded" by the group, concluding with a host of suggestions, ideas, and experience related to the specific challenge. The person in the "Hot Seat" then commits to implementing one or two suggestions within a specific time and reports the results back to the group.

LIFE AND SUCCESS

We tend to do in life that which we say aloud, write down, and then follow up. A great Mastermind will open your mind to fresh, new ways of viewing your business and your life. It will enable you to:

Brainstorm,

Share and account for your success,

Define your goals and future,

Utilize your expertise to help others,

Focus on your specific plan for business growth and/or personal development,

Increase your professional network of "advisors."

However you define success, science has now shown that the power of our own minds to get there is far greater than imagined. And the power of two or more minds focused on a single dream can dramatically increase the manifestation of that dream.

CONTAGIOUS BY EXAMPLE

Life truly is a SEA of possibilities. You have to dive in and swim like you mean it! A Mastermind group can encourage you and even give you that first push into the water if that is what you need. You can start now by asking yourself, "What will I master today?" Then find or create a Mastermind group to help you do it.

MASTERING YOUR MASTERMIND

ELLEN KRATKA

A lot of people these days are doing Mastermind work but not all of them have fully grasped that the Mastermind contains all the information there is, including how to do anything you could ever dream of doing. Imagine what it would be like to have this type of "super computer" in your back pocket! For some of you, this idea may seem farfetched. But for others who have experienced themselves as unlimited beings of energy, it will make immediate sense. Feel free to set aside or explore this piece as you wish. For those just beginning to explore the Mastermind, I'd like to offer some thoughts.

The Mastermind is easy to enter into—it costs nothing, takes very little time, and requires no advanced training. It is there for you even if other advisors or support groups cannot (yet) be found to help you do whatever you want to do, which is an additional great advantage. The hard part is creating the mindset that unlocks the door to it.

So here are some suggestions from my daily practice of consulting the Mastermind.

Take a few minutes to relax and allow your inner energies to flow. Close your eyes and breathe. Notice what your body feels like on the inside. Feel your feet on the floor and adjust your posture while focusing your awareness in your abdomen. This helps get you out of your head and into a full self-connection to the Mastermind, which is why many refer to its gifts as "gut knowing."

Now simply intend to "link up." You may choose to ask for ideas around a specific goal or problem, or you may simply receive whatever is important for you to know at this moment.

You may tune into the Mastermind as a whole or request the presence of specific beings, such as masters in your field from the present or past (like Einstein for science matters, Beethoven for music, etc.). As you play with this technique, you'll think of other ways to use it as well. Lately, I've been calling on my future self for answers to challenges I'm facing now, since that being knows what it took to move through them.

Once you have stated your intention or asked your question—and I suggest keeping it simple and concrete, especially at first—just notice whatever shows up. It could be an actual solution or innovation, an idea for where to go for help, an insight that will help you solve the problem, awareness of your next step to take, or something so vague that it can only be called a hunch. It's also possible to get nothing the first few times. It takes persistence, mainly to teach yourself how to relax fully and surrender to the process, since so many people in our culture are used to relying on limited parts of their brains for solutions. In Mastermind work, the information—and intuition—comes through less frequently used parts of the brain as well as the heart and other energy centers of the body. However, once you get the knack of it you'll never want to stop.

When I work with the Mastermind, I often hear words as answers to my questions or feel confirmation in my body. That's because I'm primarily auditory and kinesthetic. A more visual person might see an image or suggestive colors. Occasionally, I've even smelled familiar scents, which indicated to me the energetic presence of people from my past that could help me. Don't try to decide in advance how your information will come. Just enter into the process as an adventure, without expectations, but knowing that miracles are possible.

One more thing—this is a wonderful process to bring to a group. The members can either do it together silently, or individuals can bring their insights from their personal sessions to the meeting, and then bat them around for others' contributions and further development. The Mastermind loves to play big, so the more energy and consciousness involved the better.

CONTAGIOUS PRACTICE

Who are five or six people you admire, even if they are deceased? Take the time to learn everything you can about them and try to understand their personalities. Then visualize them advising you.

TRIBUTE TO MY FAVORITE MENTOR

PAULA SNYDER

As a kid, I always knew the right person to ask for help. I'd go to Mom if I wanted an answer (the only answer). I'd go to Dad if I wanted to discuss the answer. Being a creative person, Mom's black and white answers just did not satisfy me. There were so many shades of gray in between. There were always alternative options. These possibilities became more evident when talking to Dad. Although I've had several individual mentors since then, I think Dad was the most influential. Rarely judgmental, he taught me to trust my thoughts and intelligence to come up with the answers I needed. He rarely told me just what to do. He asked questions and made me think about the answers.

When I would consider a dangerous path, Dad knew how to guide me, subtly, to a more productive path (or, let's say, he asked me more questions, which made me think and then I would choose a better path). At times when I was sad, he offered an alternative action. For instance, instead of chastising me when I hitchhiked across the country to "find myself," he suggested that I write a travel journal. I didn't always listen to my favorite mentor, but I never doubted that he wanted what was best for me. He believed in me. Still, when I veered, he was always ready to talk me through it.

Dad passed away in 1992. Before he died, he let me help him in various ways, such as including me in his medical appointments and entrusting me with significant personal decisions. I was able to give back and felt good about that even though I was losing him. Now, when I have a challenging time, I talk to myself as he would have (and most of the time I do listen). When I accomplish something I think he would be proud of, I look up to the heavens and smile into his face as I visualize it, as if he were right there. "You would have really loved this, Dad," I say to him out loud.

Through the years, because of the way I was raised, I've been able to ask questions of others to find out what I needed to know. I have learned how to speak up, request, investigate, resolve problems, and even let things go. I can sometimes hear him tell me "just let it roll off your shoulders" when I am distracted with fear or anger. I remember his "mind over matter" approach to life's ups and downs, his way of remaining productive when gray clouds would shadow the sun.

Many times I will act as the mentor. I enjoy it. I've also worked hard to instill the same thinking methods and practices in my daughter, who now works (as a mentor of sorts) for a nonprofit she organized. I believe there is always something I can do, another step I can take, another decision I can make to enhance life. Though Dad is no longer with me, the memories and lessons that I learned from him remain. I self-guide by asking myself the questions that Dad would ask. I answer myself and seek the next appropriate question to ask. I feel that my favorite mentor and guide, even in spirit, will continue to nudge me forward into the future, be it envisioned or unknown.

About a year ago, I determined that I could help facilitate business growth and show support within our local creative professional community by starting a Meetup group. Our group consists of creative professionals and hobbyists from various art disciplines. The most popular meetings that we have are those in which we've implemented a Mastermind format. When we Mastermind, we each take turns sharing information about our current projects and the challenges we've encountered. Then the entire group becomes a mentor to that individual by giving feedback and solutions stemming from their experiences within their discipline and own level of professionalism. These are very powerful interchanges. We all walk out feeling extremely energized.

So whether I'm seeking answers or not, as I meet with others, I find that I learn and grow from every exchange and experience. As a tribute to my favorite mentor, now *every* person I meet becomes my mentor.

CONTAGIOUS PRACTICE

Make it a point to listen and learn from others. Everyone has the ability to share knowledge from the most trivial thing to the complex.

ASK AND ANSWER

BARBARA RADY KAZDAN

Why do we need permission to expand our horizons? Who is holding us back from spreading our wings and trying new things?

Like many families, when we went anywhere by car it was taken for granted that my husband would drive. On a road trip, although I would have gladly traded off driving shifts, he never relinquished the wheel. When we bought an RV, I could have learned how to drive it, but there was no point. He clearly enjoyed being the captain of that ship.

We were a family of four for ten years. We took our two little girls on dozens of trips from our home base in Houston to the nation's capitol, Florida, the Rocky Mountains, the Midwest, and the West Coast. In our RV, we stopped at points of interest, soaking up the local culture and our nation's history. We made memories together.

Then we welcomed our third child. We fashioned a safe space for him in the RV and continued our travels. But he was too young to remember many of the historic places I viewed as essential to the basic education of our children. He was also too young to make the kind of memories that would last a lifetime. When he was in junior high, I wanted to introduce him to many of those "must see" places, but my husband felt he had "been there, done that." He had no interest in retracing our journeys across America.

Although I had not done any long-distance driving for all

of those years, I was determined to give my son the same exposure to our nation's beauty and history that our girls had enjoyed. With some trepidation, I summoned the courage to do it myself.

In our first adventure, I drove my son from Houston to the Rocky Mountains. He was too young to drive, but he could read maps, so I drove and he navigated. Since our opinions were the only ones that mattered, having fun took priority over making good time.

We stopped at scenic overlooks and roadside stands. We ate at "ma and pa" restaurants or diners instead of fast food spots or chains. We rented fishing gear and tried our luck. We got out of the car to walk beside a bubbling creek or to visit a local attraction. We had the time of our lives. This was the first of many trips we took together. Some of my happiest memories are from moments we shared during our travels. We still talk about the place in New Mexico that had the world's best French toast. This place was on the Colorado border, near the vast, incredible landscapes that my son had never seen.

What if I hadn't given myself permission to try? What if I had let old mindsets (my own and others) squelch the plan? I was the only one with the power to say "yay or nay." I could have agreed that it was too dangerous for a woman and child to venture into unfamiliar terrain or too tiring for me to be the only driver, but I took the leap. It turned out to be the first of many "leaps" on my personal journey because I learned an important lesson: You are the only one who has the power to grant you permission.

CONTAGIOUS ACTION

Sometimes we can be our own Mastermind, our own mentor. If you're looking for someone to ask, look in the mirror. Just make sure the image you see reflects the real you. You will know if it is right. Then give yourself a green light and go!

CAN I GET
A LITTLE HELP HERE?

REBECCA FEIN

*"Freedom from effort in the present merely means
that there has been effort stored up in the past."*
—Theodore Roosevelt

I have always been a firm believer that if you ask for help, people
are more than willing to provide it. Perhaps that is because I live
my life by that standard and help people whenever it is in my
power, even at a cost to me.

I don't have a life coach or a singular mentor in my coaching
business; I have several mentors. Some are still here and some
are not.

A few weeks into my coaching certification program, I
noticed an icon on the LinkedIn website that recommended
groups that a user might like. I'm all about networking, so I
thought I would check them out. I joined three groups specific
for coaches and began starting and participating in discussions.
The discussion I started was called, "What Do You Know Now
That You Wish You Had Known When You Started?" The
outpouring of support and responses was unbelievable. I even
had a business coach call and tell me everything she wished she
had known. She also included an article I wrote in her newsletter
in order to introduce me to her client base. I was amazed and
touched, as I wasn't expecting that level of support from anyone.

Several coaches encouraged me to post on their blogs and

a few directed me to other places they thought I might want to target as well. A few weeks after this, an associate of mine contacted me and asked me to become an official coach for a project he was doing on anti-bullying. I am opposed to bullying, having survived it in many places in my family, and I consider it in line with my vision to help abuse victims move forward via coaching. I am looking to make enough as a paid coach to be able to offer free coaching at a local domestic violence agency.

If you ask for help, you will get it. The part that people usually mess up, when it comes to getting the help, is not knowing *when* to ask for it. I ask for help all the time, even before I think I will need it, just so I know it will be there.

When considering Masterminds and mentors, it is easy to remember that people usually want to have contact with those who have crossed the bridge before them. And those who have crossed the bridge already are more than willing to help others cross after them. In some cases, the person being mentored has the opportunity to build a better bridge.

Thirty people helped me make the biggest accomplishment of my life. I helped connect eleven orphans with families. I would not have been able to do that without the help of a great group of volunteers. They educated me on the process and together we made the world a better place for children that may have had no future.

The Zulu philosophy of Ubuntu states, "I am who I am because of whom we are as a community." Never doubt for a second that you are unable to get help building a coaching empire, helping a child get adopted, graduating from college, completing a master's (in the middle of a divorce), etc.

I am very passionate about mentoring people, which is why I chose to become a coach. I wish I had done this sooner, but better to be late than to never show up.

CONTAGIOUS ACTION

If you don't ask for what you need then surely you will not get it. Fear stops people from getting what they need from others. It also stops them from giving others what they need as well...let go of the fear and step into your power.

GIVE US THIS DAY

BARRY LINDSTROM

About three or four years ago I was on a project that required me to drive through a less than desirable part of town. One particular freeway underpass housed the man I would later come to know as Harley.

I think Harley was about my age, maybe even a little younger. He certainly could not have survived these conditions if he were much older than fifty. He had lost most of his teeth and couldn't seem to stand fully erect. When he walked to a car to accept a donation, his movement was restricted as though each step toward the charity caused him physical and emotional pain.

In the thirty seconds or so that I witnessed these daily dramatics, I would think about giving something to the guy. But it always seemed the light would change before this bedraggled weary figure could reach my vehicle. Sometimes I would wave and enunciate a "Catchya next time" as I drove past him. But mostly, it saddens me to say, I would just try to put the whole image behind me.

Finally, after about two months, I got up the courage to actually try to interact with Harley. If the stoplight gods would just position me appropriately, I was going to hand him a twenty-dollar bill. I approached the underpass and sure enough the light went from green to yellow to red, placing me first in the line of potential donors. I rolled down the window and Harley came up to me, smiling a hideous but somehow engaging toothless grin. I extended the twenty but Harley pulled back.

"Oh no, brother, that's too much!" he said.

"No, it's not. Please take it!" I insisted.

"I can't, my friend. I just don't need that much," he replied.

"What do you mean? Come on, I want to help," I retorted.

Just then the light changed and Harley stepped back onto the curb out of reach. "God Bless you, brother! You better get going. Five's my limit," he said as he held up the five gnarled fingers of his right hand. Cars began to honk at me so I had to drive away. How could this guy turn down twenty bucks? I thought about stopping my car and walking back to talk to him, but there was really no place close or safe enough to pull over. Besides, it would have made me late for work. So I resolved that tomorrow I would just give this guy four fives. Clearly, I reasoned, he was too addled to know it was the same as a twenty.

The next day came and the lights were with me again. I held out the four fives to the approaching Harley, he pulled one of them from my hand and said, "That will get me a meal and night in the shelter. God Bless you, brother!"

"Well, take them all so you can have three more nights in the shelter!" I replied. Harley stopped smiling, took on a more professorial air and pronounced, "I couldn't do that. If I die tomorrow then you will have wasted all that money. You just give the rest to somebody who needs it today."

Over the next few weeks, I managed to get about a half dozen more fives into Harley's hand and then he wasn't there anymore. I figured he had found a better spot to collect his daily allowance. When the homemade cross appeared at the intersection with the words, "God Bless You Harley," I knew I was right. I learned a lot from him and consider him a shining star in my life that continues to shine.

CONTAGIOUS INSIGHT

By simply pondering what is good in your life every day, you will find that you're more productive, more relaxed, and more appreciative of your life regardless of what you are balancing at the time.

THEY OPENED MY CHUTE

BARBARA RADY KAZDAN

The day began like any other. After breakfast, my husband said, "I'm going to the store" and left like usual. Several minutes later, I discovered that he was in the car, but he hadn't left the driveway. The motor was on, the windows steamed up, but the car hadn't moved. I called 911 as I ran to the car, but it was too late. He was gone and I was a widow—alone after forty-three years of marriage.

Months later, although I had strong support from family, friends, and a life coach, I joined a bereavement group. I wanted to leave no stone unturned as I learned to accept my situation and make my way toward a new reality. The first time the group met, most of us broke into tears as we told our stories. Our wise, gentle facilitator, a widow of twenty-five years, made it clear that this was a safe, supportive place where we could say or ask anything. Week by week, each of us described the person we lost, the events that led to and transpired in our loved one's final moments, and what it was like for us to carry on. We spoke without restraint, knowing that this was a safe place like no other. That weekly meeting became a priority on my calendar.

The group members drew strength from each other. We talked about the torment leading up to the death of our spouses, the painful goodbyes, and the decisions that had to be made immediately afterward—matters too delicate or maudlin to share with family or friends. We vented about how hard it was to be cast into a role we hadn't signed up for, to be solely responsible for raising children, earning an income, and managing finances. We helped each other figure out how to do mundane tasks that had been on our spouses' to do lists. And we laughed at our first experiences at the motor vehicle department, with the IRS, or keeping up our end of conversations with mysterious people like plumbers and auto mechanics. We supported each other as we held our ground with well-meaning friends and family who thought they knew what was best for us. Most important, we encouraged and applauded each other as we took baby steps forward, tried our wings, and began our new lives.

Eight weeks later at our last meeting, there were no tears. We were stronger. Not better, but better able to cope with the thoughts and feelings that swirled through our heads. We could be more patient with ourselves because we recognized that the strange phenomena we were experiencing—forgetting appointments, feeling lethargic, waking from disturbing dreams—came with the territory. Rather than disband after the formal program ended, we kept the group together. Now, once a month, we enjoy a Saturday night date. We dine, laugh, share...and survive; looking forward to the time we know is coming, when we will once again thrive.

CONTAGIOUS BY EXAMPLE

··•● ●•··

Allow others to help you during your times of need. The more stubborn you are, the more your difficult circumstances will linger.

WHAT'S YOUR BURN RATE?

BECKY WOODBRIDGE

Before I launched my real estate business in 2003, I turned to a few good friends of mine for advice. As a first-time business owner, I certainly needed the input. One of my friends, Frank Holmes, who ran a successful consulting practice, became an occasional consultant for me. Another person, Bill Bergeron, one of my original clients, became both a friend and a mentor. He said that he liked my enthusiasm and my passion for real estate.

In retrospect, I had surrounded myself with good people—one of the first tenets of running a successful business. The problem was that I wasn't listening to them. I was in over my head—and sinking fast. I remember calling Bill in a total panic and blurting out that I seemed to be drowning in debt.

"What's your burn rate?" Bill asked.

"What?" I said. I'd never heard of such a term. Bill explained that my burn rate was the breakeven point on my expenses.

"Drop everything you are doing," he said, "write down the amount of every bill that rolls in on a monthly basis. Don't guess. Be as accurate as possible then call me back."

It's a good thing I was sitting down when the reality of my business dealings hit me right between the eyes. My financial picture was even worse than I had imagined. I needed forty thousand dollars each month just to cover my business and home expenses. The income coming in could barely cover half of that.

I was shocked. Moreover, I was embarrassed...and humbled. There was no passing the buck in this situation (not that I had any bucks to pass!). This was my fault. I quickly realized that my biggest mistake, from the beginning, was turning a deaf ear to the sound business advice I was receiving from my consultant and mentor.

I allowed my ego and my arrogance to stand in the way of listening—and learning. My ego spoke loud and clear when I was creating a vision to the point where I thought I knew what was best for my business. That's nothing but insecurity talking. Deep down, I wasn't comfortable not knowing everything, so even when I received sage advice, I tuned it out. This contributed to a variety of costly rookie mistakes. I grew the business too fast. One office was more than enough to accommodate the clients we had, not three! I didn't even take the time to develop a business plan. I was so caught up in the early rush of having my own company that I let this fundamental part of a business model fall by the wayside, even though I had smart people advising me.

Sometimes a little humble pie is good. I realize now that I am blessed to have mentors in my life who are wise beyond my years. I'm equally fortunate to know so many people with wisdom that influenced my life both personally and professionally. More importantly, I realize that there is great learning in listening—really listening.

I learned that a company doesn't have to be big to be successful. Income doesn't mean anything if it can't cover your expenses. And don't put the cart before the horse—be patient and be wise. Had I held my ego in check and opened my ears to what my bright and experienced mentors were telling me, I might still have my real estate business. Instead, I have the value of a lesson learned...the hard way.

CONTAGIOUS PRACTICE

Lessons learned: Find a mentor. Use your own experiences to mentor a friend or group. Understand the importance and responsibility of being a mentor to someone else.

SAVING STRIDES

MYRTLE NEWSAM

In 2007 I was sick with what was later diagnosed as diabetes, congestive heart failure, and hypertension. My feet had become so swollen from my illness that it was difficult for me to walk. Unable to work, I moved in with my cousin temporarily.

Three weeks later I sought residence at a local homeless shelter. I could not believe this had happened to me. Other family and friends no longer had room for me. After my first night in the shelter I woke up to a rainy morning. Breakfast was served early and then everyone living there was asked to leave until three o'clock when the shelter reopened its doors. At this time my feet had become more inflamed and I was only able to wear wide slippers.

I called a friend, Teresa. With my garbage bag of clothes and my soaking wet feet she took me to her house where I took a warm bubble bath and was treated to lunch. We then prayed together before I returned to the shelter.

The next morning I went to see an advocate to address the swelling in my feet and legs. The advocate quickly sent me to see a doctor to get the medication I needed. The doctor put me in respite and I thanked God that I had three meals a day and somewhere to rest. He then approved me to work through Vocational Rehabilitation. The two-block walk to the bus stop was excruciating, but if I could not get to the bus I would have no way to get to the job. Determined to make it to work, I prayed every morning for the strength to walk. The bus driver would see me coming and waited for me to get there. I always thanked him. Little by little I started walking faster.

One Saturday, Redeeming Love Missionary Baptist Church supplied our lunch and they asked me to come to their church for a visit. I decided to go and I enjoyed the singing. The church van started picking me up every Sunday. Four months later, I joined the church. There is a lot of love expressed there and I finally felt at home.

In April 2008, my Disability was approved after I was turned down twice before. I moved in with a friend from the shelter. She had three bedrooms and two children. I then prayed and asked God for my own apartment. In August 2008, he answered my prayer and I moved into my own place. The week before I moved out of my friend's apartment, the song "It's Your Time" was played at dinner—confirmation!

God took good care of me when I was in that shelter from 2007 to 2008. I know who he is and what he can do. I know that I would not have gotten the care I needed if I had lived with anybody else during this time.

CONTAGIOUS COMMITMENT

A force in your life, whether it be God, a friend, a mentor, or a higher being, is always there for you. Remember that when you are down, and focus on your appreciation. It will deliver but you need to recognize and acknowledge.

> *"The most disabling condition: ATTITUDE.*
> *The most enabling condition: ATTITUDE!"*
>
> —Adero Allison

CHAPTER EIGHT

YOU HAVE ARRIVED!

Nothing is impossible in terms of achievement.

Embracing and appreciating "now" reminds you of what it took to get here.

Make it a goal to radiate enthusiasm, confidence, and optimism to others. This energy will improve their lives and add even more value to your own.

This final chapter serves two very important purposes. The first is a piece of good news for those struggling. It simply says, "You will arrive!" So, instead of being down or frustrated with your life, just know that you will arrive at your preferred destination. I am living proof that the ride to the destination, no matter how bumpy, can be just as happy as the destination itself, if you let it (as explained in the "Goal Analysis" chapter). You just need to hold that optimism in your heart throughout the process.

The second purpose is to remind people who "have arrived" that they should appreciate the adventure it took to get there. They should consider "paying it forward" as the saying goes by reminding others that optimism, perseverance, and faith in yourself, and the universe, will ultimately deliver your goals.

David

"I have arrived! I didn't think that was the case when I learned I was having triplets a few years ago but these children and my wife are the best things in my life. Couple that with the wonderful addition of a baby girl, thus bringing the total to four children within two years. Of course the support of our families has made managing the pack a little easier. To summarize my forty-two years: I am complete, even with the hard work, agendas, and upcoming tuitions!"

—Joseph Coppola, Trumbull, Connecticut

"I read a great article by Robert Frank in the Wall Street Journal Wealth Report. He states, 'Why the huge spending on old cars when the rest of the economy is sputtering? The wealthy would rather put some of their money into real things they can enjoy rather than watch it erode in the financial markets. You can't take gold coins for a ride with the top down on a summer night.' There is a lot to be said for enjoying the finer things in life when you finally can. Not everything is an investment."

—Brett Murphy, Jupiter, Florida

MAKING MY MARK IN THE WORLD

MONA MACDONALD TIPPINS

My life journey has always taken me down paths that allowed me to help others. For example, I frequently rescued stray cats and dogs, I helped people in communities where I lived, and accomplished many things that reflected an altruistic lifestyle. Several years ago I started to think about my life in another way. Once my children were grown I decided that I wanted to be remembered for something unique. A "bucket list" did not appeal to me, and my award-winning pineapple upside-down cake was not enough! Admitting to myself that I was too old to win an Olympic medal and not talented enough to win an Academy Award, I thought about somehow getting into the Guinness Book of World Records. This was not an easy task as I quickly found out.

Then, about two o'clock one morning, it hit me like a ton of bricks. I jumped out of bed and called the Guinness people in London. I realized I could combine my love of train travel with a Guinness record. I offered to stay on the same train for a year if there would be a way to take showers. I was told that the best way to get into the book was to beat an existing record.

After searching the Guinness book I found the one I wanted to try. There was a record of the most unduplicated miles traveled by train. I got the approval from Guinness, but not a promise of being in the book (even if I broke the record).

I got more adventure than I had bargained for. Although some of my travel was easy and without mishap, I was robbed in Bucharest, beaten in Berlin, and then mistaken for a beggar, a prostitute, and other unsavory characters. I was also lost several times but many strangers helped me along the way. I traveled through thirty-three countries and my mileage was enough to have circled the globe three-and-one-fifth times. Each kilometer had to be verified by a conductor. Any retraced kilometers would not count, which is more difficult than you think.

The hardest part of the journey was being a vegetarian. There were times I thought of giving up but too many people were counting on me, including the various "sponsors" that had donated rail passes and cash to my plight. I could not disappoint them. Traveling low on cash and being a woman alone was easy compared with the difficulty of being a vegetarian. The world eats meat!

I beat the record near the borders of Russia and Kazakhstan. The hotel in Kazakhstan had kept my passport and visa, so I was worried about traveling into Russia without my documents. With the help of others on the train I managed to appease the border guards and made it back to Moscow.

After several months, I finally heard from the Guinness people. My record had been accepted for the 1998 Guinness book. I cried when I saw my name in that book especially due to the fact that I was one month away from my sixty-fifth birthday when I beat the record. Yes, I was proud of myself and my family was proud of me as well. I have made my mark in the world as an author and a world record-holder!

CONTAGIOUS COMMITMENT

Remove the statement, "I can't do it," from your mind and agree to never say or think it again.

THE ROAD LESS TRAVELED

MICHAEL DELIA, ESQ.

I completed high school with honors in chemistry and received the chemistry award upon graduation. Thus, it was a fore-gone conclusion that I would major in chemistry in college. Following my college graduation, I was accepted as a research assistant in the research laboratories at Columbia University where I was able to work toward my graduate degree. The work was exciting since, at the time, James Watson and Francis Crick were working out the configuration of DNA and a whole new world of science. It was at this time that I met the love of my life, whom I eventually married.

I was faced with a dilemma. I was reluctant to abandon my work in science but I also realized I could not support a wife and family while working as a research assistant. I had to find a new career. Life had been tough up to this point. My father had died when I was ten and my mother struggled for many years to make ends meet. I wanted to take all the necessary steps to give my family a good life and also to allow my mother to enjoy her retirement years.

Help came from an unexpected source. An old friend that I seldom saw had suggested I go to law school and specialize in patent law where I could combine both law and science. I felt this was sound advice. Although I never considered law as a profession that I would be interested in, I decided to give it a try. I went with my hunch that this old friend had given me great advice.

Following four years of law school in the evenings, and studying for the New York State and Patent Bar Examinations, I was ready to start my new career. But, again, I was faced with a dilemma. Very few companies and intellectual property law firms were inclined to hire inexperienced attorneys. "Time is money" was the common saying during the arduous interview process.

I experienced numerous disappointments but finally landed a position with a chemical engineering company where I practiced general law and a smattering of patent law. After several years of exploring numerous other opportunities, I was fortunate to secure a position in the patent department of a major pharmaceutical company where I was able to utilize my biochemical training combined with law. This was clearly the point I had hoped for when I initially decided to go to law school back in 1955.

My career with the pharmaceutical company took many rewarding turns among which was the good fortune to serve with Dr. Watson, the Nobel Prize winner I mentioned earlier regarding DNA, on our company's cancer grant program for promising researchers. I spent many years traveling the world to defend our company's patents as well as to protect our business interests worldwide. I worked my way up "the corporate ladder" and have a lot to be thankful for. Personally I also feel rewarded; I am happily married fifty-five years and have three great children and seven grandchildren.

I often wonder what direction my life would have taken had I not had that casual talk with my old friend.

CONTAGIOUS INSIGHT

Consider how many times you have gone down an unexpected path and were glad you did. The more you focus on that, the more you can accept when paths cross unexpectedly in the future.

FAITH IN MYSELF

FAITH CAMPBELL

There are so many different aspects of my life that I could share. I could tell you that just four short years ago I was beginning my road to recovery after twenty years of drug abuse. I could tell you that being HIV-positive for the last eighteen years has been a blessing, not a death sentence. I could also tell you that I am a testimony of hope and a living miracle. So, what I will do is tell you a little about myself and hope that anything I say will encourage others.

I was born June 19, 1968, the only girl and last born to a single mom of four. I guess my mother knew that I was going to need a strong name. There were a lot of things that went on in my childhood, but my mom never stopped believing that I would succeed. So I never stopped believing. Although I spent most of my preteen years in a household filled with physical and mental abuse by an older brother, I never stopped believing. Even after being kicked out of one of the most prestigious prep schools in the country two months before graduation, after being there four years on a scholarship, I never stopped believing.

After having four children out of wedlock, being diagnosed with AIDS, and battling drug addiction, I never stopped believing. When my eldest son was shot and left for dead, I never stopped believing. When I had to show my children (the people I love most in the world) tough love, I never stopped believing.

My life took a wonderful turn when I was able to attend

Grace Institute, a school in New York City for disadvantaged women. Grace provides free education and training in business along with developing personal skills necessary for improving the quality of life. I graduated with honors and received awards for academic excellence and leadership. From this wonderful opportunity and hard work, I was able to become an administrative assistant for a nonprofit organization, a mentor at a business school for women, and a peer trainer for a financial organization. I have become an advocate for HIV and AIDS and give motivational lectures as well.

In all that I have been through I have never stopped believing that I was destined for great things. Four years ago nobody wanted to know my name. Today, people want to hear my story. Four years ago I was ashamed to say what I had done hours before. Now I can stand with pride and tell people, from all walks of life, the many achievements that God has allowed me. Not only do I have certificates and awards, but I also have the respect and trust of family and friends. I have the admiration of those that I meet. I am in a leadership position in my church. I have a decent job, my own home, and I am in excellent health. My mother is proud of me. My children, although they may not always like me, love me. My job commends me.

It hasn't been easy and not every day is a good day. But every time I can give someone else hope, my struggle becomes so much more meaningful. Every time I can give inspiration to someone who thinks they can't accomplish their dreams, my life becomes so much more fulfilling. Every time I can encourage someone who says, "I won't" to say, "Yes I will," my life becomes worthwhile.

Thank you for this honor to share my story. I will never stop believing. I am proud of the woman God has allowed me to become. It is an honor and a privilege to be where I am today and know I dare to dream of where I'm going to be tomorrow. I have arrived! Faith—the substance of things hoped for, the evidence of things not seen.

CONTAGIOUS INSPIRATION

· · ● ● ● ○ ● ● · ·

Always look beyond yourself for answers and have faith in what you receive, whether it comes from religion, the universe, or another power that offers you solace.

I AM ENOUGH

DR. COLLEEN GEORGES

Life is funny. It's unpredictable, and just when we think we understand ourselves or others, something unexpected happens that throws us off. The thing is, we are always changing and evolving. Life is a fascinating journey of constant exploration. And there are not always going to be clear answers to all the questions we ask along the way. I have learned a lot from the people that I've encountered on this journey so far. I think most of us are trying to figure out who we are and how to best be that person. In this process, we try to be lots of different people, taking on all kinds of characteristics. We behave in different ways, interact with all kinds of people, and try to see what works and what doesn't—what feels right, what fits with what is at the core of who we are. We step outside of ourselves and watch and listen for our true feelings. Hopefully, we try to listen to the people we encounter as well. It's amazing what you can learn about yourself and others simply from listening.

During the second year of my counseling practicum in graduate school, a very wise client ended our final session together by saying, "Thank you for teaching me that I am enough." That statement has stayed with me ever since and has changed the way I understand people. I began to listen to people with particular attention to areas in which they believed they were lacking. I started wondering more and more, "Could that be what it's all about?" If we could all learn to embrace ourselves as we are and come to understand that we are enough, would we live healthier lives? Since my client made that wise statement, I have used this wisdom in my work with clients and in my interactions with all those I encounter. Additionally, I have used this belief to guide me on my own journey toward self-understanding.

So what does it mean to believe that we are enough? How do we do this? And how will we benefit from it? How does it affect our life quality? When we come into this world, we all start out in different places. Some of us have greater resources, whether it's a supportive family, economic security, or a quality education. Some of us start out with less of these resources. Nonetheless, we all possess the ability to become better at being who we are. Some parts of our journey toward this goal are simple; other parts are more complex. However, if at the end of our journey we are better able to embrace who we are—strengths, limitations, and all—we have fulfilled the greatest of personal goals.

CONTAGIOUS PRACTICE

Don't tell yourself that you're not good enough. Acknowledge and address areas for growth, but always know that you are enough to love and to be loved—fortunes and misfortunes, talents and flaws, mistakes and triumphs.

RESILIENCE

EILEEN LICHTENSTEIN

We can all benefit by listening to each other's resilience stories, resilience meaning "the lifting yourself up after a fall" that has caused you to "lie low" for a while.

My husband Steve and I, college sweethearts, have been through a lot together and it hasn't always been smooth sailing. We have been married for forty years and have two beautiful daughters. They both left the nest long ago; Jess (thirty-three) is living in London, Ariel (thirty-one) is in Madrid. Jessica attended graduate school in London and decided to stay with her British boyfriend; they've now been married for seven years. Ariel first went to Europe for adventure and ended up settling down there. She teaches English and lives with her Spanish boyfriend.

Well, I was devastated with their individual decisions to stay in Europe. I'd been "empty-nested" through their college years but this was different! I just didn't get it. We've always been close with open communication and now, every time I wanted to have an evening chat, they would be sleeping. Before this turn of events I'd been really good at visualizing positive outcomes, meditating, and moving on from negative thinking. In the past I was able to "detach" and not be disappointed with the decisions my daughters made. These times were different and my "visualizations" weren't right. Then there was 9/11, which compounded my concerns.

Finally I got it! Jess and Ariel were doing what each had

visualized for themselves and I needed to be fully behind them as I had been in the past. I knew that Steve and I had brought them up to think things through and to be aware of problems that may arise from their actions. We had to trust their wonderful judgment, a quality that makes us so proud. Knowing this, I was confident that they were making wise choices for themselves. It was me who needed to shift so that I could be supportive emotionally. I kept coming back to an old proverb about child rearing: "Give them roots and wings!"

My "aha" moment helped me to bring my extreme sadness of that period into perspective. Now we travel across the "big pond" and see each other three times a year and video chat often. I think of them every day, send my positive thoughts, and visualize their happy scenarios in my meditations and dreams. At the same time, I'm enjoying being best friends with Steve again! We have found a new passion for life and are enjoying many great hobbies, activities, and travel!

CONTAGIOUS BY EXAMPLE

Resilience is part of our chemistry. We just need to find it, take advantage of it, and let it get us through tough times when necessary. Sometimes the best way to do that is to listen to other people's resilience stories.

WELL DONE

JANET BALES

"Whatever you decide to be in life, be the very best at it."

—Theodore Marlette

These were the words my father would say over and over when we were growing up. My dad wanted all of us to succeed in everything we did; he also wanted us to be happy.

I am the youngest of five. My oldest brother Mike died in an automobile accident at the age of eighteen. He was valedictorian of his class and only days away from graduation. My parents began to search for meaning in it all; if there was any purpose in his death they wanted to know. They decided to take all of us back to church, something they used to do with the family before I came along. It seems disillusionment with a quarrelling congregation pushed them away from any further fellowship years prior, but, now, in this time of sorrow, they sought the only place they knew could give them solace.

We lived in a small village in northern Wisconsin. Ironically, we moved there to escape the hustle and bustle of city life and to give Mike the opportunity to really thrive in a smaller community for his last years of high school. My brother did find favor in this tight-knit community; he was fun and likeable so it was no surprise.

We went to a warm and welcoming church in what I would

apprehensively call downtown New Auburn; population was approximately three hundred if you counted the dogs and cats. I remember the services being meaningful and intimate. I also recall our family taking up a whole pew, sitting attentively as if we were waiting for someone to quiz us at the end. Our young priest was genuine and caring; it was the only place I really felt welcome. I carried that memory for years.

Not surprisingly, my parents could not stand passing the site where my brother died on a daily basis. It was only a mile from our home. They decided to move us back to the city we had moved away from; my father passed a few years later.

Those were formative years. I dealt with more loss than most, less than some. I learned where to turn for answers and the peace I was looking for through my parents' example. I married in 1980 and shortly after that my husband was diagnosed with diabetes. I became a caregiver along with the various other titles the average person acquires as a wife and a mother. We started attending a local church where we started to serve quite actively.

Years later my husband passed with complications from diabetes. I remarried to a wonderful man who was also a widower. He was familiar with loss, as he became a caregiver after his wife was diagnosed with breast cancer. At this point I thought life couldn't get any better. We collectively had six wonderful children and five grandchildren, with more on the way, when suddenly my life took a different turn and I was diagnosed with colon cancer. It was easier for me to be the caregiver than the care "recipient." It may seem like a dark statement but it was all I knew. Being vulnerable, in need of another's help was not something I ever wanted to experience; however, it was necessary. I liked being self-reliant, something I was soon to find out was not healthy. Now I was receiving the meals that so many times before I would bring to others.

I had to accept help, and, to my horror, even had to ask for it.

Throughout a period of eight months during surgery, tests, and chemo, I received a word of encouragement daily, either by mail, phone, email, or face-to-face. It was incredible. In a time when most people don't know the names of their next-door neighbor, I was experiencing a kind of community few are privileged to be a part of.

I recall a number of years ago; it was a particularly wet spring. The rain kept coming and saturated the soil, so much so that the large oak trees fell because they couldn't release the moisture quickly enough and the ground couldn't hold their weight. Many times our lives mirror nature. Too much of anything is not good; it does not bring a healthy balance, and can bring our demise. I only saw one side of community before I got sick; I couldn't receive, only give. With this view I didn't really value community but I didn't see the full picture. My appreciation now is much more encompassing.

My husband and I are starting a nonprofit mission that is dedicated to helping missionaries, something we talked about prior to my diagnosis. Our hope is to "serve those who serve," giving them longevity in the field.

My life has taken a full circle. Still the desire to please my father runs deep. I can still hear him say, "Whatever you decide to be in life, be the very best at it." Through life's turns I've learned to be patient, kind, and long-suffering, although I still have a lot to learn. I have a heavenly perspective I would not have had otherwise. I never would have imagined the road taken or the time it took to get here, the place where I feel I have arrived. Life is funny, but thankfully God is good. I look forward to the day I reach the other side of eternity and I can hug my earthly and heavenly fathers, and I hope to hear them say, "Well done."

CONTAGIOUS INSIGHT

We meander in different directions, many of which are out of our control. Take a personal inventory and know that shifts in our life are usually healthy, necessary, and part of the growth process.

BRIGHTEN THE CORNER WHERE YOU ARE

MARY ANN DAVIS

As a child, one of the many songs we sang was "Brighten the Corner Where You Are." Whatever road you have been on, there are probably others whose road was even more difficult or treacherous. I think sometimes we forget that and want to think that we are the only person who has had a rough go of things. But if you can wake up in the morning, manage to get out of bed and get dressed, and move into your day, you are more fortunate than some. For those of us who recognize our many blessings, we not only need to be grateful, but to demonstrate that attitude so others can recognize it.

It costs nothing to put a smile on your face and share it with others as you go through your day. It only takes a moment to speak to passersby. It may take a few minutes more to ask about their health or their well-being, but sometimes you need to do that, especially with family and those you consider friends. But imagine the joy you could bring to a complete stranger who seems to be having a "down" day if you simply ask how they are. Maybe no one else has asked them that. Yes, they may actually tell you, but that may also be just what they needed. This might be just the type of kindness they needed.

Even in such small ways we can help to brighten someone else's day, which should be a good feeling for you, as well.

CONTAGIOUS COMMITMENT

Make it a point to say hello to at least one stranger per day. And, also make it a point to say hello to someone you see frequently but never said hello to before.

THE STORY OF GEORGE

DAVID MEZZAPELLE

Driving along the water on a beautiful afternoon in Southern California, I was en route to a dinner lecture when I hit massive traffic. I pulled over at a marina to ask the security guard for alternate directions. This marina was full of magnificent yachts, which had caught my eye.

The security guard, George, was a friendly Eastern European gentleman roughly between sixty-five and seventy years old. George could not have been any nicer and we started discussing his life in America. My single request for directions became an hour-and-a-half conversation.

George moved to the U.S. thirty years ago with nothing except his wife and a few dollars. They came to Southern California where she could use her nursing experience to get a job in healthcare. George had warehousing and logistics experience and had visualized some sort of opportunity where he could excel. As hoped, he landed a position as a laborer at a local distribution facility and worked his way up to supervisor.

Over the course of thirty years and raising a family, George amassed $150,000 in cash, which they nested away for retirement along with several rental properties. This nest egg of cash and real estate was built from his employment as well as various side jobs he took on. It also included money saved from his wife's job. George's thought pattern, when he purchased the rental properties, was to preserve capital and to bring in an additional income stream. Back in Eastern Europe he was always told, "Go to America. Buy property."

George's long-term plan was to retire, enjoy a small pension from his job and his wife's job, and have income from rental properties. George finally did retire and everything started out as planned. His wife reduced her hours to part-time—she loved her job. George's daughters were now married and had homes of their own.

George found retirement boring and decided to make real estate a new career. He started buying and flipping properties during the real estate bubble. He bought several "good deals" using their nest egg for deposits along with pension dollars, equity loans, and conventional bank financing.

Within two years George had turned the $150,000 into more than $300,000 from these activities. Now, between the cash, rental properties, and primary residence, George had eliminated most of the debt.

Their retirement was looking better and better as their net assets were over half a million dollars at this point. However, George was now bitten with the "bug" of speculation and was determined to continue. What he overlooked was the grossly overvalued real estate market. It was clear that a real estate correction was in sight, many areas throughout the U.S. were already experiencing it, but George was determined to keep going.

Later that year George found a raw land deal that would cost him $300,000 (his entire cash pile). His plan was to purchase the property for cash and subdivide the lots. At that point he would leverage the property in order to entitle the land and sell lots for a profit. He would also build homes in partnership with a local general contractor for additional profit. To make a long story short, he lost the entire nest egg on this deal. The real estate bubble burst and he was stuck in the middle. He was forced to borrow against all the remaining equity he had in his rental properties and his primary residence. The rental incomes did not come close to the carrying costs and they lost every asset they had, including their home.

Why did I choose to put this in a chapter titled, "You Have Arrived"? Because George is as happy as can be! Broke, now living with his daughter and new granddaughter and working full-time as a security guard, George told me that he has arrived. George works nights so that he can help raise his granddaughter while the daughter, son-in-law, and his wife work full-time during the day.

George and his wife are so focused on their family that they consider working full-time during their retirement years to be a pleasure. Plus, living in the U.S. makes them proud and they wouldn't live anywhere else. When I asked George about the lost nest egg, foreclosed home and rental properties, his response was, "That's just money. It is fun to earn and it will come again, God willing. There is only one life and I have been blessed with a path that led me into my daughter's home. My wife and I get to be part of raising another beautiful child."

Needless to say, I was late for the lecture but certainly gained a refreshing perspective.

CONTAGIOUS PRACTICE

•••●•••

You learn a lot when listening to people. Always keep your ears open. You never know the impact they will have on your life.

THE BEST IS YET TO COME

ALAN MALIZIA

A major difference between us, and the beasts that make this planet our home, is awareness. We, unlike our counterparts, have a conscious awareness of our mortality. When a person wakes up in the morning from a night's sleep he or she may give thanks for another day of life. A pet of that same household will not, because pets do not possess the ability to do so. We know that there are forces at play, be they illnesses, accidents, or other threats, that could deter us from being around to wake up the next morning. Our pets are not burdened with this concept. They only are, at any particular moment in time, responding by instinct to the environment around them. Man's sense of mortality instills wonder of death's purpose, as an end or a means to another.

Purpose may be defined as something set up as an end to be obtained or an action in course of execution. The Hubble Telescope has proved the universe is expanding. And since this is true it has not yet reached a static state, if it ever will. Therefore, the universe has purpose. When we enter this world through birth we too have purpose. For we will affect not only the lives of our parents and siblings, but all who we come in contact with in life—for better or worse. It is as though a pebble were dropped in a pond. The rings of rippled water will continue to radiate outward from the center for as far as the size of the pond allows. Now, if other pebbles were dropped into the pond, they too would have a similar effect. There would be an endless crisscrossing of ripples influencing one another. This is an example of both our unique independence and dependence based upon the effect we have on others and they on us.

So now we have this life that is set up to obtain some end and a course of execution to achieve that end. What, then, is that end? It is happiness. For happiness is sought by all humans. What then is the true course that leads to happiness? It is as clear as day and night, light and darkness, good and evil. The absence of one opens the way to the other. At dusk day ceases and night begins. As two objects cannot occupy the same space at the same time, neither can the aforementioned. Which course then to choose? By choosing one we must abandon the other.

In Oscar Wilde's *The Picture of Dorian Gray*, Dorian has his portrait painted by an artist whose hedonistic view is adopted by Dorian. In fear of losing his youth and beauty, he makes a pact to sell his soul in return for his agelessness. The portrait is to take on the effects of age and his debauched acts as he remains young. In time, the gruesomely transformed portrait gives Dorian a view of what has become of his soul by his sinful actions. His inflated ego led to the selfish use and abuse of those around him as a means to the end he pursued, self-satisfaction. As time passed his numerous heinous acts increased upon the portrait and incessantly tortured his conscience. In an attempt to free himself from the torment, he tries to destroy the horrifying portrait and all his corruptions, which he felt unforgivable, along with it. He slashes it with the knife he used to murder his former friend. In the end, this act ironically kills him. All the embodiment of his sinfulness, which once adhered to the portrait, is now transferred to him. The portrait is restored to its youthful beauty. Dorian's choice determined his tragic end.

There is a story, found recently in our church bulletin, of a woman who was one of the oldest members of her church and also one of its most faithful. One day she shared the news from her doctor that a previously undetected tumor would take her life in six months. Just as the minister was expressing his sorrow, she interrupts and she tells him not to be sorry because God has blessed her with a long life and she was ready to go. They talked about appropriate Scripture readings and her favorite hymns that would be incorporated into her service. When all was decided upon she requested one more thing: that when she is buried she wanted a Bible in one hand and a fork in the other. He understood the Bible but why the fork? The woman said she had been thinking about all the church dinners she had attended over the years, especially at the end of the dinners when the waitress removed the used plates. "So when they told me to keep the fork," she continued, "I knew the best was yet to come...Dessert! That's why I want the fork. So people will talk about it, along with remembrances of me, at my funeral. As they walk by my casket, I want them to ask, 'Why the fork?' And I want you to tell them, I kept the fork because... the best is yet to come!"

Dorian Gray used others to make himself temporarily happy. The faithful woman made herself useful to others to find her eternal happiness. Dorian's life would end in violence and solitary despair. The faithful woman's life would end in peace and hope among those she loved and who loved her. Dorian's greatest sin was that he felt he was beyond forgiveness. Bishop Fulton Sheen wrote, "We all are walking in heaven or hell, here and now. All we need do is die. Where we are at that moment we will be forever."

Our choice not to do as we should separates us from our true purpose. Without true purpose we cannot attain true happiness. Death serves its purpose one way or another. For Dorian Gray, death's reward is desolation and hopelessness.

Death for the faithful woman is nothing more than a rebirth into the warm eternal light of love. There is no fear of death in a life lived well.

CONTAGIOUS EFFECT

You may not be on a course that you are comfortable with at the moment. It is important to make an examination of conscience. Be honest with yourself. From here make those changes that will restore the course you are meant to travel. But don't overlook a change of course that may have happened for a good reason. In the process, the result will be happiness. In the end, joy.

WHAT TO DO WHEN YOUR WORLD ENDS

LISA ROTHSTEIN

I had been living in Paris for the past ten years of a twenty-year career, working for ad agencies as a copywriter and creative director on products like toothpaste and fabric softener. By this time, I could do the job with my eyes closed, and at this point I was completely burned out. So I was only mildly and dolefully surprised when after only six months at my most recent job, I was fired for the first time in my life.

On balance, it had not been a great year so far. My fiancé, the only decent guy I had met in ages (or so it seemed at the time), met someone else online using my laptop, and somehow made me believe it was my fault. My beloved dog stayed around to comfort me for as long as he could, but passed on at sixteen. Having willfully remained overseas longer than was prudent for my career, I was so far out of the Madison Avenue loop that I was in another galaxy. I would turn forty before the end of the year and here I was, childless, manless, dogless, jobless, and clueless. It would have been comical had these events been part of one of the screenplays I had been toying with writing. But this was real life, and it was pretty clear that I had messed mine up.

Now I was on my way to Hawaii, my refusal to cancel the trip was one of the reasons cited for my firing. As part of a leadership team, I was leading a group of French speakers to a Tony Robbins seminar called "Life Mastery." The irony was not lost on me.

That week, as I and my team swam with sea turtles, rappelled off of telephone poles, and shuffled across hot coals, my mind kept asking the question, "What the hell are you going to do now?" I really had no idea.

The next morning, late for the day's kickoff session, my European friends stopped me and said, "You'd better look at the television." "I don't have time," I argued. But they insisted. It was September 11, 2001.

That day and the remainder of that week the world turned upside-down for everyone. Many of the two thousand seminar attendees were from New York, and some worked in the World Trade Center. There were many tears, impromptu prayer sessions under palm trees, and long lines for landline phones. As I looked out over the peaceful ocean, I tried to fathom the unthinkable violence that had just occurred six thousand miles away. And then, I felt a wholly unexpected rush of gratitude. I'm alive; I can start over. I'm going to be all right. It's OK not to know what's next. I had hated that job and I silently thanked my boss for liberating me, as I never would have allowed myself to quit. My fiancé had been a critical jerk who would surely have cheated on me after we were married. I felt so lucky. My former life was indeed over. But now I had a second chance. Suddenly, my unknown future seemed full of promise, rather than a gaping void.

When I returned home, I went through my mail. A letter had arrived from a screenwriting contest I had entered months before. My first screenplay had won a prize and they were flying me to Hollywood to accept it.

I now live in Southern California, and while my "big break" in Hollywood has been elusive, I do have an agent and I am married to my best friend and biggest fan. When I'm not writing, I coach others in exploring what great things they might do with their creative talents and ideas. I use my advertising skills to help them market themselves. Life is good. It's interesting. And it's certainly not over.

CONTAGIOUS INSIGHT

The next time you feel that your life is falling apart, ask yourself whether it may just be falling together. Sometimes you've got to lose everything you think you need in order to receive what you really deserve.

ACHIEVING THE IMPOSSIBLE CARROT

FAYE LEVOW

My life has been all about the carrots. I'm one of those people who are driven toward the carrot, no matter what. Sometimes I get the carrot I was looking for; sometimes I get something very different. Either way it's a learning experience.

I always look for the lessons in each situation. What worked? What didn't work? What did I learn? You might call it "The Rapid Growth Method." Others might call it the "Being OK With Looking Foolish Method." Same thing, different perspective. If you care too much about what others think, it can hold you back from all sorts of wonderful experiences and opportunities.

One time, I was determined to go to a business conference for entrepreneurs taking place on the other side of the country that I felt would further my life and my business. The conference was about six weeks away when I learned of it and decided it was a must for me. The program included young people with an entrepreneurial spirit, so I determined that my daughters would benefit too. It was going to cost thousands of dollars between tuition, airfare, hotel, and incidentals for the three of us. And I only had about a hundred dollars to my name!

I enlisted the support of the sponsoring organization to learn the fine points of raising capital and immediately began contacting everyone I knew to raise the funds. I was on the phone day and night. My daughters, then about ten and fifteen, would come home every day from school and check in to find out the amount that had been raised. "Where are we at today, Mom?" They were my biggest cheerleaders and this was a *huge* carrot.

I made our plane reservations by phone (pre-Internet) and, for an entire month, called every twenty-three hours to re-reserve them in order to preserve the lower pricing. We were doing all of the recommended preparations to maximize the value of this endeavor.

As our departure day grew closer, the girls began packing their bags and I laid my clothes out on the bed for packing—but never stopped making calls. On the day we were supposed to leave, a business friend of mine, who had been watching my progress, showed up and extended his credit card limit at my kitchen table so he could loan me the money for our hotel and other trip expenses! After thanking him profusely, I dashed to my room and threw my clothes into a suitcase.

My husband drove us to the airport. The girls and I literally ran with our bags all the way to the gate. Once we boarded and buckled our seatbelts, the three of us looked at each other and said, "We did it!" We had a group hug and I started to cry.

It was the most intense six weeks of my life. I had achieved what appeared to be impossible at the outset and something that most people wouldn't even attempt. The rewards were great, even long after the conference had ended.

Because I was so determined and refused to accept anything less than being at that conference with my daughters, it made a huge difference in our lives. My kids learned that if they put their mind and actions to something, no matter how difficult or impossible it may seem, they can achieve it. They both chose difficult careers that have tested their resolve in many ways and will continue to do so. My older daughter is a real rocket scientist. My younger daughter is an actress, destined to walk the red carpet someday. As for me, I learned that I can achieve the "impossible" when I go after it all the way. I believe this is true for anyone!

One more little tidbit: Stay away from the naysayers. I actually never told my mom about my plans because I didn't want to combat the negativity. I needed every bit of energy and concentration to remain focused on the goal.

CONTAGIOUS COMMITMENT

The keys to achievement are: 1. Be clear about what you want. 2. Know you will achieve it. 3. Take dedicated and determined action. 4. Never give up. 5. Go for it!

THE NOW OF YOUR LIFE

IRA SCOTT

Yes, now you have arrived. You empower yourself to be the greatest version of yourself you can be—and that enables you to be a resource to those around you.

Last December, a week or so before Christmas, I was at a local shoe store and went in for a free shoeshine. As I sat and waited for the one employee of the store, who was assisting another customer, I simply relaxed and was in the present. I was not thinking about where I had just come from or where I needed to go next. I was simply there, in that moment, relaxing. When the other customer left, the employee turned to me and said, "Hi, my name is Ron, how may I help you?" He had a big ol' smile on his face and seemed to also be in the moment. In addition, he clearly had a lot of gratitude for being able to have a job and being able to assist me, the customer. So he took my shoes and started shining them—taking great pride in his work. At that point we started talking.

Ron admired my Gucci shoes and told me he had always wanted a pair and found them for twenty-five dollars at a thrift store. I smiled and said, "Well, I need to shop there and start saving money!" I admired his demeanor and passion for life. He told me it all started when he was in the military. He had joined the Navy decades ago and was able to travel to foreign lands, learn new cultures and languages, and at the same time protect and serve his country. I told him about my cousin who has been in Iraq multiple times and how much I admired him and was thankful for his service.

Ron then told me how he spent much of his time reading so that he could strengthen his mind and teach others. All the while he was shining my shoes with a glowing smile. He then told me how he also works in a youth center and tries to help kids reach their full potential. He mentioned that he taught using the theory behind the poem "The Dash" by Linda Ellis. I knew it well. He then said, "You seem like a teacher or something." I replied, "Right now, listening to you, I feel like a student."

Living in the moment is something that everyone can, and should, do. You never know what you will miss in life at any given time. When you live in the moment you open the possibility for those great experiences and interactions to happen. Dale Carnegie called this "living in day-tight compartments."

CONTAGIOUS INSPIRATION

••●• ● •●••

Remember, happiness is never about what someone or something from the outside gives to you, rather, it is always about what you give to yourself on the inside. The answers are within you—simply look and you will find.

FATIGUE NEVER STOOD A FIGHTING CHANCE

BRENDA SUTTON JONES

After fourteen years of running a successful promotional marketing company, I found myself growing tired of the products that the industry had to offer. As a result, the industry felt stale and if I saw one more engraved sticky note holder or stackable set of highlighters, I was pretty sure I'd go crazy! Our clients deserved more and I knew that it was my company's responsibility to give them more. In order to change the landscape and make our business stand out from the pack, we developed a mantra: "Innovate to Differentiate!"

We concluded that the best way for exciting new products to get to market was for us to develop them ourselves. So we did. After all, creative energy is what made our business successful in the first place; we just needed to take it to the next level. Once we decided to trade our "sourcing" hats for "inventor" hats, we instantly became energized.

Then we hit our first obstacle, negative thoughts—some bubbled up from within us, others were thrust upon us by friends and family, and another set was provided by our industry contacts. We entertained all thoughts of doubt; "Can't," "Don't Know How," "Fear of the Unknown," and "Will Not Work" all lived with us for a short while. We learned that defeating ourselves early on would be easy to accomplish and overcoming fears to reach our goals was going to take real work. We decided that what we sought to gain was more critical to our success than what we were risking to lose. Committed to our vision, things began to fall into place and challenges became hurdles rather than walls. From this point on we were innovators, period!

We began by building our "Dream Team." We tapped into our local universities and enlisted talented product designers and design engineers. Ideation was 24/7—brainstorming paired with thoughtful analysis. My two sons joined me on the leadership team, helping to bring concepts to the table and motivating the rest of our team to test them, and to be visionary. We pushed each other and we were fearless.

We also had our "ace in the hole"—our ability to survey current clients about what they wanted to see developed. A serious paradigm shift! The industry typically developed products and then pushed them out to the buying clients. Instead, we polled our clients and learned more about their needs.

It worked. We innovated and designed products that we knew would be successful. That said, there were plenty of challenges. In order to produce certain items and get them to market at competitive prices, we needed to embrace Asian manufacturing. So began the process of learning how to do business in the Far East. As you could imagine, some of our learning experiences were costly and time consuming. In time, we became mostly fluent with regard to negotiations, International Customs, and transportation issues. Nonetheless, the travel and jetlag were brutal, but we were driven by our mission to innovate and bring clients the products they wanted, within their budgets.

Thirty-three patents later (and a few still pending), we produced and brought to market over seventy-five one-of-a-kind pieces. We established ourselves as the go-to gurus of promotional advertising items and we operated offices in Raleigh, North Carolina, New York City, Hong Kong, and two in Mainland China. We established partnerships with some of the world's largest companies, including Target, Michaels, Pfizer, and GlaxoSmithKline.

The financial success was gratifying, but the best part of the journey was working with my sons, and, as the business grew, we employed other relatives and friends. When we look back at the obstacles we overcame and tell stories about the early days, it sounds tiring. The truth is that we were so energized by our inspiration and commitment to our mission, that fatigue never stood a fighting chance.

CONTAGIOUS ACTION

Innovation, energy, and design are vital. Change your approach and change your outcome. Be the change that you want to see in the world. Passion and success go hand in hand. Obstacles are a problem for those less committed to a vision. Transformation is powerful.

ABOUT DAVID MEZZAPELLE

DAVID has been motivating others to be positive since his childhood. In most aspects of life he has been living his vocation of making others feel good about themselves, the world around them, and what lies ahead. David is a major proponent of optimism. He has served a variety of roles to mentor others and to assist people of all demographics in appreciating their current life as well as in building a foundation for the future.

David was inspired to write this book based on his life's experiences, his contagious optimism, and the encouragement of his Alma Mater, Fairfield University in Connecticut. A portion of each sale will go to the school.

David was the founder and director of marketing for Goliath Technology from 1990–2007. Goliath Technology became a leader in data center infrastructure. His company supported corporations, schools, and government agencies worldwide. In addition, David orchestrated one of the most innovative internship programs ever created. Prior to 1990, David was an intern for IBM while attending school at Fairfield.

Goliath Technology was sold in 2007, and David pursued the next level of his passion, building employment tools for schools, students, and alumni via GoliathJobs, a marketing and consulting organization he created in 2006, and retained after the sale of his company. He also launched a niche portal for Baby Boomers and retirees, JobsOver50.com, which has become the number-one employment resource in North

America for the age fifty-plus demographic.

In 2009, David's company, Goliath LLC., formed a joint venture with SilverCensus and David became their marketing and development advisor. Within one year the new Silver-Census grew from a Florida-based directory to a leading senior living and health services resource in the U.S. under his guidance. Today, David consults on various projects and initiatives along with serving on several public and private boards.

Throughout David's life he has encountered great peaks and valleys, all of which he is thankful for. He never lost sight along the way and has kept his positive attitude and confidence at 110 percent. He has influenced many people with his outlook and this book is his way of offering optimism to others.

David has been a guest on various radio and televison programs. He is also a frequent contributor to the *Wall Street Journal* and various other publications and websites around the globe.

ABOUT DANIEL TULLY

 DAN TULLY is Chairman Emeritus of Merrill Lynch & Co. Inc., the worldwide financial services corporation. Mr. Tully has spent his entire business career at Merrill Lynch, which he joined in 1955 in the accounting department. Within two years he was named operations manager of the Stamford, Connecticut, office. After this grounding in the firm's operations, he entered the Merrill Lynch Training School and in 1959 returned to the Stamford office as an account executive. He was appointed manager of the Stamford office in 1970 and the following year he was elected a vice president of the firm.

In 1976 Mr. Tully was appointed director of individual sales. One year later he was elected to the Board of Directors of Merrill Lynch, Pierce, Fenner & Smith, the firm's principal securities subsidiary, becoming chairman and chief executive officer in 1985. He also served as president and chief operating officer of the parent company, Merrill Lynch & Co., Inc. Mr. Tully then served as chairman of the board and chief executive officer of Merrill Lynch & Co., Inc. from May 1992 to April 1997.

Born in New York City in 1932, Mr. Tully is a graduate of St. John's University where he received a bachelor of business administration degree, and has completed Harvard Business School's Advanced Management Program. He served in the U.S. Army from 1953–1955.

Mr. Tully served as vice chairman of the American Stock

Exchange from 1984–1986 and as vice chairman of the Securities Industry Association from 1985–1986. He also served as President of the Ireland United States Council for Commerce & Industry from 1990–1992 and as director of the New York Stock Exchange, including a term as vice chairman from 1994–1995.

In April 1996, Mr. Tully was appointed to the Board of Governors of the NASD and was named chairman in July 1996. He also served on the Board of Trustees for the New York Racing Association. Mr. Tully is a member of the Board of Incorporators of the Stamford Health System and a former chairman of its board. In 1999, Mr. Tully was elected to the Board of Elan Corporation, PLC. Mr. Tully was appointed a commissioner of the National Pensions Reserve Fund in April 2001 and in October 2002 the NYSE and NASD appointed Mr. Tully a member of the newly formed IPO advisory committee reporting to the SEC. Mr. Tully has retired from all boards with the exception of the Stamford Health System.

Mr. Tully and his wife, Grace, have four children and fourteen grandchildren. The family resides in Hobe Sound, Florida.

ABOUT MARSHALL GOLDSMITH

DR. MARSHALL GOLDSMITH has recently been recognized as one of the fifteen most influential business thinkers in the world in a global study sponsored by the London *Times*. Other acknowledgments include: American Management Association—top fifty thinkers and leaders who have influenced the field of management over the past eighty years; Institute for Management Studies—lifetime achievement award (one of two ever awarded); *Wall Street Journal*—top ten executive educators; *Forbes*—five most-respected executive coaches; *Economic Time* (India)—top CEO coaches of America; and *Fast Company*—America's preeminent executive coach.

Marshall is one of a select few executive advisors who have been asked to work with more than 120 major CEOs and their management teams. He is the million-selling author of numerous books, including the *New York Times* best seller *What Got You Here Won't Get You There*, a *Wall Street Journal* number-one business book and winner of the Harold Longman Award for business book of the year. His newest book, *Mojo: How to Get It, How to Keep It, How to Get It Back if You Lose It*, is a *New York Times, Wall Street Journal, USA Today,* and *Publishers Weekly* best seller. Learn more at www.marshallgoldsmithlibrary.com.

MEET OUR COAUTHORS

AUDI OF AMERICA, INC. Headquartered in Herndon, Virginia, Audi of America, Inc. and its U.S. dealers offer a full line of German-engineered luxury vehicles. Audi AG is among the most successful luxury automotive brands globally. Audi was a top-performing luxury brand in Europe during 2011, and broke all-time company sales records in the U.S. Through 2016, Audi AG planned to invest about seventeen billion dollars on new products and technologies. www.audiusa.com

RICHARD ANTHONY. Rick is founder and managing director of The Solutions Network, Inc., a management consulting firm specializing in business advisory services, human resource management, and performance improvement. He is also founder of The Entrepreneurs Network, a venue for aspiring and serial entrepreneurs and accredited angel investors. His book, *Organizations, People, and Effective Communication*, is available on Amazon. He can be reached at 610.225.0277 or r.anthonysr1@verizon.net.

JANET BALES. Janet is a mother of three, a stepmother of three, a "nana" of ten grandchildren, and a newlywed to her husband of three years. Janet is a musician and at an early age traveled on tour with America's Youth in Concert, Janesville Symphony Orchestra, and recorded in Carnegie Hall in 1976 with the BBC. Her musical talents were useful in the local church where she served for twenty-three years as a worship team leader, in the choir, and leading various art teams. In

2000 she was hired full time as the programming music and arts minister at a church in Wisconsin where she served until retirement. Soon after handing in her resignation, she developed colon cancer. The following year was spent in chemo until she successfully beat the disease.

Janet is now serving as the director of Tychicus Ministries, Inc., an organization she formed with her husband, Peter. They travel extensively supporting missionaries in the field, keeping them healthy so they can be effective in the areas they are serving. www.tychicusministries.org

CAROLYN BATES. Carolyn is an International Coach Federation (ICF)-certified personal life coach, expert contributing author for *Selfhelp* magazine and *Boomer Living*, and a Top 50 expert with *Self Growth* magazine. Coach Carolyn is also a member of Coach U, Coachville, and the Highland Lakes Health Partnership.

Her organization, Coaching Life Design, offers personal coaching and workshops with a focus on the challenges of caregiving, dealing with adult children, divorce after fifty, supporting a serious diagnosis, career changes, retirement decisions, and death and dying. They also write a newsletter and create customized teleclasses and e-books on the challenges of *creating life, before life creates itself.* www.coachinglifedesign. com, carolyn@coachinglifedesign.com

INEZ BRACY, MS, CNLP, CGC. Inez is a lifestyle transitions coach, speaker, award-winning author, and radio and TV personality who helps Boomer women rejuvenate, reinvent, and redefine their lives. Inez started her coaching business in 2005 to help Boomer women deal with the sometimes overwhelming prospect of starting a new life in their boomer years. Through the medium of TV, radio, web, etc., she has helped tens of thousands deliberately create a life by design.

As the creator of "SPICE" (Sassy-Phenomenal-Inspired-Conscious-Empowered) woman, Inez believes that each woman has the right to unleash her femininity and live the life of joy she desires. Inez has been featured on Lifetime TV's *The Balancing Act*, giving tips on how to start a home-based business. She is a frequent guest on the Fox 4 *Morning Blend* as their career coach, giving tips to help Boomers successfully navigate the workplace. She is a columnist for the *Coastal Breeze* Newspaper, Senior Stuff and former columnist for *The Island Voice*. www.thebracygroup.com

MICHAEL BRAGA. Michael is a marketing and development manager for Morse Life in West Palm Beach, Florida. Formerly from Tiverton, Rhode Island, Mike was trained in healthcare therapies, management, and marketing at Quinsigamond College in Worcester and University of Rhode Island in Narragansett. Michael has been married to his wife Carrie for ten years and they have two children, Zach and Isabelle. They reside in North Palm Beach, Florida.

DALE BUSS. Dale is a veteran automotive journalist, based in Rochester Hills, Michigan. He is a major contributor to industry coverage by Forbes and Brandchannel. Dale also has covered the car business for *Chief Executive Magazine*, Edmunds.com, *Automotive News*, *Advertising Age*, Auto-Trader.com, and the *Wall Street Journal*, where his coverage of General Motors earned a Pulitzer Prize nomination by the *Journal* for him and his colleagues. dalebbuss@aol.com

LISBETH CALANDRINO. Lisbeth is an award-winning author, activist, and entrepreneur. Lisbeth has spent over twenty years developing custom tailored training programs in team building, sales, and customer service. Today she is cofounder and vice president of Peachtree Communications and associate publisher of *Fabulous Floors* Magazine, an international flooring consumer publication.

Lisbeth recently published *Red Hot Customer Service: 35 Sizzling Ways to Heat Up Your Business and Ignite Your Sales* and hosts a radio show by the same name. Her awards include the executive of the year award from the International Executive Association, and first-place honors in an international marketing contest for alternative medicine. Lisbeth has spoken extensively about her experiences with cancer, offering words of comfort and inspiration. She has worked with at-risk youth, spoken out against injustice, and advocated for and helped to build resources for women. www.lisbethcalandrino.com, redhotcustomerservice@nycap.rr.com

FAITH CAMPBELL. Faith is a mother of four who lives in Bronx, New York. She is an administrative assistant for a nonprofit organization, a mentor at a business school for women, and a peer trainer for a financial organization. Faith attended Grace Institute where she graduated with honors as well as receiving awards for academic excellence, leadership, and attendance. Over the years Faith has accumulated various certificates and awards ranging in areas from academics to HIV/AIDS advocacy. She loves giving motivational talks, helping others, and ushering in her church.

JOSEPH CARBONE. Joe is president and chief executive officer of The WorkPlace, Inc., an innovative workforce development board, which helps people prepare for careers and develops the workforce for employers in southwestern Connecticut. It also has projects that cover the entire state of Connecticut, several states across the nation, and in Latin America.

Joe's unique perspective grows from his experience working in the private sector, government, and nonprofits. He holds a B.S. in economics from Quinnipiac University. jcarbone@workplace.org

DEE CASCIO, LPC, LMFT, ACC. Dee founded the Professional Counseling and Life/Retirement/ReCareer Coaching Center in 1986. She works with individuals, couples, and groups to achieve healthier and more satisfying lives now and as they transition to a more fulfilling lifestyle.

Dee is a private practice licensed psychotherapist who successfully entered the coaching arena as a certified life coach and a certified retirement and ReCareer coach. Dee writes a retirement planning newsletter on various aspects of creative lifestyle planning. She makes presentations about life planning to financial planners, professional groups, church and civic associations. She is also a member of Rotary International and the Dulles Chamber of Commerce, and she volunteers in her community. deedeelpc@aol.com

MARY ANN DAVIS. Mary Ann has over twenty years of experience providing coaching, counseling, and advising individuals through various life transitions. Mary Ann is a licensed professional counselor and is certified as a master career counselor, a life/work counselor, and is a Distance Credentialed counselor. She is a resourceful coach, empathic counselor, and an experienced guide on life's journey.

Mary Ann has been an associate with Holistic Counseling Care of Cincinnati since 1995. She launched "Your Career Plan," an online practice for coaching and counseling in 2007, and she teaches a career development workshop. www.yourcareerplan.com, yourcareerplan@cinci.rr.com

MICHAEL DELIA, ESQ. Michael was born in 1931 and raised in Brooklyn, New York. He moved to Connecticut when he was thirty years old. He currently has three children, seven grandchildren, and resides in Connecticut and Florida. Michael is still active in legal consulting as well as golf, swimming, and various community organizations.

DR. BRIAN DENHOFFER, DC. Brian is a holistic practitioner who discovers and helps to gently remove any interferences in your nervous system to allow your body the opportunity to heal itself. His training has given him the ability to get to the core of people's imbalances and to help them have overall health in a very expedient manner.

He works with infants, children, and adults, with all levels of disease (lack of ease) and those who are seeking higher levels of function and performance in their lives. He also works with those on the autistic spectrum, ADHD (attention deficit hyperactivity disorder), depression, anxiety, mind and body performance enhancement, pregnancy, fibromyalgia, MCS (multiple chemical sensitivity), and RDS (reward deficiency syndrome), including addictions of food, shopping/hoarding, drug and alcohol addiction. Many healthcare professionals consult Brian for their own physical well-being, which has aided them in better serving their communities.

Brian holds a doctorate degree in chiropractic studies from Life University; has been in practice since 1999; holds certification in addictionology and obsessive compulsive disorders from St. Martin's College, 2005, and a bachelor's degree in physics from Skidmore College. www.drbriandenhoffer.com, drsoulsoother@gmail.com

JED DIAMOND, Ph.D., LCSW. Jed is founder and director of MenAlive. Though focused on men's health, MenAlive is also for women who care about the health of the men in their lives. Jed is a member of the International Society for the Study of the Aging Male and serves as a member of the International Scientific Board of the World Congress on Gender and Men's Health. He is the only male columnist writing for the National Association of Baby Boomer Women.

Jed has been a licensed psychotherapist for over forty-five years and is the author of nine books including the international bestselling book, *Surviving Male Menopause,* which has thus far been translated into twenty-two foreign languages, *The Irritable Male Syndrome: Understanding and Managing the 4 Key Causes of Depression and Aggression,* and *Mr. Mean: Saving Your Relationship from the Irritable Male Syndrome,* which has recently been published. He is currently working on two new books: *Tapping Power: A Man's Guide to Eliminating Pain, Stress, Anger, Depression, and Other Ills Using the Revolutionary Tools of Energy Psychology* and *As Civilization Sinks: Making the Transition to a Better World.* www.menalive.com

MARTIN DIANO. Martin is a leader in helping Baby Boomers use social media to find, access, and consume high-value content. He is founder and CEO of the Boomer Authority Association and publisher of the Baby Boomer Knowledge Center. Martin is a veteran of international business, held senior staff positions at Eaton Corporation, Thunderbird—the American Graduate of International Management and the National Institute for World Trade. He is managing partner of the social media and public relations consultancy Martin Diano Agency LLC. A native of New York, he has a B.S. in business from City College of New York and lives with his wife of forty years, Annette, in Arizona and New York. www.boomerauthority.org

SCOTT DUNCAN. Scott is from Renfrewshire, Scotland. After discovering that he was dyslexic in his early twenties, Scott realized there was a reason for his struggling at school. Eventually he discovered a passion and strong ability to relate to people also facing multiple barriers in life.

Scott learned Tai Chi (Chi Kung), thought field therapy, neuro-linguistic programming, relaxation techniques, and active learning. Since graduating with a degree in community education, Scott has focused in areas such as business development, social enterprise, social media, Internet marketing, and project management. He has written and published a number of e-books and also loves writing song lyrics. Scott believes in the idea that there should always be something to look forward to in life, appreciating what you have today, and spreading laughter and joy to those who need it most. scottieduncanio@gmail.com

JERI HIRD DUTCHER. Jeri is a certified professional career coach, resume writer, and interview expert who inspires executives and professionals to envision, attract, and achieve the career of their dreams. Jeri has more than twenty-five years of experience as a professional writer; ten of those years writing resumes that have resulted in interviews in nearly every industry. She specializes in resumes for candidates for positions in computers and technology, communications, creative arts, and sales/marketing. Career highlights include being the senior editor of ResumeEdge.com, the premier online resume provider along with numerous industry awards. Having attained a B.A. in English (summa cum laude) with a concentration in writing, she taught composition at the college level. www.workwrite.net

DR. ANDREW FAGELMAN. Andrew is a board-certified internist. He completed his internal medicine residency at

St. Vincent's Medical Center in Bridgeport, Connecticut, an affiliate of Columbia University, College of Physicians and Surgeons. During his training, Andrew did extensive research into the clinical efficacy of Sildenafil. He attended medical school at the University of Buffalo School of Medicine in Buffalo, New York, and business school at the Zicklin School of Business in Manhattan where he earned an MBA in healthcare management. Andrew has received several honors and awards including being recognized as the Critical Care Resident Physician of the Year. He currently is an attending physician at Beth Israel Medical Center in Manhattan. www.sohohealthny.com

REBECCA FEIN. Rebecca has always been drawn to helping people live better lives. After a lot of soul searching, she decided to become a life coach and specialize in relationship transitions. The core of Rebecca's practice is working with people experiencing divorce. In addition to these efforts, she has helped people work through other transitional issues in business and business start-ups. Rebecca believes that people aren't broken; they just have to unlock the answers they seek to bring out more of their own potential. Her greatest joy is watching people flourish and reinvent themselves.

Rebecca completed her certification as a relationship coach at the World Coach Institute in 2010. She completed her MBA degree in healthcare management at University of Phoenix in 2007 and a B.A. degree in political science at Hope College in 1999. Rebecca is the mother of four children adopted out of the U.S. Foster Care System in 2005. Contact her at 720.523.3346, rebeccaa.fein@gmail.com

NANCY FERRARI. Nancy shares her life lessons in an energetic, vivacious spirit with messages of the importance of healthy living in all aspects, which she lives by example. Nancy celebrates that her college major in communications and journalism has come full circle as she is now a contributing author, currently writing her first book, a motivational speaker, and proudly hosts her popular BlogTalkRadio Show, *Feel Free in the O.C. with Nancy T.* She had the honor of broadcasting live as a guest speaker at the 2010 AARP convention speaking on the subject of "life energy," and has enjoyed numerous guest appearances on various radio shows. Nancy unveiled her new company, The Ferrari Energy Network, on January 1, 2011, and looks forward to expanding and sharing her messages.

Nancy's life is abundant as she has shared thirty-two years of marriage with her husband Dominic, her three children, and her seventeen-month-old granddaughter and has a deep desire to help others attain their health and wellness goals, to inspire others to find their authentic self, and to live their most abundant life. www.nancyferrari.com, nancy.t.ferrari@gmail.com

DR. COLLEEN GEORGES. Colleen has been working for thirteen years as a counselor and coach. She has come to find that true contentment and balance are possible only after we are able to embrace ourselves—gifts and flaws. Over the years, she has found immense joy in helping to guide individuals through self-discovery and personal and career goal attainment.

Colleen received her bachelor's, master's, and doctoral degrees in psychology from Rutgers University. She is a certified professional resume writer, certified professional career coach, certified JobsOver50-Boomer Authority career coach, certified professional life coach, certified professional NLP practitioner, NJ licensed professional counselor, and a member of the Professional Association of Resume Writers and Career Coaches (PARW/CC). Her professional background has included work as a psychotherapist, career counselor, university department director, and college instructor. She currently owns Colleen's Career Creations and Concentric Life Coaching. She teaches Psychology and Women's and Gender Studies courses at Middlesex County College and at her two alma maters—Douglass College and the Rutgers University Graduate School of Education. www.colleenscareercreations.com

DR. CARLOS GONZALEZ. Carlos is a nationally board-certified chiropractic physician and has been in private practice since 1991. His postgraduate training includes: chiropractic orthopedics, pediatrics adjusting techniques, motion palpation, sacral occipital technique, whiplash and spinal trauma, sports chiropractic, extremity adjusting, holistic healing, Ayurvedic medicine, bio-energetic synchronization technique, and geriatrics. He has also served and participated with the Texas Workers' Compensation Committee, Aging to Perfection Conference, Healthy Living Expo, and the alumni board of directors for the Parker College of Chiropractic.

Carlos produced and hosted the live radio talk show program *All About Your Health*, which aired every Saturday for three consecutive years. He has also appeared on Spanish and English local TV talk shows. He is a wellness consultant for local businesses in helping them reduce workplace injuries, and presents on wellness, injury prevention, stress management, and anti-aging to name a few. Carlos has written over one hundred articles on wellness, fitness, weight loss, holistic healing, pain relief, women's issues, preventative care, and more. He has authored the soon-to-be released e-books, *Hanging Out for the Health of It* and *Hanging Out Pain Free*. www.hangingout-forthehealthofit.com, drcmgonzalez50@yahoo.com

ELISA HAM. Elisa, adjunct professor and writing consultant in the English Department at Brookdale Community College, Lincroft, NJ, has also worked independently as a writing tutor and graphic freelancer. Elisa graduated magna cum laude from Fairfield University with a B.A. in English and received her teacher certification from Georgian Court University, where she earned her M.A. in education. Elisa and her husband, Steve, live in Fair Haven, NJ, with their sons, Stephen and David.

JOEL HELLER. Joel worked in the insurance industry for twenty-five years in various underwriting and management positions. He left the insurance industry in 2010 to open a retail clothing, jewelry, and gift shop in Vermont. Joel holds a B.A. degree from Fairfield University and resides with his wife in New Hampshire.

ROSEMARY H. Rosemary lives and loves in Florida. She has God, her husband, three married children, one granddaughter, one grandson, one step-grandson, her mother, two married sisters, three granddogs, and a good man named David to thank for the inspiration to do this writing. She enjoys family time, volunteering, boating, fishing, movies, and social time with friends.

BRENDA SUTTON JONES. Brenda started her marketing career in 1981 selling promotional advertising products to some of the nation's largest pharmaceutical clients. In 1990 she opened her own company, Adstracts, Inc., where she served as CEO for twenty years. Adstracts's portfolio holds over thirty patents and has offices in Raleigh, New York City, Hong Kong, and China. Pharmaceutical clients included Pfizer, AstraZeneca, GSK, Novartis, Bayer, and Merck along with retail partnerships with Target and Michaels.

Brenda is also passionate about helping to fight our nation's obesity problem and its associated diseases. Over the past two years, she has been successful in launching a pilot study at ECU Brody School of Medicine, dietetics and nutrition department, using her patented BMI (body mass index) wheels and the proprietary nutrient analysis software. These studies will target health improvement in poverty-stricken areas. Brenda resides in Pine Knoll Shores, North Carolina. She has two sons, and one precious granddaughter.

CHLOE JONPAUL, M.Ed. Chloe has published the following two books: *What Happens Next? A Family Guide to Nursing Home Visits…and More* and *Entering the Age of Elegance: A Rite of Passage and Practical Guide for the Modern Maturing Woman.*

Chloe's many achievements include being Ms. Maryland Senior America 2003; receiving the Fulbright Fellowship Seminars Abroad Award to South Africa in 1996; serving during the 2005 Maryland legislative session as a Legacy Leadership Institute graduate; being lead facilitator for the Alternatives to Violence Project in prison; and also running community workshops on conflict resolution for ten years. She is a state representative for the National Family Caregivers Association Caregiver Community Action Network 2006–2008 and an advisory board member for the Maryland Health Care Commission and the Interagency Commission for Aging Services: Maryland Dept. of Aging. She volunteers for hospice and the local homeless shelter. Chloe is also the coordinator for the Good Samaritan Project at her church. She has traveled extensively and has a strong philosophy on life: find a need and fill it. www.enteringtheageofelegance.com

KAREN LYONS KALMENSON. Karen is a poet, blogger, animal and human rights activist, who has contributed her rhymes to many places, many causes, and in the process, made friends worldwide and touched many hearts.

In Karen's eyes, the world is a vibrant palette and a limitless source of inspiration in its most beautiful and saddest of incarnations. She finds a rhyme and a laugh almost everywhere she looks. And she is always looking; heart, mind, and smartphone ready for whatever so she can share with her thousands of compatriots circling the orb. fayely10@aol.com

BARBARA RADY KAZDAN. Barbara is widely known for her leadership of Ashoka-U.S. where she built a fellowship of outstanding social innovators. In 2009, she launched Achieving Change Together to spark social change. She directed new initiatives for Generations of Hope, a unique intergenerational program model. Barbara also presented a "nuts and bolts" workshop for innovators at the 2010 Purpose Prize Summit and is actively engaged in The Transition Network. Earlier in her career she created a regional literacy awareness campaign that became a national initiative, and chaired city, state, and national planning entities. She founded the Houston READ Commission, a mayoral literacy-coordinating agency. At READ she pioneered instructional strategies, transformed adult literacy services at thirteen new technology-assisted learning centers, and helped shape federal policy to direct literacy funding to community-based initiatives. She then cofounded InFOCUS to help indigent people access affordable quality eye care. Barbara earned a B.A. from the University of Michigan and a certificate from the management program at the Jones Graduate School of Administration, Rice University.

In 2010 Barbara earned certification as a JobsOver50-

Boomer Authority career coach to help accomplished individuals pursue socially significant careers. www.achievingchangetogether.com, barbara@achievingchangetogether.com

ELLEN KRATKA. Ellen is an Integrity Coach who helps people realize the power of unconditional self-love for healing and growth and then aligns the essence of who they are in their soul with its expression in life and work. Trained in multiple modalities of heart and energy-based healing, she brings fifteen years of research into energy, manifestation, consciousness, esoteric philosophy, and holistic healing to her work with individuals and groups.

Ellen has also been a student of physics, a high school teacher, a journalist (in Nicaragua), a factory worker, an entrepreneur, and an activist for social justice, peace, and sustainability. In addition to her work in the arena of personal evolution, she also works with leaders by offering tools, systems, and consulting to help them make more of a positive impact on the world. www.theloveandlight.net

FAYE LEVOW. Faye, president of Launch Pad Publishing, Inc., has been a freelance writer and editor for over thirty years. As a book writing coach, she assists upcoming authors in seeing their way clear to completing their manuscripts. Her further background includes business, sales and marketing, as well as personal development, hospitality, and theatre. She has appeared on NBC's *South Florida Today* with Trina Robinson and James Chladek's show *The New Yorkers*.

She was contributing author to *Sprout the Life You Love*, published in 2008 by Sprout Publishing in Australia, and has authored hundreds of poems. Her upcoming book, *OMG! My Parents Are Getting OLD!*, is scheduled for release in the upcoming months. www.launchpadpublishing.com

EILEEN LICHTENSTEIN, M.S. Ed. Eileen is a keynote speaker, seminar leader, Peak Performance Success Coach, and consultant-trainer. Her unique style blends mind-body modalities including EFT (emotional freedom techniques) with traditional coaching training competencies and strategies to facilitate success. The founder of Balance & Power, Inc., Eileen has been in the training and coaching arena for over twenty-five years, facilitating trainings and workshops for the corporate and private sectors. Eileen believes inner strength and being centered are keys to life and business management. A former biofeedback therapist and faculty at Hofstra University, she is currently a trainer for CUNY schools. Eileen has been featured in print, TV, and radio media and has recently published the book, *SOAR! with Resilience.* www.balanceandpowerblog.com

SAMUEL LIEBERMAN. Sam is president and CEO of Rothschild Lieberman LTD., a broker dealer founded in 1981; Rothschild Lieberman Capital Management Corp., a money management firm; and Rothschild Lieberman Partners, L.P., a hedge fund. He has helped to fund, and served on the board of directors of several large organizations across various industries. Prior to 1981, he was a partner at Rothschild Securities Corp., and began his career as an over the counter trader at Goldman Sachs & Co.

Sam has received significant attention from both national and local media. He has been interviewed and called upon as a repeat expert source in media outlets, which include the *Wall Street Journal*, the *New York Times*, and several television networks. Furthermore, he has been actively involved in numerous charities throughout his career, and has served on several committees for the National Association of Securities Dealers (NASD), as well as the Cincinnati Stock Exchange. Sam holds a B.S. and B.A. degree from Boston University, College of Business Administration. www.rothschildlieberman.com

BARRY LINDSTROM. Barry is a maverick adaptive design scientist offering unique and innovative solutions to individuals and organizations. His career spanned nearly forty years. He went from cleaning tables for a dollar an hour in Gary, Indiana, to mopping up process failures at major corporations throughout the country. He has authored hundreds of nonfiction papers, user manuals, and presentations for those confused by complexity and wearied by the pace of change. Barry's first significant work of fiction is *Considering SomeplacElse.*

He continues to count his blessings with his life partner, Melinda, in suburban Arizona and places thirty-nine remarkable years of marriage, three outstanding children, and six wondrous grandchildren at the top of his list. www.soiwrotethisbook.com

ALAN MALIZIA. Alan attended Sacred Heart University in Bridgeport, Connecticut, and earned a B.A. in mathematics and a M.A. in education. His professional experience included corporate positions with companies such as Walden Books and then he shifted gears to teaching, his true passion.

Alan taught at Our Lady of Fatima in Wilton, Connecticut, and then at Stamford Catholic High School in Stamford, Connecticut, where he ultimately became a renowned coach for the girls' volleyball team. Under Alan, the team earned four state championship titles, one county title, and numerous city and division titles as well. Many of Alan's players earned athletic scholarships. Alan earned Connecticut Coach of the Year in 1988 and was selected for the Connecticut Volleyball Hall of Fame in 2007.

Alan self-published two books: *The Little Red Chair*, an autobiography about his life experience with polio, and *A View from the Quiet Corner*, a selection of his poems and reflections. Alan received book awards from the USA Book News National in 2009 and was the International Book Award finalist in poetry for the inspirational category and winner in the religious category in 2010. amalizia1@ct.metrocast.net

DAVID MARTIN. Born into a Wall Street family, David began his financial career in the mailroom at the Paine Webber offices in Boston, Massachusetts, in 1988. Later, after completing his B.S. degree in finance at San Diego State University, he joined his father at the Paine Webber offices in Stamford, Connecticut, in 1994. David then became a financial advisor at Smith-Barney in Stamford from 1995 to 1998. Later he joined UBS Financial Services as vice president of investments in 1998, where he managed portfolios for over two hundred high-networth families. There he used a combination of derivative strategies and careful selection of outperforming asset managers to enhance portfolio returns.

David's approach was naturally synergistic with the quantitative mathematical methods being developed by one of his clients, physicist Kevin Monahan. In late 2006 David left UBS to become a branch manager for LPL Financial Services. In 2007 he formed a partnership with Kevin Monahan and together they cofounded Quantflow Strategies, LLC, in 2009, a registered investment advisor (RIA). www.indxstrategies.com, david@indxstrategies.com

LAURIE MARTIN. Laurie has been teaching self-love and personal empowerment for over ten years. Her indomitable courage pushed her to transition from her corporate job as a vice president to follow her heart. As a professional speaker, certified life coach, author, advice columnist, and writer, Laurie passionately shares her wisdom, tools, exercises, and visualizations to help others connect with their infinite powerful being. She is the author of the published book, *Smile Across Your Heart: The Process of Building Self-Love,* and audio downloads, *The Conscious Breakup Guide: Navigating Through the End of Your Relationship* and *Becoming Your Own Best Friend.* www.SmileAcrossYourHeart.com, LaurieM@ SmileAcrossYourHeart.com

J. C. MONROE. J. C. began her career as a copywriter trainee at a large U.S. mail order company. She quickly learned that corporate life was at odds with her entrepreneurial spirit. At age twenty-five she asked herself, "If not now, when?" J. C. answered her own question by striking out on her own to establish a direct marketing creative agency. Within two years, however, her innovative boutique shop was generating several million dollars in annual client billings.

TINA MONTEZ. Tina is a business advisor to entrepreneurs in California and a distinguished media professional. She was recruited to assist in the development of AIDS awareness campaigns by the Centers for Disease Control (CDC), selected as a public affairs production fellow, WGBH-TV and the Corporation for Public Broadcasting, and won the Orson Welles Award for creative media.

Tina was raised in Mount Vernon, New York. Her father was a Navy veteran. Her mother was a talented songstress and vocalist in The Chantels. Tina has a master's degree in business administration from Dominican University of California and a bachelor's degree in journalism from Duquesne University. She spearheaded collaborative relief efforts in the wake of the earthquake in Haiti and Hurricane Katrina in New Orleans.

Her philanthropic objectives were met through educational scholarships and literacy programs in Solano County, California, as well. tina.montez@hotmail.com

MYRTLE NEWSAM. Myrtle, a resident of Raleigh, North Carolina, is a gospel songwriter and is currently in the process of recording a gospel CD. In 2010, three of her gospel songs were selected for her church's Christmas album. Besides pursuing her music career, Myrtle is busy writing children's and young adult stories as well as doing freelance work in the commercial and jingle writing industry. She is also an active member of BMI, Central Carolina Songwriters Association, and Writers-Unite.com.

MICHELE NUZZO, M.A. Michele inspires Baby Boomers to recharge their batteries and take positive action. Her specialties include career transitions, retirement life planning, and caregiver support. Michele earned a master's degree in clinical psychology and is certified in various coaching areas. Personal medical challenges, family caregiving crises, and her own midlife reinvention taught her the importance of focus, resilience, and self-care. She weaves her professional training with her personal experiences to bring insight, compassion, and humor to her writing and coaching practice.

Michele is the author of a caregiver booklet, *Keeping Seniors Safe: Tips for Boomers and Their Parents*, and a career transition booklet, *Keeping Hope Alive: Success Strategies for Mature Job Seekers*.

ANABELA OLIVIER. Anabela grew up in Connecticut and completed her bachelor's degree in history at California State University, Los Angeles. She then went on to complete her law degree at Suffolk University Law School in Boston. Anabela, her husband, and their five-year-old son live in the San Francisco Bay area.

SUSAN ORTEZ. Born in Mexico, Susan came to the United States to attend college. She is an alumna of University of Colorado and earned a bachelor's degree in business administration along with a minor in law. In addition, Susan earned her U.S. citizenship. Susan resides in Denver, Colorado, and has one daughter. She is an administrator at a law firm and still hopes to attend law school someday.

MICHAEL POLLOCK. Mike is a freelance writer in Ridgewood, New Jersey, focusing on investment topics. He has more than thirty years of experience as a business and financial reporter for The McGraw-Hill Companies and Dow Jones & Co. michaelapollock1@gmail.com

HARVEY REPHEN, Esq. Harvey is an attorney and founder of the law firm M. Harvey Rephen and Associates, P.C., with the main office located in New York, where he concentrates his practice in all areas of consumer debt law. Within this area of practice he handles a variety of matters including disputes, Fair Debt Collection Practices Act claims, debt resolution and management, debt elimination, and Fair Credit Reporting Act issues. Harvey is a dedicated advocate that received his law degree from Pace University School of Law in 1995. www.mharveyrephenlaw.com, consumeradvocatenyc@gmail.com

SUSAN ROSS. Susan's career spans twenty years in business education, new business launch and development, business growth consulting, sales training, speaking, and team building. She has worked with over five hundred businesses and coached one-on-one with numerous clients.

Susan's work began in college teaching kindergarten, then teaching college. Later she launched a private business college, which achieved national accreditation and approval from the U.S. Department of Education. The college specialized in training people to become entrepreneurs and sales professionals, a journey that allowed Susan to participate in hundreds of career and business launches. After selling her business college in 2005, Susan shifted her passion from students to business by founding Blue Ocean Business Coaching and Masterminds. www.blueoceancoaching.com

LISA ROTHSTEIN. Lisa is a former Madison Avenue creative director and copywriter whose campaigns for IBM, Hanes, Johnson & Johnson, and many other Fortune 500 companies have run worldwide. She continues to consult for select clients such as Capital One Bank, Samsung Electronics, and Lenox. Lisa's first screenplay, *Brit or Miss,* was the winner of the comedy genre prize in *Creative Screenwriting* Magazine's Screenwriting Expo Screenplay Contest and a top finalist in several other competitions. Lisa is represented as a screenwriter by the Bohrman Agency in Beverly Hills, California.

Lisa is a cartoonist, a singer with the San Diego Master Chorale, an occasional stand-up comedian, and a certified coach for creative entrepreneurs. She is the coauthor of the upcoming book, *The DaVinci Dilemma™: How Multi-Talented People Can Get Focused, Get More Done and Get More Joy Out of Life.* Lisa holds a B.A. in Semiotics from Brown University, is a graduate of Anthony Robbins Leadership Academy, and is a certified coach through Life Purpose Institute. www.thedavincicoach.com

JACQUELYN SAAD. Jackie is president of Inter-Change Consulting Inc., a full-service human resources and organizational development consulting firm specializing in change and problem management. Projects have included human resources program development, coaching of key executives, business closure, merger and acquisition support, employee fraud investigation, organizational redesign, team building, and employment dispute mediation in the U.S. and Canada. inter-change@rogers.com

TERRI SCHANKS. Terri is a healer, visionary teacher, writer, and affirmative life coach based in St. Louis, Missouri. She offers a nationwide practice and works with adults, children, and businesses to heal, empower, and transform lives and challenging situations. Terri holds a master's degree in social work from St. Louis University and is a licensed clinical social worker. She is the owner of Blessings Enterprises, LLC, a holistic healing and coaching business dedicated to honoring all the path of life brings with mindfulness and giggles. www.blessingsenterprises.com

IRA SCOTT. Ira is a certified master practitioner of neuro-linguistic programming, certified in "Belief Craft ™" (Knowledge Engineering and Sleight of Mouth), an American Board of Hypnotherapy board-certified hypnotist (Neo-Ericksonian Hypnotherapy), and has studied Human Needs Psychology, Strategic Intervention, and Havening (a Psychosensory Therapy). Ira empowers clients to find their answers that are inherently within themselves and to take measurable action for positive, lasting, empowering, and fulfilling growth leading to deeper connections with self and others. Ira is a member of the International Coach Federation as well as The Long Island Coaching Alliance. www.leanintolife.org

DR. BARBARA SEIFERT, CPC. Barbara is the president

of Committed to Your Success Coaching & Consulting in Orlando, Florida. She helps individuals take charge of their careers. She coaches organizations to enhance employee engagement and leadership. Barbara has held various positions in the corporate world in both corporate and nonprofit organizations. In her twenty-five years of business experience, she has mentored and trained employees and business providers to become successful and to achieve personal and organizational goals.

Barbara is a certified professional coach as well as a licensed clinical social worker. She is an adjunct professor at two universities teaching both management and human resources courses. Barbara is also certified in neuro-linguistic programming. She is a writer for The Work at Home Woman and Forbes Woman. www.cyscoaching.com

LEE SHILO. Lee holds a nine-to-five job and, in his free time, enjoys a passion for writing. He has a variety of published books and e-books. Contributing to this book has been a pleasure for him and he hopes there will be a sequel that he can also contribute to! He lives on Vancouver Island in Victoria City, British Columbia. www.shilocom.com, leeshilo@yahoo.com

LYNDA SMITH. Lynda is a wisdom preserver and connection specialist in South Africa. Her current role is building The Refirement Network in South Africa. This network is helping organizations and Baby Boomers to understand the opportunities and challenges that the future holds for this demographic. Lynda is a certified retirement coach with Retirement Options in the U.S.

Lynda is a social entrepreneur and has a passion for understanding how South Africans can unlock skill development and help grow the economy. Lynda would like to encourage

Baby Boomers worldwide to play an "encore" role in helping with skills, development, and growth by engaging virtual, and live, travels to South Africa. www.refirementnetwork.com

PAULA SNYDER. Paula has been songwriting and performing coast to coast over a forty-year span. Generally expressing her heart through poetry and song, Paula also enjoys writing articles, stories, and marketing copy. Though she started songwriting in her early college years, Paula waited until recent years to record and publish some of her music. Paula recently started a new poetry and songwriting gift service, "Verses to Go," for special occasions. You can also find Paula on iTunes.

Paula is a graduate of Eastern Michigan University. She currently resides in Raleigh, North Carolina, with her husband Marc. www.pcsnydermusic.com

KIM SOLOMITO. Kim is married to Jon Malkmes. They have been business partners for twenty-five years as floral designers. Their business, Kim Jon Designs, is located in Water Mill, New York. Kim is also active in yoga and other wellness activities. www.kimjondesigns.com, kim@kimjondesigns.com

MONA MACDONALD TIPPINS. Mona has two children and four grandchildren. She has lived in several states but now resides in Arkansas with her husband. Mona is the author of *Tomorrow the Train: Journey to the World Record* and *European Train Travel Tips*.

MARINA TONKONOGY. Marina is a psychotherapist practicing in Thousand Oaks, California. She has a M.A. in psychology in the field of marriage and family therapy, certification in psychoanalytic psychotherapy, and is a member of California Association of Marriage and Family Therapists.

She offers individual and marital therapy, support groups for those going through divorce or those recently divorced, and for those dealing with their partner's infidelity. Marina has a passion for making psychological education open and accessible to the general public and gives lectures and presentations on a variety of psychological topics. www.mtmft.com, marina@tonkonogy.com

LEONARD VELASQUEZ. Leonard graduated from high school on a Thursday and was drafted for Vietnam the following Monday. He chose the Navy; he wanted to serve his country and to also travel abroad to see what he had read in books. Leonard realized that however poor he thought he was, he was rich by the living standards he saw abroad.

Leonard's work experience commenced as a Navy postal clerk. After the service he landed a temp job with the Bank of America, which eventually became full-time. He worked his way up the corporate ladder. His roles along the way included computer operations midnight shift manager, mainframe operations (the new IBM platform), cash management lockbox services, account reconcilement services, mortgage and enterprise-level server operations. He was blessed with great teams from Hawaii to New York. Together they found continuous ways to improve the business. He has now worked for the Bank of America for over forty years and is proud of his accomplishments.

RICKY WADE. After leaving Jamaica and a career in aviation, Ricky took a corporate position with McDonald's in 1981 and became a franchisee in 2001 along with his wife Lissette. While operating high-performing restaurants, the Wades are extremely involved in regional and national McDonald's leadership and as role models in their community. Ricky is known as a business leader and as a mentor for youth throughout his community. He has devoted his talents to fifteen community boards, from the Urban League and Hispanic Chamber of Commerce to United Way, The Arc of Palm Beach County, and Ronald McDonald House Charities. He is a frequent speaker at youth-oriented events and was honored to meet George W. Bush at the White House in 2007 as a McDonald's representative for Black History Month.

The Wades have three children and live in West Palm Beach, FL. The couple recently received the coveted McDonald's Golden Arch Award, an honor bestowed on less than one percent of franchisees. www.mcflorida.com/32726

PAUL AND CHARLENE WALKER. The Walkers reside in South Florida. They are proud parents of five children—Nicholas, Frederick, Michael-Lerner, Michael, and Angela—and have fifteen grandchildren.

JOANIE WINBERG. Joanie is the CEO of the National Association of Divorce for Women and Children and the founder of Single Again! Now What? She launched several mentoring programs for women and men on how to survive after a loss or a divorce. Joanie's mission is to provide educational programs to empower single parents to regain their confidence, build self-esteem, and create a foundation of life skills to enhance their quality of life—for themselves and their families. Joanie is a certified human behavior consultant, author, speaker, corporate trainer, and mentor specializing in divorce. www.freshstartafterdivorce.com

BECKY WOODBRIDGE. Becky, founder of Becky Woodbridge & Company, is a motivational speaker and coach. Based on her philosophy of "community + care = results," Becky's platform develops personal development and organizational training tools for clients throughout the United States. A Newfield Network and Education for Living graduate, Becky specializes in ontological coaching, the study of being. Becky recognizes the importance of giving back by supporting many nonprofits in her community. Becky currently resides in Delray Beach, Florida, with her dog, Benney. She is a member of the Florida Speakers Association and the International Coach Federation. www.beckywoodbridge.com

KAREN WRIGHT. Karen coaches individuals seeking clarity and assists corporations in transforming ordinary into exceptional. In *The Sequoia Seed: Remembering the Truth of Who You Are*, Karen speaks knowingly of life's hardships—fires that can ravage and entrap, but also strengthen and free. This profound little book packs a powerful punch of inspiration and guidance for those who have lost their bearing on life's spiritual journey home. Her bimonthly e-zine, *Waking Up*, gives a precious moment's sanity to a world in chaos. www.wrightminded.com

BARBARA WULF. Barbara is a professional career and life coach, speaker, and writer. She brings twenty-five years of experience in education and career consulting to her business, Beckon Call. With a master's degree in counseling, Barbara completed her professional coaching certification from the Coaches Training Institute, holds the designation of associate certified coach by the ICF, and is a certified ReCareer coach. She lives in Wisconsin with her husband and miniature schnauzer and is a mother of two young working adults. www.beckoncall-coach.com

SUSAN YOUNG. Susan has a B.S. in business and a M.A. in education. One of her greatest strengths is getting people to share their stories with her. She asserts that everyone has the desire to feel loved and appreciated for the person they are and not the person others need them to be. Having coached hundreds of people, Susan understands how personality type affects every aspect of a person's life.

Susan has developed a teaching system where a person can be better prepared for college, a career, or even finding the right partner. Susan's goal is to enlighten millions of men and women on what makes them unique and to follow their passion and focus on their strengths. www.selfevaluationsystem.com, susan@selfevaluationsystem.com

ACKNOWLEDGMENTS

I thank Fairfield University not only for their involvement and efforts in copyediting this book but for the education and experience this wonderful school offered me years ago. I am an eternally grateful alumnus and a proponent of this fine university.

Fairfield University

Tom Baden, editor in chief of the *Connecticut Post*, a Hearst Newspaper. Tom served as adjunct professor for the advanced publishing class that copyedited this book.

Dr. James Simon, English department chair.

Dr. Wook-Sung Yoo served as chair and professor for the school of engineering that assisted in various aspects of this project along with the students of the software engineering program.

Copyediting team: Danielle Anctil, Eric Bernsen, Christina Callahan, Drew Fauser, Jennifer Fiorillo, Kerilee Horan, Bryan Houlihan, Daniel Leitao, Mary McCormick, Amber Nowak, Desiree Pina, Anne Rooney, Allison Schuster, Carly Sutherland, Chelsea Whittemore.

Learn more about Fairfield University at www.fairfield.edu.

Marshall Goldsmith

We appreciate the foreword written by Marshall Goldsmith and are honored by his support. In business and in life, Marshall has the ability to motivate, educate, and set things in perspective for anyone that has the benefit of reading his works or attending one of his lectures.

Dan Tully

We thank Dan Tully for taking the time to write the preface to this book. Dan is a major proponent of optimism and has led his personal and professional life supporting it. His affinity for positive thinking, living and working by principle, and respect for others, has been apparent in all aspects of his life. We are honored to have him on board the *Contagious Optimism* team.

Sharon Donovan

Sharon is our literary agent and consultant. We appreciate the confidence she has in this project and her ability to move us forward. From her initial read of the draft manuscript to the relationship she facilitated with our publisher, she has been great.

Brenda Knight and Viva Editions

Brenda and the team at Viva Editions have been terrific. We greatly appreciate their confidence and vision for *Contagious Optimism*. This relationship is the perfect match; their optimism and uplifting mission parallels our mission. Working with them is as motivational as the wonderful books they produce.

SHARE YOUR STORIES

Thank you for reading *Contagious Optimism*. We hope you found it helpful and inspirational. We are proud of the hard work and efforts that went into this project. Our team of authors, copyeditors, and contributors gave this 110 percent.

We are looking forward to future volumes. Our goal is to continue delivering stories from around the globe that remind people that any cloud can have a silver lining and that positive forward thinking is available to everyone.

Please tell a friend about *Contagious Optimism!* Our books and e-books are available in any bookstore and online at www.lifecarrots.com.

Should you have a story or reflection that you wish to share which offers a lesson of hope and inspiration please send it to us at submissions@lifecarrots.com. We will consider it for a future edition and would love to have you onboard.

Stay positive and make it contagious!

David Mezzapelle and the *Contagious Optimism* Team

TO OUR READERS

Viva Editions publishes books that inform, enlighten, and entertain. We do our best to bring you, the reader, quality books that celebrate life, inspire the mind, revive the spirit, and enhance lives all around. Our authors are practical visionaries: people who offer deep wisdom in a hopeful and helpful manner. Viva was launched with an attitude of growth and we want to spread our joy and offer our support and advice where we can to help you live the Viva way: vivaciously!

We're grateful for all our readers and want to keep bringing you books for inspired living. We invite you to write to us with your comments and suggestions, and what you'd like to see more of. You can also sign up for our online newsletter to learn about new titles, author events, and special offers.

Viva Editions
2246 Sixth St.
Berkeley, CA 94710
www.vivaeditions.com
(800) 780-2279
Follow us on Twitter @vivaeditions
Friend/fan us on Facebook